CHRISTIANITY AND THE SHONA

LONDON SCHOOL OF ECONOMICS
MONOGRAPHS ON SOCIAL ANTHROPOLOGY

Managing Editor: Anthony Forge

The Monographs on Social Anthropology were established in 1940 and aim to publish results of modern anthropological research of primary interest to specialists.

The continuation of the series was made possible by a grant in aid from the Wenner–Gren Foundation for Anthropological Research, and more recently by a further grant from the Governors of the London School of Economics and Political Science. Income from sales is returned to a revolving fund to assist further publications.

The Monographs are under the direction of an Editorial Board associated with the Department of Anthropology of the London School of Economics and Political Science.

LONDON SCHOOL OF ECONOMICS
MONOGRAPHS ON SOCIAL ANTHROPOLOGY
No. 36

CHRISTIANITY AND THE SHONA

BY

MARSHALL W. MURPHREE

UNIVERSITY OF LONDON
THE ATHLONE PRESS
NEW YORK: HUMANITIES PRESS INC.
1969

Published by
THE ATHLONE PRESS
UNIVERSITY OF LONDON
at 2 Gower Street, London, WCI

Distributed by Tiptree Book Services Ltd
Tiptree, Essex

Australia and New Zealand
Melbourne University Press

Canada
Oxford University Press
Toronto

© *London School of Economics,* 1969

485 19536 4

Library of Congress Catalog Card No. 68–18053

PRINTED IN GREAT BRITAIN BY
ROBERT CUNNINGHAM AND SONS LTD
ALVA

PREFACE

This book is concerned with an analysis of the relationship sustained between the different forms of religious life found in contemporary Shona society. Shona society today presents a heterogeneous religious situation, and the analysis has focused on the particular circumstances existing in this society which have led to this type of religious situation. To some extent the answer to this question lies in factors which in the first instance were external to Shona society and which intruded upon it. Attention has therefore been given to the history of the European occupation of Shona territory, the extension of Western economic, cultural and political forms among the Shona and the history of missionary expansion in Southern Rhodesia. The answer also lies in factors intrinsic to Shona society and culture which have made Christianity since its introduction a viable alternative form of religious expression. The identification of these factors was the main objective of the field-work period. The book combines, therefore, the results of historical research with the findings of a period of anthropological field work.

It is perhaps wise to point out that I do not regard the sociological orientation of this study as being the only valid perspective from which to view the phenomena of Shona religion. This is a qualification perhaps not necessary for my colleagues in anthropology, most of whom are well aware of the limitations as well as the potential of the discipline. However, because of the wide interest in the subject of this study it is possible that some who are not anthropologists will read this book; it is hoped that in a similar recognition of the qualified claims of sociology they will also recognize its value and validity in the study of religious phenomena.

The data on which this analysis is based was collected during a field work period in the Mtoko Reserve, the home of the Budjga peoples. This is therefore primarily a study of Budjga religion. Since Christianity arrived in Mtoko later than it did in many areas of Rhodesia, the Budjga may not be typical in every respect of the general Shona religious picture. However, since the Budjga share with other Shona tribes the common cultural and historical background which is described in the first part of this book the term Shona has been retained in the title, and the material presented here has a general, if not specific, application to all the Shona area.

Within Mtoko Reserve much of the field research was carried out in one community of the Nyamkowo Chiefdom, an area containing a population of 2955 people in which all four principal forms of Budjga religious life were found in close proximity. A religious census of the entire community was carried out to determine the connections between residence, kinship and religious affiliation. Most of the other data collected was acquired through three channels: observation, interviews and quantitative surveys. A variety of religious rituals was observed, but observational attention was also placed on the daily activities of various individuals identified with different religious orientations, with special reference to the networks of association and activity in which they were involved. Interviews of both directive and nondirective types were carried out, the first yielding a considerable number of comprehensive life histories, the second a variety of information. Techniques yielding quantitative data included an attitudinal survey involving the use of multiple choice questions, and a prestige rating test. Having been born and brought up on a mission station in Manicaland, I had the advantage of having learned Shona as a child, and practically all of the investigation was carried out in this language.

Field work was carried out at various periods between August 1962 and November 1964. It had been my intention to make extensive use of Shona research assistants during the investigation, but unfortunately during the entire period of research the Reserve—as indeed the whole country—was in a state of extreme political tension, and sociological investigation of any kind tended to excite suspicion and hostility. The basic cause of this tension was the conflict between the divergent and apparently irreconcilable objectives of an awakened African nationalism and those of the incumbent European Government, but the hostilities and frustrations generated by this situation were manifested in Budjga primarily by a conflict between adherents of the two African nationalist parties. Since it was difficult for any African to prove his party allegiance (the carrying of cards indicating membership in the banned nationalist parties was, of course, illegal), an outsider in any community was regarded with suspicion as a potential spy or infiltrator for whatever party was in local disfavour. In this situation it was, paradoxically, easier for a European investigator to work in the Reserve than an African, and consequently most of the material had to be collected by myself. In January 1964 an attempt was made to place eight research assistants in selected communities throughout the Reserve, but several narrowly escaped physical violence, their presence was an embarrassment to those who entertained them, and the project had to be abandoned. I was able to use local Budjga—particularly teachers on duty—as assistants with some success, but since they invariably were closely involved in the local situation their value was limited.

Since the commencement of this investigation the former Federation of Rhodesia and Nyasaland has been dissolved, some of the constituent territories have been granted their independence and all have changed their names. Other terminology has also changed; in Southern Rhodesia for instance what were 'reserves' are now 'tribal trust lands', and what were 'native purchase areas' are now 'African purchase areas'. To avoid possible confusion, however, terminology in use at the time of the field investigation has been preserved in this report.

This book is a condensation of a Ph.D. thesis submitted to the University of London in November 1965. The Central Research Fund of the University provided a grant which helped in expenses involved in field work. My academic supervisor during the research period was Professor I. Schapera, for whose encouragement, patient assistance and valuable insights I am very grateful indeed.

Dr Paul Geren, sometime American Consul General in Salisbury, kindly provided a grant toward the employment of research assistants. I am grateful to Dr M. Blake, Bishop R. E. Dodge, Miss M. Deyo and others in the Administration of the Methodist Church who granted me the time and co-operation necessary to complete this study. I wish to express my appreciation to Professor George Fortune of the University College, Salisbury, who provided me with useful introductions to authorities of the Roman Catholic Church and to Father Simon Tsuro and his colleagues at All Souls' Mission for their hospitality and warm-hearted co-operation in this project. To the leader of the Vapostori

Church, Mr Abel Ngomberume, and to the many Vapostori leaders who gave me their time and friendship I am equally grateful.

In both Salisbury and Lusaka I shared with many other research students the valuable direction given by the field seminars arranged for our benefit by Professor J. C. Mitchell, a privilege greatly appreciated. Among others who have provided the opportunity to discuss items of this study and given me their valued advice and criticism are Professor V. Turner, Professor J. Middleton, Dr M. Gelfand and Dr K. Garbett. To the many people in Budjga, including various personnel in the Government and tribal administrations, I owe a special debt of gratitude. I am also grateful to Professor R. Firth for permission to refer to unpublished material and to Mr Robert Kauffman and the editors of the *Journal of the African Music Society* for permission to reproduce the Wabvuwi text appearing on pp. 73–4. I am greatly indebted to my wife, Betty Jo, for her help in the preparation of the text and to Mrs Dominie Herman for the preparation of the typescript.

To Dr Marshall Gamble I owe the inspiration to start this study. For the help and encouragement needed to complete it I am indebted to the late Mr Dewey Stallard and to his wife, Mrs Geneva Stallard. To these people I am especially grateful.

University College,   M. W. M.
Salisbury

CONTENTS

MAPS

I

Introduction

The social sciences have in recent years produced a wealth of material relating to the religion of various African societies. Some studies have dealt with traditional religions, others have concentrated on modern Christian or semi-Christian movements which have had a development independent of mission control, while still others have attempted a comprehensive religious survey within a restricted area. Studies of the last two types, taking into account the Christian factor in contemporary religious situations, have been carried out in South Africa, Swaziland, Bechuanaland, Northern Rhodesia, Nyasaland and the Congo.[1] Yet in spite of this profusion of research in countries on or near the borders of Southern Rhodesia, no major work of this type has yet been carried out among the Shona tribes who live between the Limpopo and the Zambesi and who, with over two and one-half million members, constitute one of the largest cultural groupings among the Central and Southern Bantu. The religious studies which have been done on the Shona have been primarily concerned with aspects of their traditional religion, and only a few short articles have been published which examine the place of Christianity in their contemporary religion.[2] This omission has been noted by Sundkler, Shepperson and Ranger, and has led to various speculations concerning the character of the separatist and independent groups in their midst.[3]

This book is the report of a study which was undertaken to obtain some of the data necessary to fill this ethnographic gap. It is also an attempt to analyse these data in terms of the relationship between the contemporary religion of one Shona society and its

---

[1] Among the more important of these may be cited: Andersson, 1958; Kuper, 1946; Pauw, 1960; Rotberg, 1961; Schapera, 1958; White, 1961; Wishlade, 1965.

[2] Of these, the articles by Aquina (1963) and Ranger (1964) are perhaps of the most interest to the anthropologist.

[3] Such as Worsley, 1957, p. 235 and Shepperson, 1963, p. 89.

other present-day institutions, and to examine the interconnections between the different forms of religious life. The society selected, that of the Budjga of north-eastern Southern Rhodesia, presents a heterogeneous religious situation involving four principal types of religious expression: Catholicism, Protestantism, Budjga traditional religion and an independent African Christian group. The analysis has been focused on the circumstances which have permitted these four types of religious expression to co-exist.

Recent anthropological studies of religiously heterogeneous societies in Africa have utilized various schematic perspectives in their analysis of the data. One, which we may call the 'categorical' approach, sees the situation essentially as one of conflict, in which two (or more) religious systems compete for the loyalties of the society. Trend and direction are usually conceived in terms of the subsidence of one system and the ascendancy of the other.

There is also the 'layer' or 'veneer' approach, which sees the earlier religion of the society as still forming the basic sub-stratum of the contemporary religion, and the more recent ideological and ritual intrusions as accretions to this. In this approach conflict and competition between the different religious modes are also regarded as important, but are seen as taking place primarily within the individual, not in the society, so that each individual represents in his faith a species of religious phylogenetic recapitulation.

There is, finally, what we may call the 'synthetic' approach, which sees a dialectical interchange between the traditional, local religious organization and the immigrant religion (or religions) and focuses in particular on such independent religious groups as may arise as being the synthetic end of this process.

It is the contention of this study that this last is the most useful for analysing the Budjga religious situation, though useful only when applied not only to the Independent African Christian group, which would normally be assumed to exhibit syncretistic ingredients, but to the whole range of Budjga religious behaviour, be it 'traditional', 'orthodox' or 'independent'. The changing conditions of Budjga society have greatly enlarged the range of situations calling for religious solution. The result of these conditions is a high degree of religious mobility and heterodoxy. An examination of the relations between the different religious groups is perhaps the best way to understand the place of religion in Budjga society today.

THE SHONA BACKGROUND

The Budjga are one of the Shona tribes, a group of peoples who live immediately south of the Zambesi River, most of them in Southern Rhodesia and Mozambique, and who today number more than three million. Many of these tribes as we know them today are only autonomous fragments of what were at one time more centralized units, and in certain instances of different origin. They therefore exhibit tribal variations which make it dangerous to generalize about 'the Shona' as a whole, particularly in respect to religion. On the other hand, they do exhibit sufficiently marked linguistic and cultural conformity to set them off from the neighbouring Bantu peoples.[1] Perhaps even more important for this study is the fact that the tribes living in Southern Rhodesia have shared a common history of Nguni invasions, British conquest and missionary occupation. Improved means of communication and transportation, and the agglomeration of members of the different tribes in urban industrial complexes such as Salisbury and Bulawayo, have accelerated the trend to homogeneity and, as Holleman has pointed out with regard to tribal law, inter-tribal contact has been free and frequent during the last fifty years, and what may once have been exclusive features of different sections are now common to different communities living in the same locality.[2]

In 1890 the British took possession of Mashonaland, incorporating it into one political unit with Matebeleland, and set the

[1] Mitchell places them in the 'northern' group of the 'Southern Bantu' in his general classification of the Bantu of Central Africa, characterizing them as 'patrilineal, cattle-keeping, weak chieftaincies, rain cults'. (Mitchell, 1960, p. 178.)

[2] Holleman, 1952, p. 1. The complex question of inter-tribal relationships among the Shona lies outside the scope of this study. That European occupation has led to an increase in inter-tribal contacts can be accepted as generally true, but it should also be noted that in some aspects of tribal life it had the opposite effect. One result of legislation introduced by the colonial government was that tribal territorial boundaries were fixed, inter-tribal wars ceased, the incentive to inter-tribal alliances was removed and significant inter-tribal political activity in effect came to an end. The spirit-mediums of the Shona tribes (*infra*, pp. 45-8), who played an important part in inter-tribal political activity, ceased to activate the trans-tribal network they had previously maintained, and religious contacts of this type are now rare.

border with the Portuguese along the Inyanga and Chimanimani Mountains which was to divide the Shona-speaking peoples. The few legal arguments that the settlers had as a justification for their occupation were based on negotiations not with the Shona but with the Ndebele. It soon became apparent, however, that, regardless of the proprietary attitude of the Ndebele, there were several Shona groups in the eastern part of the country that would have to be dealt with individually. Some—including the Budjga—entered into agreements with the British. The treaties concluded were of the same type as the Rudd Concession made with the Ndebele: in return for 'protection' the chiefs conceded mineral rights only. But soon large grants of the best farming land were made to the settlers, a shock to the Shona compounded by the unfriendly and superior attitudes of the Europeans, the imposition of an alien legal system and the introduction of taxation and of a police force made up largely of Nguni elements.

As a result of these pressures the vague sense of unity that the Shona had already acquired in the face of Ndebele pressure crystallized, and when in 1896 the Ndebele rose in rebellion the Shona, encouraged by the tribal spirit mediums, joined them. The rebellion was soon put down by the British. The Shona lost such land rights as they might previously have claimed, and the policies of the European Government began to impinge more directly on them. The powers of the chiefs were weakened as they were stripped of their ability to impose severe punishments, and many of their administrative and judicial functions were taken over by the European Administration. At the same time some central-ization took place through the creation of reserves exclusively for Shona settlement. These reserves were developed in accordance with a policy of modified territorial segregation, especially desired by the European farmers, who did not want tribal methods of agriculture adjacent to their own. Reserves were demarcated one by one, and by 1913 they covered about twenty-two per cent of the entire territory and accommodated about forty-five per cent of the African population.[1] Ethical justification for the system was sought in the argument that they provided a sanctuary for the African until such time as he would be ready for assimilation into the Western community, but in practice they became permanent.[2]

[1] Brelsford, 1960, p. 71.
[2] The history of this policy is discussed by Mason, 1958, pp. 255–94.

Closely linked to the land policy was that of African taxation. The whole economic structure of the country rested on a base of unskilled African labour, working either on European farms or in the developing urban and industrial areas. Taxation created a demand for ready money that recurred year after year, and helped to even out the supply of labour. For many years the experience of wage labour was peripheral to the life of the Shona, and their culture continued to find its impetus and scope in the reserves. Later a permanent African population began to develop in the urban areas and rural-urban mobility began to increase, a process accelerated at the end of the Second World War. The influences of urbanization thus affected the rural Shona in an increasingly wide context. Garbett's study[1] has shown that the period of time spent by Shona men in towns between visits home has decreased significantly in recent years. 'Month-ender' visitors have become 'week-enders' as commuting problems have been eased by a vast increase in the number of buses, most of them African-owned, which run between the towns and the reserves. The number of trading stores, bakeries and butcheries in the reserves has increased noticeably. While many of these are owned by local men, others are branches of urban businesses, and the delivery lorries of these firms as they ply between the towns and the reserves are now a common sight. These vehicles often carry with them the daily or weekly productions of the urban press, which together with radio form a news medium closely linking the urban and rural populations.

An important change in the land tenure system was effected by the Native Land Husbandry Act of 1951. Among its far-reaching provisions was the registration of tribal reserve land in the names of individual African owners, making them responsible for its proper cultivation and at the same time giving them the right to dispose of it by sale. Since the implementation of this Act has been delayed in many areas, it is difficult to assess its precise implications for Shona society, but that it represents a complete break with tradition is obvious, and therefore its effect must be profound. The Act has met with great opposition in certain places, for some of the demarcated plots in areas of high population density are economically below the subsistence level. Furthermore, many urban Shona have opposed a measure which deprives them of the

[1] Garbett, 1960, pp. 8, 19, 49–51.

economic security given by their communal rights in the reserves. These facts, along with the strong feeling of spiritual attachment to the land, have made the Act (however economically and agriculturally sound) a politically sensitive issue.[1]

THE INTRODUCTION OF CHRISTIANITY TO THE SHONA

The first attempt to introduce Christianity to the Shona was made by a Portuguese Jesuit missionary, Fr. Gonzalo da Silviera, at the court of the Monomotapa dynasty until he was murdered as a result of court intrigues in 1561. Subsequent Portuguese alliances with the dynasty kept alive the influence of the Church at the king's court, and several of the later Monomotapas, some of their chiefs and many of their people were baptized. During this period Portuguese and Catholic influence were greater than is generally realized; a list of churches in 1640 names twelve in three groups, following lines along the Mazoe River to Mt Darwin, south of Zumbo on the Zambesi to the present Sipolilo, and from Beira to Manicaland.[2] How deep this influence was is problematic, for when the Portuguese withdrew from the area (by 1667) they left no discernible trace of Christianity in any of what is now Southern Rhodesia. The fact, however, that they penetrated into Shona territory and stayed there a considerable time should be kept in mind, since it may have influenced Shona religion in ways not easily ascertained today.

The modern history of Christianity among the Shona dates from the occupation of their country by the British South Africa Company in 1890. The same year saw the establishment of the Christian missionary enterprise among the Shona from which the present Christian Church in their midst takes its origin.[3] The two

[1] The promulgation of the Tribal Trust Land Act of 1967 has, in fact, abrogated many of the provisions of the Land Husbandry Act.

[2] Devlin, 1961, pp. 149–50.

[3] Prior to this date the L.M.S. had established mission work among the Ndebele in the territory which is now Southern Rhodesia, but Christian missionaries had been prevented by Lobengula from establishing work in Shona areas. Shona territory was the chief hunting ground of the Ndebele *impis*, and as such was carefully guarded by Lobengula. The Anglican Bishop of Bloemfontein, Bishop Knight-Bruce, after repeatedly attempting to gain permission from Lobengula to enter Shona territory, sadly decided to hold the introduction of Christianity to the Shona in abeyance and to circumvent their territory and work north of the

events were closely related, and this relationship has placed its stamp upon the subsequent development of the Christian Church among the Shona and their attitude towards it.

The close association between Church and Company was not discouraged by the Company. Rhodes approved of it, and even encouraged it. He seemed, in the words of Bishop Knight-Bruce of Bloemfontein, to have 'an ardent desire to get the co-operation of the Church, if possible, or if not possible, to prevent any hindrance on her part to such plans as they (the B.S.A. Co.) may not wish reflected on'.[1] After Colquhoun's expedition to Chief Mtasa of the Manyika in September 1890, the Company promised to 'aid and assist in the establishment and propagation of the Christian religion and the education and civilization of the native subjects of the King, by the establishment, maintenance, and endowment of churches, schools and trading stations . . .'.[2]

To give concrete support to this policy Rhodes and the Company encouraged missions of various denominations to settle in the Shona area by offering them large grants of land for this purpose, and by the year 1900 land grants covering 325,730 acres had been given out to ten different denominations.[3] In addition to these grants, a large number of plots were acquired by the various missions in the townships that were being set up for African occupation near European industrial and urban centres.

It was not, however, in the urban areas but on the mission stations that the Church was first to grow. The policy of concentrating mission effort in a few centres so strong as to become self-sufficient communities, largely independent of the society at large, was of course common to missionary enterprises throughout Africa and Asia, but the degree of independence in Southern Rhodesia was unusual for a number of reasons. We have already mentioned the extent to which land was made available to the missions. Not only was Rhodes generous with his grants, but in some cases he even suggested where the missions could best establish themselves. With these large tracts of land at their

Zambesi. He rejected the idea of breaking the Ndebele power as a means to the evangelization of the Shona, holding that 'the probable evils resulting from that at present would be greater than the benefits'. (Fripp and Hiller, 1949, pp. 101-2, 130.)

[1] Knight-Bruce to Tucker, 25 Nov. 1889. U.S.P.G. Archives, London.
[2] *British Parliamentary Paper C 6495 of 1891*, p. 27.
[3] *Report of the Native Education Inquiry Commission*, 1951, p. 3.

disposal, and with official government policy urging development on them to hold them, it was natural that the missions concentrated their efforts at these places.

Another reason in many cases for this concentration of mission effort was an estrangement between the Missions and the tribal leaders at this critical initial stage. Prior to the Rebellion the Shona chiefs appear on the whole to have been friendly to missionary enterprise. Reporting on a trip made through Shona territory in 1891, Knight-Bruce said, 'Not only did the Chiefs receive the Missionaries in nearly every case, but they offered help in some form or another . . . the number of tribes under the Church's influence is very great. Besides this there are a large number of tribes who are only waiting for us to supply them with resident teachers.'[1] The Rebellion, however, brought about an alignment which in many instances opposed the chiefs to the missionaries. The missionaries' position during the Rebellion was ambivalent. They found the very existence of their organized work to be dependent upon the law and authority of the Company, and furthermore they shared the white settlers' views on the superiority of Western Culture. Yet at the same time most of them conceived of their purpose as being primarily to help and benefit the Shona, and as time went by they saw this come into increasing conflict with settler interests. This ambivalence has marked the attitudes and policies of the Church in Shona country to the present day.

Government policy stipulated that the consent of a chief was necessary before any mission body could enter and work in the territory of his people. A number of chiefs refused this permission, some being openly hostile, while others simply delayed their answers indefinitely. These refusals were not, however, accepted as conclusive and where they were denied entrance the usual tactic of the missionaries was to acquire freehold property from the Company on land adjoining the reserves and establish missions there. They could thus work independently of tribal authority. As a result, Christianity in its early stages developed outside the main stream of Shona life. Instead of directly influencing Shona society, it segregated its adherents in largely dependent sub-societies based on the mission centres. Many of these mission holdings were large—in some cases nearly as large as the native reserves they bordered; their inhabitants were outside the direct control of the

[1] Pascoe, 1901, pp. 365–6, pp. 366a, 366b.

tribal authorities, and it is not too much to say, as Taylor does in the context of Northern Rhodesia,[1] that some of the missionaries, by dint of long service in one place and the force of their personalities, came to function, at least psychologically, as substitute chiefs. Thus a pattern was set in this important incipient stage that was different from the evangelization of, say, the Tswana.[2] Here Christianity had won the support of a significant number of chiefs, whose people had followed them in what amounted in some cases to group conversions. Among the Shona, with few exceptions, this was not to happen. Conversion to Christianity was usually individual, and at conversion the individual frequently moved out of his tribal milieu into the society of the mission station.

Yet this pattern did not lead to the radical cleavage in Shona society that might have been expected. This was due to a number of factors:

(a) The cognate qualities between the traditional Shona religion and Christianity, to be mentioned,[3] enabled the Shona converts more easily to adapt the Christian ethic to their own society.

(b) The mission station pattern to some extent segregated the missionaries and their more radical demands from the Shona people. At the same time it provided a training ground for a corps of African Christian workers who, when the time came for expansion from mission stations out into the reserves, could to some extent mediate the conflicts between Christianity and their society.

(c) The acceptance on the part of many Shona, particularly of the older generation, of the inevitability of the advance of Western Culture and the decline of their own traditional one. They could tolerate the promulgation of an alien faith among their children in the name of Christianity, since they conceived it to be more adaptable than their own to the demands of the new society.[4]

It was when the missions became involved in the programme of education among the Shona that Christianity moved away from the mission centres and out into the reserves. Only after this can it be said to have taken root in Shona society in any significant way. Until that time Shona Christians were primarily adherents of a

---

[1] Taylor and Lehmann, 1961, pp. 18–20.
[2] Schapera, 1958, pp. 3–9.   [3] *Infra*, p. 59.
[4] It is a common experience to hear an old Shona individual, by way of explanation for not being a Christian, make the statement, 'The new way is not for us who are old, but it is all right for our children, because their life is different.'

religious system external to their society and touching it only
through their own personal mediation.

The missions were the pioneers of the present educational
system among the Shona, and for many years they and the people
bore almost all the cost. The missions discovered that chiefs who
had previously been unwilling to admit them for purely religious
activities would allow them to enter if they undertook educational work, since it was becoming apparent that only through
education would the younger generation be able to cope with
the new society that had been introduced to the country.
This attitude gave them a means of taking Christianity into the
reserves.

The pattern that usually evolved was for a local group or
village, with the permission of their chief, to approach a mission
with the request for a teacher. The mission would then stipulate
its conditions, usually involving the erection of school buildings
and a teacher's house of a simple type, and often also the provision
of at least a part of the teacher's salary. The teacher sent would be
a convert of the mission, with some elementary education, plus
training as a catechist.[1] He would use the school building through
the week as a class-room, and on Sundays as a church. Considerable pressure would be brought on the school children to attend
church and accept Christianity; but the parents could not be
brought under the same control, and those who did become
Christian did so from individual choice. Yet even though most of
the adult population did not join the Church they became closely
identified with it through the new common interest. They would
form a school committee under the missionary's guidance, and
would frequently meet with church officials, both in the village
and in the mission, to discuss matters of common interest. Soon
it became usual for the villagers of a given community to
identify themselves as 'Methodists', 'Anglicans', or some other
denomination by virtue of their association with that Church in
the education of their children. When their children had gone as
far as they could in the local school they would frequently go
on to the mission station for further education, and thus links
between community and Church were further strengthened.

It was from the ranks of these students who went on to the
Mission schools that most of the Churches built up a corps of

1 Often these men were referred to as 'pastor-teachers'.

Shona workers, teachers and ministers, who progressively took over the task of the direct presentation of Christianity and who more recently have been the main mediators of its doctrines.

Since 1920 the Government has moved increasingly into the field of African education, especially in the spheres of secondary and technical education and primary schooling in the towns. In the country primary education is still almost entirely under Mission supervision, and it is estimated that 94 per cent of those Africans in Southern Rhodesia who have received any formal education have obtained at least a part of it in a mission-related school.[1]

For many years, since education was almost completely in their hands, the Missions avoided that close identification with the Government that had compromised them in the eyes of the Shona with regard to land. But as the demands for education rose it soon became necessary for the Missions to accept government subsidies which progressively involved more state control although the administration of their schools was left in Mission hands. The Missions retained the privilege of using the schools as a medium of religious instruction, but their academic and financial arrangements came to be rigidly regulated.

A noteworthy result of this Government involvement in primary rural education came from the legislative provision that no village school could be started except under the aegis of an approved mission group. Many of the religious groups who arrived later on the scene, particularly churches of the 'Bantu Separatist' type,[2] never won this approval. This became an important factor inhibiting their growth in the rural areas.

Other factors also operated to prevent the tremendous proliferation of sects and denominations that has been evident in, say, the Republic of South Africa.[3] The strong organizational position in which the pioneer denominations were placed by the land grants they received was such as to discourage other denominations from entering their areas. Comity agreements were arranged between most of the major Protestant denominations, and were largely effective. Thus the tendency in rural areas was for geographical division; some areas were 'Anglican', others 'Wesleyan', others

[1] Parker, 1960, p. 99.
[2] For a definition of this term, see Pauw, 1960, pp. 41–2. Also Sundkler, 1961, p. 18.
[3] Where, in 1961, Sundkler reported over 2030 of these groups. Sundkler, 1961, p. 374.

'Roman'. Competition, where it did arise, was usually between the Roman Catholic and Protestant groups, who had no comity agreements.

The greatest multiplication of denominations was found in the urban areas. When members of the various churches left their homes to work in the towns they set up congregations of their own denominations in their new environment. Thus, those which had been carefully separated by comity agreements in the rural scene, found themselves side by side. Conflict between them, however, was not particularly severe since they drew their adherents from distinct tribal and geographical units, and there was no great tendency for their members to cross the lines of demarcation set thereby. The strongest conflict was between these groups as a whole and the younger proselytizing denominations which did not draw their membership from a rural base.

There was also a tendency in the towns for individual ministers to split off from parent denominations and start independent churches. Two factors contributed to this: the fact that in the urban situation, free from the restrictions of traditional authority, personal ability and ambition had more scope for expression, and the fact that new church groups could more easily grow than in the country where their members would have to negotiate with the parent church concerning the education of their children.

Between 1920 and 1935 this fissiparous development in the towns (comparable with what Sundkler refers to as Ethiopianism) was paralleled by the rise in several rural areas of independent African Christian movements of what Sundkler has called the 'Zionist' type.[1] Some of these were introduced in the first instance by Europeans, others by Shona who had been at work in Johannesburg and come in contact with similar movements there. The Government viewed this development with disfavour; the movements were restricted, though not prohibited, and they gained a slow but steady growth in spite of the fact that they were not allowed to open schools in the reserves.

NATIONALIST POLITICS

For over fifty years national political activity in Southern Rhodesia was almost entirely in the hands of the whites, who in the

[1] Sundkler, 1961, pp. 38–50.

Referendum of 1922 voted against union with South Africa and became a self-governing colony. But after the Second World War African political activity, having developed beyond the limitations of the traditional political structure, has not contented itself with local government. From the time of the fall of the Todd Government in 1958, African political activity in Southern Rhodesia has taken the form of an essentially black nationalism, disillusioned with any thought of substantial concessions on the part of the whites and determined to win control of the government within the near future. This activity derives much of its support and guidance from the Pan-African movement based in African countries already politically independent, with which the activists feel a strong sense of unity. This unity is also in evidence in the relationship between the Shona and Ndebele, who, at least for the time, have modified their tribal differences in their common cause against the whites.

A significant development was the emergence of a second nationalist political party, led by a Congregational minister from the Ndau area of Manicaland. This organization has gained a reputation of being the party of the African intelligentsia and having a Manica bias.

Since the declaration of independence by the Rhodesian Government in November 1965, the leaders of these two nationalist parties have been prevented from giving overt leadership to the nationalist movement. Whatever the connotations that African political control would have for Shona society, African leaders are intent on pursuing a deliberate policy of 'Africanization' for both political and sentimental reasons. They glorify the specifically African past—the name of the country is to be changed to 'Zimbabwe'—and intend to renew specifically African forms of culture:

We do not want to be Europeans; we want to be Africans. The Whites thought that they could destroy our African culture, but they failed; it has only gone underground. It is still there, and we shall resurrect it. We shall take from the European culture that which can help us, but we shall blend it with our African culture, and the end result will be *African*.[1]

These sentiments, which are widely held, at present derive their strength primarily from negative reactions to white political and

[1] A résumé of a statement made in London, 17 February 1962, by the leader of the largest nationalist party, and recorded by the author.

economic domination. They cannot therefore in and of themselves be regarded as indications of the continuity and development of Shona culture in a changing society. Only an intensive study of the institutions of Shona society in their developing and contemporary aspects can identify the characteristics of this process, a study to which this present work hopes to contribute.

2

Budjga Society

BUDJGA HISTORY

BUDJGA TRADITIONAL HISTORY

The Budjga[1] live in a 760-square-mile tract of land in north-eastern Southern Rhodesia which they call 'Budjga' and the Government calls the Mtoko Native Reserve. The name is said by old Budjga men to mean 'Great Land taken by the Conqueror', and reflects the traditional history of the Budjga peoples. According to this history, the ancestors of the present-day Budjga lived in Mungari, a remote area in the Zambesi Valley near Tete in Portuguese East Africa, probably until the sixteenth century. At that time one of their leaders, Nohureka, ranging to the south-west, came upon the well-watered highlands now known as Mtoko and determined to possess them. To this end he had to dislodge the incumbents, a people of whom little is said except that they were ruled by Makate, a chief with great magical powers. Conquest was achieved only by the exercise of magic by Nohureka himself; Makate and his people fled to the east, where it is said that they disappeared into a large stone mountain never to be seen again.

In his occupation of the territory Nohureka was assisted by two other leaders, Zvimbiru and Nyakutanda. Victory having been achieved, the three of them divided up the land, Nohureka taking

[1] Properly in Shona usage *VaBudjga* (sing. *muBudjga*). In general the Shona prefixes will be omitted from this text. No consistent spelling of the name has yet evolved. Holleman, the only trained social anthropologist who has actually worked with these people, has it as 'Budya' (1953, p. vii) while Bell (1961, p. 52) uses 'Budga'. Kuper (1955) is not consistent, spelling the name 'Budja' (pp. 10, 11, 12) at times and 'Budga' at others (pp. 18, 32, 33). Mitchell (1960, p. 180) uses 'Budjga' and this is the spelling used here as being closest to the Budjga pronunciation of the word.

for himself the western and central portions, Nyakutanda taking the eastern section and Zvimbiru taking the northern portion.[1] In this way the three principal tribal sections of Budjga were established, although not under their present names, the designations in current use being the names of the chiefs reigning at the time of British occupation. The patrilineages of these three founding ancestors provide the genealogical framework for political control in each section. On their death each of the three—Nohureka, Zvimbiru and Nyakutanda—became the principal *mhondoro*, or tribal spirits, of their respective areas and are considered to exercise their influence on the welfare of the Budjga to the present day.

An interesting aspect of this traditional history with regard to Nohureka's area reflects a situation unique—to my knowledge—among the Shona tribes. According to the story, Nohureka after his great victory found his position of leadership threatened by Mapatwe, variously suggested to be either his brother or a Budjga hero of the war of conquest. Rather than involve himself in open conflict with Mapatwe, Nohureka abdicated his position in favour of Mapatwe and withdrew to the far western section of the Budjga area, but at the same time established his ritual superiority over the whole area. At his death he became the tribal spirit for both sections, whereas Mapatwe never became such a spirit. In theory Nohureka himself continues to rule directly over the area to which he withdrew through a chieftainess, Charewa, a woman who is the guardian of his spirit medium. Reciprocal relations developed between the two areas, Nohureka's approval was required for the installation of a new chief of Mtoko (the chieftainship established by Mapatwe), and the latter had to nominate a woman to the post of Charewa.[2]

---

[1] There is evidence to indicate that the section led by Zvimbiru was of Korekore origin, while that of Nyakutanda was of Mbire origin. It is possible that, contrary to popular Budjga history, their occupation of Mtoko was not simultaneous with the Budjga invasion described here. Occupants of the Nyamkowo Chiefdom (Zvimbiru Section) occasionally refer to themselves as VaNgawhe, while those of the Chimoyo Chiefdom refer to themselves at times as VaSewhe. Currently, however, it is usual for these people to identify themselves as Budjga, and as there is no significant variation in religious belief or practice between them and the Budjga of the Mtoko and Charewa Chiefdoms they are accepted as such for the purposes of this study.

[2] This description of traditional Budjga history has been distilled from various Budjga accounts, none of which agree in all details.

THE BUDJGA AND THEIR NEIGHBOURS

The history of the past 100 years is more easily verifiable from first-hand records,[1] and is particularly useful in shedding light upon the relationship between the Budjga and their neighbours.

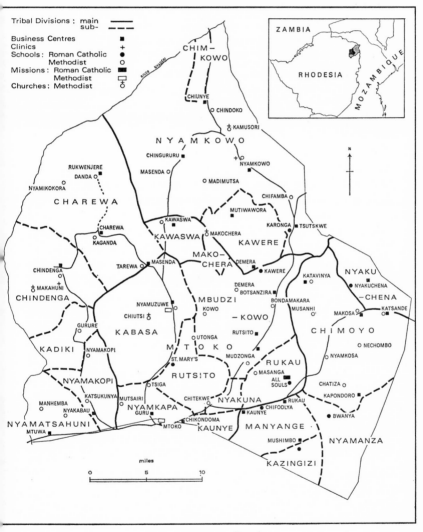

MAP I: Divisions of Budjga

[1] cf. Brendon, 1959, pp. 19–25.

In the last two decades of the nineteenth century a Goanese adventurer, Manuel Antonio de Sousa, established himself as a military power in the area south of the Ruenya River, in what is now Portuguese East Africa, with the blessing of the Portuguese authorities. About 1885 he occupied the territory of the Tonga chief Katsuru on the banks of the Mazoe, and also what is now the Mkota Special Native Area in the extreme north-east of the Mtoko District.[1] Control of this area was of great interest to the Portuguese, since the banks of the Mazoe at this point yielded considerable alluvial gold. In 1887 de Sousa (known throughout the area as Gouveia) attacked the Budjga. His attack was repulsed by Chief Mtoko, aided by men from the Charewa area.[2] A hero in the battle was Gurupira, one of Mtoko's sons. Gouveia attacked the Budjga again the following year, this time from the south. To do this he had to pass through the territory of their Shona neighbours, the Nhowe under Chief Mangwende, and he enlisted their aid by the promise of firearms. After an inconclusive battle he was forced to retreat without achieving the conquest of Budjga.

About 1891 Gouveia attacked the Barwe chief Makumbe, to the east of Budjga. Makumbe appealed to the Budjga for help, which they gave. Gouveia was captured and killed. The Budjga did not forget the assistance the Nhowe had given their enemy, and in the Rebellion of 1897 joined forces with the British against them. The Nhowe rebels were surrounded on Mt Zhombgwe, and in an attack on their position Gurupira was killed. When the Nhowe later surrendered it is reported that the Budjga, incensed at the death of their leader, killed large numbers of them in the mopping-up operations.[3]

The antipathy felt by the Budjga for the Nhowe was evidently reciprocated, for as late as 1924 a Methodist lady missionary, in a report to the Methodist Conference urging the establishment of a girls' school at Mrewa (Nhowe territory) rather than send Nhowe girls to Nyadiri Mission on the borders of Budjga, said, '. . . Wazuzulu [i.e., in this case the Nhowe] feel towards the

---

[1] See Map 1.

[2] Mtoko, the incumbent of the chieftainship established by Mapatwe, mentioned earlier, is said to have been given the name 'Mtoko' by his people for his liking of the drug dagga, which he habitually smoked through a bubble-pipe, called in Shona 'mutoko' (Simmonds, 1964, pp. 62–3). The name was used by the British to designate the District, the Native Reserve and the administrative and trading post which was established on its borders.   [3] Tendenguwo, 1964, p. 5.

Wabudgwe [VaBudjga] somewhat as the Jews did towards the Samaritans and the Native Commissioner says that girls from Mrewa will not go to Nyadiri for school'.[1]

With the arrival of the British in 1890 the Budjga found themselves with a new set of neighbours, the whites. As we have seen, relationships with the whites were more amicable than in the case of some other Shona tribes. The coming of European administration led to the establishment of a small settlement of white traders and government officials at the Mtoko Centre. Some European farms were created in the extreme south-east of what is now the Mtoko District, but on land that was not traditionally Budjga. These farms were separated from the Reserve by a belt of Purchase Area land,[2] so that the Budjga have never experienced the friction over the boundary with farm land characteristic of other parts of Southern Rhodesia. The Mtoko District is essentially an African area, and Budjga contacts with Europeans are mainly confined to those whites who live in it as missionaries, traders or Government servants.

HABITAT, SUBSISTENCE AND ECONOMY

HABITAT

The habitat of the Budjga, the Mtoko Reserve, covers an area of 486,000 acres. Its western and north-western border is the Nyadiri River, beyond which lie the tribal areas of the VaZumba and VaPfungwe, Shona tribes with whom the Budjga have traditionally been at peace. To the north-east and east, beyond the Tsutskwe and Susamoya Ranges, lie two large tracts of flat, uninhabited bush land, known to Government as 'Area C' and 'Area D'.[3] Beyond them, on the borders of Portuguese East Africa, lie two small tribal enclaves of Tonga peoples, the Mkota and Chikwizo Special Native Areas. Before the Budjga moved into their present Reserve, their territory extended into Areas 'C' and 'D'. The intention of Government was evidently to create European ranches in these areas, but the rainfall was low, surface water nonexistent and the plan was abandoned.[4] More recently dams have

---

[1] Miss Pearl Mulliken, *Methodist Conference Journal*, 1924, p. 47.
[2] *Infra*, p. 20.   [3] See Map 1.
[4] The writer has observed the Mudzi River, which rises in the Budjga highlands and flows north-east into this area, to have on several occasions a surface flow in Budjga and no surface water further downstream in Area 'D'.

been built in these areas and Budjga and others are being allowed to take occupancy under modified tribal conditions.

To the south of the Mtoko Reserve is an area devoted to small African farms averaging from 150 to 400 acres and held freehold by African farmers from all over Southern Rhodesia who qualify for occupancy under stipulated standards of agricultural achievement. This is known as the Budjga Native Purchase Area.[1]

Viewed from the air, or from the north on the highlands of Pfungwe across the Nyadiri River, the Mtoko Reserve is a spectacular sight, the oustanding visual feature being the profusion of granite hills rising above the plateau on which they stand. Some of these hills, commonly known throughout southern Africa as *koppies*, consist of piles of granite boulders, while others are solid mountains of granite, here and there peeled by exfoliation. This type of hill formation is variously known by geomorphologists as a 'sugar loaf' dome, inselberg or bornhardt, and Floyd has suggested that since it exists in classical form in Rhodesia the Shona name for this type of formation, *ruwari*, be adopted as the standard scientific name.[2]

Geomorphologists attribute all these hill forms to scarp retreat and the growth of pediments, a process known as pediplanation.[3] The pediplanes at the base of the *ruwaris* and *koppies* provide the arable areas of Budjga agriculture. Most of the soils on these pediplanes are derived from granite, and are leached coarse-grained sands of low fertility. Richer doleritic contact soils occur in a few places, mostly in the north and east.[4]

Most of Budjga lies at an altitude of between 3,000 and 4,000 feet above sea level; it is therefore considerably higher than the low veld areas to the north and east. The annual rainfall is correspondingly higher, averaging about 29 inches over a number of years. Rainfall is confined almost entirely to the five months

[1] See p. 45. The native purchase areas introduce new and interesting social conditions into the Shona scene, aspects of which are currently being studied by Mr Roger Woods.

[2] Floyd, 1959, p. 31.   [3] Floyd, 1959, p. 32.

[4] Many of the Shona reserves exhibit these combined characteristics of granite outcropping and light *sandveld* soils. In view of the fact that the Shona found the granitic *koppies* a useful refuge from the marauding Ndebele and found the light soils easier to work with their simple hand agricultural implements, it is not surprising that the Europeans found them in occupancy of these areas. The fact that the Europeans thereby occupied the richer loam and clay lands is now an added source of inter-racial friction in Rhodesia.

November–March, and it is only during this period that crops can be grown. Amounts of rainfall can fluctuate widely, and in poor years can be insufficient to produce a good crop. Excessively heavy rains can flood the fields and ruin the crops. Moreover, the onset of the rains is not regular; they may start late, or make a 'false start', when a few heavy showers are followed by several weeks without rain. In such conditions the problems of when to plant and how to secure adequate rains throughout the growing season naturally occupy the attention of the people and assume, as we shall see, great religious significance.

The natural vegetation of Budjga comprises a variety of woodland interspersed with a tall grass (*Hyparrhenia spp.*) which is used for thatching. Among the more common tree types are *Brachystegia boehmii* (*Mupfuti*), *Brachystegia spiciformis* (*Msasa*), and *Isoberlinea globiflora* (*Mnondo*). *Parinari curatellifolia* (*Muhacha*), a tree which has an edible fruit much prized by the Budjga, is found throughout the Reserve and is a prominent feature of many cleared areas, where it is allowed to remain in the middle of the fields.

Game is scarce in Budjga itself, although it abounds in the uninhabited areas to the north and east. Large troops of baboons inhabit the *koppies* and cause considerable crop damage. Leopards also live in the hills, and occasionally raid domestic livestock.

SUBSISTENCE AND ECONOMY

Agriculture is the principal mode of subsistence. Maize (*chibahwe*), sorghum (*mapfunde*), finger millet (*rapoko*) and bulrush millet (*munga*) are the staple crops, supplemented with groundnuts (*nzungu*) and cowpeas (*nyemba*). Maize and groundnuts are the principal cash crops. Various vegetables are grown near the *vleis* or rivers, where water is available for hand irrigation. Fruit trees of various types are plentiful, and a large number of mangoes are now produced for sale on the Salisbury market.

There is no fixed division of labour between the sexes, although the men mostly do the heavy ploughing and threshing, while the women perform the more routine tasks of cultivating and harvesting. Work parties, called *nhimbe*, are sometimes organized at threshing time, when neighbourhood groups of men move from field to field, the only 'payment' being the provision of ample home-brewed beer.

Cattle, goats and chickens are held in considerable numbers, and since the establishment of butcheries in the Reserve meat has become a more important item of diet. Regular stock sales are also held throughout the Reserve, and the sale of cattle has become a significant source of income. Formerly, cattle were held only for marriage and ritual purposes, and beef was only consumed on ritual occasions.

Grain and groundnuts which are not consumed locally must be marketed under the auspices of the Grain Marketing Board of the Government at set prices. In each township[1] there is at least one trader who is authorized to purchase produce under the regulations of this Board; the townships therefore become centres where Budjga farmers can obtain cash for their crops and spend it on the goods the traders offer.

LAND PRESSURE

Budjga as has already been stated covers an area of 486,000 acres, or 760 square miles, but less than one-fourth of this is available for cultivation. The area of arable land was estimated in 1964 to be only 98,773 acres.[2] The population numbers 55,941, giving a ratio of 73·6 persons per square mile, but the more significant fact is that there are 363 persons per arable square mile, so that for each man, woman or child in Budjga there are 1·76 acres of arable land.

Robinson has calculated that under traditional methods of shifting agriculture Southern Rhodesia had a carrying capacity of approximately twenty persons per square mile (based on 25 per cent usability),[3] a figure comparable to that given for Northern Rhodesia by Allan in 1945.[4] Obviously Budjga could not carry its present population with these methods. An attempt was made in the late 1930s and 1940s to centralize and stabilize arable holdings, bringing them together to form large blocks of cultivated land separated by continuous stretches of grazing. Villages were relocated in lines along the arable blocks. Relocation has made necessary the construction of new homes, and many houses are

---

[1] See Map 1. Township areas have been designated by the Government, and the establishment of stores, mills, carpentry shops, etc. is permitted only in these areas. They are known in Government parlance as 'Business Centres', and, by a curious transposition of the word into Shona, as 'shipitowni' by the Budjga.

[2] Figures supplied by the District Commissioner's Office, Mtoko.

[3] Robinson, 1953, p. 3.   [4] Allan, 1945, p. 14.

now built of sun-dried brick instead of by the traditional pole-and-mud method.[1]

However, even with improved methods Budjga is no longer able to sustain its growing population by agriculture alone; overstocking and overcropping have damaged the agricultural potential of the land to the point where many of its inhabitants must seek an income from other occupations. The older people do not see the explanation of their difficulties in over-population and poor husbandry; they speak of the 'good old times' and blame the present misfortunes on 'Chirungu', a term used to cover various aspects of the white man's culture, including his religion. They see as the remedy a return by all the Budjga to their traditional worship.[2]

Some Budjga have successfully turned to various forms of entrepreneurial activity in Budjga itself as store-keepers, tea shop operators and transport vehicle owners. But by far the largest number supplement their income by periods of wage-earning activity in the towns, especially in the capital city of Salisbury, 94 miles away. Although precise figures are not available, the District Commissioner's estimate that approximately 45 per cent of Budjga men are away at work in urban areas or on European farms at any given time is roughly consistent with the results of surveys made by Garbett at Musanhi (46·4 per cent)[3] and Floyd in Uzumba (46·7 per cent).[4] It should be pointed out that, although these men may be employed away from Budjga for long periods of time, few go with the intention of staying away permanently; they remain very much a part of Budjga society, commuting back and forth at week-ends via the frequent bus services and making an active contribution to tribal life.[5]

[1] In 1951 the Native Land Husbandry Act was passed by the Southern Rhodesian Government, which sought to improve African agriculture in the country by the abolition of tribal tenure of land and the introduction of individual tenure. Garbett, 1961, and Floyd, 1959, have written extensively on the implications of this Act. It was never implemented in Budjga, and appears to have been tacitly abandoned there, at least for the present, for political reasons.

[2] A situation not unique to Budjga. An exellent example of similar sentiment in modern Tanzania is described in 'Letter from Mbugwe, Tanganyika', *Africa*, Vol. xxxv, No. 2, pp. 198–208, by G. Mbee.   [3] Garbett, 1960, p. 16.

[4] Floyd, 1959, p. 151. Mitchell (1958, p. 2) has estimated that 57 per cent of all able-bodied men between the ages of 15 and 54 in Southern Rhodesia are employed outside their own tribal area.

[5] A situation closely parallel to that described for the Tonga of Malawi. (Van Velsen, 1961, pp. 230–41.)

C

LOCAL POLITICAL AND JUDICIAL ORGANIZATION

THE TRIBE (*nyika*)

Budjga tribal organization conforms generally to what has been described by Holleman for the central Shona.[1] The largest territorially defined unit is the *nyika* (tribe, chieftaincy, tribal domain). It is controlled by a hereditary chief, the *ishe*.[2] Succession is collateral in the male line of descent from the founder. Collaterals on one generation level must be exhausted before any member of the next generation can succeed. The chieftainship is supposed to rotate among a number of lineages (*imba*). In the frequent succession disputes the medium (*svikiro*) of the tribal spirit is called upon to indicate the right successor.[3]

The tribe is divided into the important minority belonging to the patrilineage of the chief, and the bulk of the population, usually made up of other lineages. The latter are sometimes given important political responsibilities, and in return acknowledge the political superiority of the chief's lineage. The political unity thus achieved operates within the limits of a common territory. This territory is held by the tribe as a body; individual members share in its resources under the control of the chief or his representatives. It is believed that the ancestors who established the tribal occupancy of the land are still its spiritual owners and that their spirits still in a real sense govern its affairs.

The *nyika* is sub-divided into wards (*dunhu*) which are frequently, but not always, under the hereditary control of members of the major segments of the chief's lineage, called *sadunhu*. This word has definite territorial connotations, and the ward functions primarily as a land unit.

Although Budjga local organization conforms in general to the Shona pattern, it has several atypical features. Map 1 shows the

[1] Holleman, 1952, pp. 15-22.
[2] Sometimes in Budjga the term *tenzi* is used, a word which is used in the standard Shona New Testament for 'Lord'.
[3] Such succession disputes are now endemic in much of Shona country. It can be argued that they are a function of the modern Reserve system. The history of many Shona tribes is one of segmentation and migration, a process which prevented the formation of deep genealogies. Now that this is no longer possible, the range of collateral aspirants becomes so large and their genealogical credentials so difficult to evaluate, that dispute is inevitable.

division of Budjga. Disregarding Nyakuchena, which is a little enclave of various groups located by the Government in one corner of the Reserve, we have four chiefdoms: Mtoko, Chimoyo, Charewa and Nyamkowo. The ruling clan of Nyamkowo has *nzou* (elephant) as its *mutupo*, *mukotami* as its *chidawo*.[1] The ruling clan of Chimoyo has *tsoko* (monkey) as its *mutupo*, *chirongo* as its *chidawo*. The ruling clan of Mtoko has *shumba* (lion) as its *mutupo*, *nyamuziwa* as its *chidawo*. But note that the ward heads of Charewa are of the same clan; their *mutupo* is *shumba*, their *chidawo nyamuziwa*. Thus in this case we have two sections of the same clan, claiming descent from a common ancestor, acting in political autonomy but observing the reciprocal ritual responsibilities already described.[2]

Attention is also called to the Kawere ward of the Nyamkowo chiefdom. The ward head Kawere is of the Mtoko clan, but Budjga traditional history has it that the original Kawere fought with another son of Mtoko, who therefore sent him to live in Nyamkowo's country. Thus, the soil of this ward belongs to Nyamkowo, and land disputes are judged in Nyamkowo's court, while the people are Mtoko's, so disputes concerning inter-personal relationships are taken to Mtoko's court.

The only other ward in the Nyamkowo chiefdom is Chimkoko, a small area in the extreme north. Thus in effect Nyamkowo rules directly over most of his chiefdom.

Roads, schools, cattle dips and business centres have developed in the Reserve with little regard to tribal boundaries. A school situated near these boundaries will draw people from two or more chiefdoms and/or wards. These factors tend to minimize the significance of tribal divisions for the Budjga in a wide range of social situations. The role of the chief is most important in matters relating to traditional ritual, land allocation and judicial procedures; it is of less consequence in matters involving marketing and non-traditional religion. The structural position of the Budjga chief in itself carries with it little power, only the potential for it. Chimoyo is known as a 'weak' chief, Nyamkowo as a 'strong' one. The one has utilized his position to create a situation of power and influence, the other has not.[3]

---

[1] For the meaning of these terms, see p. 27. [2] *Supra*, p.16.

[3] At the beginning of my research in Budjga, being unaware of these subtleties of the power structure, I arranged directly with Chief Chimoyo for some assistants

THE VILLAGE

The village is usually composed of a nucleus of agnatic kinsmen of the headman with their wives and children, several cognatically related households, and perhaps a small number of unrelated friends and their families. Patrilocal marriage, in the sense that the wife moves to her husband's residence and not vice versa, is the rule.

The Budjga village used to be a rather unstable unit, changing in size and composition as some families split off and others attached themselves to the headman. There was no fixed boundary; the village could extend its area until it met the fields of another village. With the increase in population and the establishment of centralization this pattern has changed. Villages are now built on surveyed lines[1] along the edges of the fields, with definite boundaries.

Budjga villages can comprise anything from 15 to over 100 persons. The headman is often, though not always, a member of the lineage of the ward head or chief. He has the responsibility of providing land for his people to cultivate, and of arbitrating minor disputes. He also has the onerous task of collecting the head tax levied by the Government from each of the tax-paying males registered in the book in his possession. The use of these tax books has led to the replacement of the headman's traditional title, *samusha*, by the term *sabuku*, literally 'keeper of the book', and possession of one is the badge of office. Succession to the position and title of *sabuku* is often from father to son. Frequently a man finds the duties too burdensome, or wishes to go and work in town; he may then pass the office on to a brother or son. As with the position of chief, the power involved in the office of *sabuku* depends a great deal upon the man holding it; to some it is a burden carried grudgingly, others seek to use it as a springboard to wider political power by encouraging the establishment of schools, churches or anything that will increase the influence of their 'name'.

to do research in his area. One of the ward heads opposed their activity, and as his influence was greater than that of the chief in the area the project had to be abandoned, even though it enjoyed the blessing of the latter. More will be said about Chief Nyamkowo in a later chapter.

[1] Villages are now sometimes referred to as 'maraini', i.e. 'lines'.

LEGAL SYSTEM

The legal system is hung on the same framework as the political one just described. Disputes between members of the same village are arbitrated by the village headman. Those which cannot be settled at this level are referred to the ward headman's court, and appeals from this are referred to the chief. Under traditional law he had full jurisdiction over members of the tribe and dealt with matters considered so serious as to affect the whole community, such as homicide, witchcraft and offences against the chief's person. Under the present Government this power has been severely curtailed, although considerable jurisdiction remains in civil cases.

Budjga political leaders have few religious functions; indeed religious and political offices are rarely combined in the same individual. The village headman, ward headman and chief, apart from their individual responsibilities to the ancestral spirits of their own clan, do have the important duty of initiating arrangements for certain seasonal rituals. But the actual management of these occasions, the organization of the local manifestations of Budjga religion, and religious leadership in times of crisis, are in the hands of individuals other than political leaders.

KINSHIP ORGANIZATION

The Budjga are divided into exogamous patrilineal totemic clans, which are identified by the *mutupo* (clan-name) and *chidawo* (sub-clan name). The significance of the clan (*rudzi*) is twofold: it regulates marriage and it provides the genealogical framework for the politically dominant lineages.

The *chizwarwa*, a group of greater ritual significance, consists of the sons and agnatic successors. Holleman defines it as: 'People belonging to one *rudzi* (patrilineage) who live together and come together for ritual purposes (*kupirirana*).'[1] At ritual gatherings of the *chizwarwa* it is the spirit of the common *tateguru* (father's father) that is called upon for support, and is expected to be the intermediary between the living and the hierarchy of the ancestral spirits.

A smaller functioning kinship group in Shona society is the *mhuri* (kindred, family). This is a group of kindred living together in such a way as to have a sense of cohesion. Its head (*samhuri*)

[1] Holleman, 1952, p. 24. The assertion that the members of a *chizwarwa* always live together is not currently true for the Budjga.

exercises an *ad hoc* authority based on the esteem of the members; his position does not carry the political or genealogical superiority of the office of *samusha*, 'headman'.

Holleman describes the functions of a comparable kinship system of the central Shona in the following terms:

(a) it provides a definite pattern of social order in which any two persons or classes of persons of the same sex, closely or remotely related by blood or by marriage, are placed in a position of relative superiority or inferiority;

(b) it regulates the reproduction of unilineal and exogamous kin-groups, with due respect to Native conceptions of incest, and the existing order referred to above.[1]

The first of these aspects he calls the 'rank aspect' of the system, the second the 'organic aspect'.

The rank aspect, faithfully reflected in its terminology, is the more significant for this study. As between agnates of the same sex there is always an element of relative superiority or subordination. The hierarchy of the living links up with that of the dead, whose spirits also have their places in the agnatic order. Budjga religion is thus firmly linked with the lineage system, and through it with the society as a whole. Furthermore, through it a man's ritual status and function are defined and assured, and he becomes an indispensable link in the hierarchy himself.

As regards affinal relationships, lineages are ranked as 'wife-providers' or 'wife-obtainers', the wife-providers being higher. Both affinal and cognatic relationships between lineages are significant for the spirit of a dead man, particularly when they are called upon to perform the *bona* ceremonies which would involve ritual danger to his agnatic kin. The most prominent cognate is the uterine nephew or cousin, who does not share in this potential danger, and is furthermore in a position of close intimacy with the deceased, since in the Budjga system the relationship of maternal uncle and uterine nephew is particularly close. Analysis thus reveals a close relationship between the kinship system and both the ideology and ritual of Shona religion.

BUDJGA MARRIAGE

Of special significance for this study are certain aspects of Budjga marriage. The transfer of bride-wealth cattle for women acquired

[1] Holleman, 1952, p. 30.

in marriage has already been mentioned. Budjga bride-wealth includes money as well as cattle and is paid in two parts, *rutsambo* and *rovora*. *Rutsambo*, consisting of money, clothes and other items, confers marital rights, while *rovora*, preferably consisting of cattle, confers rights of paternity. After the transfer of *rutsambo*, (and perhaps also a small instalment of *rovora*), a conjugal relationship can be initiated[1]; it is only later when children are born that the full amount of *rovora* is paid, and if there are no children the man and his family will sometimes withdraw from the contract. Budjga marriage has thus traditionally involved a cumulative series of events rather than a single procedure as in Western and Christian modes.

That the transfer of *rutsambo* and *rovora* has a stabilizing effect upon Budjga marriage is well recognized by them. Older Budjga today lament the rise in *matorwa*, whereby young people elope to the towns and live together without the consent of their parents or any transfer of *rovora*. Often vague promises are made to pay in the future, but since such unions are often not permanent the promises are never fulfilled.

On the death of a husband of a woman for whom *rovora* has been paid she should be inherited by one of the man's brothers, preferably one whose uterine sister has provided by her marriage the *rovora* cattle which brought the woman into the family. Should the woman refuse to be taken by any of the rightful heirs a claim may be lodged against her agnates for the return of the *rovora* cattle, especially if she is still of child-bearing age.

usavira

A prominent feature of Budjga social life, found to a greater extent among them than in the other Shona tribes, is *usavira*, a formalized pact of friendship contracted between non-related friends, especially men. Partners in an *usavira* pact are supposed to render to each other unlimited assistance and generosity. This relationship becomes especially important at the death of one of them, when the other has an obligation to perform the necessary undertaking duties. The relationship is supposed to perpetuate itself in the children of the contracting parties.

[1] Great value was placed on the virginity of the bride at this point. Garbett states that this is not so for the Zezuru (1960, p. 14).

3

Budjga Traditional Religion

The traditional religion of the Budjga is still to be found among them today, a functioning system of beliefs and rituals to which a large number of them adheres. It is difficult to assess what the proportion is; at this point the student encounters the problem that plagues the study of religion generally, that of establishing adequate criteria for determining 'adherence' to any system of ideas and/or ritual. In a later chapter we shall present quantitative material based on a survey of a representative Budjga community which shows that over 70 per cent of the adult population have no official connection with any Christian group; this figure is probably roughly correct throughout Budjga. But we cannot therefore automatically assume that all these people are practising adherents of Budjga Traditional Religion. Although there are no other organized religious systems in Budjga apart from the Christian groups,[1] it is important to recognize that to some Budjga, particularly of the younger generation, personal commitment to any given religious ideology has little significance, and they rarely participate in any religious ritual, except as spectators. It is perhaps sufficient to note at this stage that the religious system described in this chapter is that practised with a high degree of conformity by a significant section of Budjga society, and that it extends its influence even to those Budjga who are not its faithful adherents.

I have avoided the word 'paganism' as a name for the traditional religion of the Budjga. To the Budjga themselves the word carries derogatory connotations, and etymologically it has little useful meaning for our analysis. Nor can the system simply be called 'Budjga Religion', since this is a study of the contemporary situation, and the inclusive term 'Budjga Religion' contains many other elements. The term 'Budjga Traditional Religion' has

[1] Budjga are aware of Islam since many of the migrant labourers from Nyasaland who pass through Mtoko on their way to Salisbury are Moslems, but this faith has never established itself in the area.

therefore been used to refer to the religion to which the Budjga adhered exclusively for several hundred years before the introduction of Christianity, and to which many of them now own allegiance. Those who are active adherents of this faith are referred to in this text as 'Traditional Religionists' or 'Traditionalists'.[1]

A Traditional Religionist, if asked what his religion is, would probably reply, 'Ndinonamata midzimu', 'I pray to the spirits'. No concise term distinguishing an adherent of the Traditional Religion from a Christian is available in the Shona language. When asked to classify people by religion Budjga will sometimes speak of a man as *munamati*, 'one who prays', meaning thereby that he is a Christian. This illustrates that traditional Budjga Society has not been highly 'ritualistic'; ritual activity has never formed part of a regular daily, weekly or even monthly sequence. This kind of regular ritual sequence, which Christianity provides, conveys to Budjga such an impression of religious intensity as to result in the award of the term *vanamati*, 'those who pray', to its adherents.

On the other hand the Budjga could certainly be termed a 'religious' people. The human life-cycle, the vagaries of personal health and good fortune, the success of agricultural enterprise and the political life of the tribe are all given supernatural interpretation. The phenomenon of spirit possession is a common occurrence. The beliefs connected with these phenomena are not codified, nor is there an elaborate body of myths to incorporate and transmit them. Instead they find symbolic expression in the rituals that do occur from time to time and occasional interpretation by the few ritual specialists—the diviners and spirit mediums —that do exist.[2]

MAN AS SPIRIT

The Budjga recognize that in every person there exists that unique combination of characteristics that constitute a human personality.

---

[1] These words, it should be noted, are *not* used as inclusive terms to designate all non-Christian Budjga, since, as has been pointed out, many in this group are not active adherents of the Traditional Religion. Elsewhere in the text the useful term 'Gentile' is used for this purpose. This word does not have the pejorative connotations for most Africans that the term 'pagan' has, and has a history of application by various religious groups (i.e. the Jews and the Mormons) for those 'outside the faith'.

[2] Some of the material presented here was obtained from such specialists, but most of it came from Budjga 'laymen', often under the stimulus of ritual conditions.

To this psychic entity they give the name *mweya*, which can be roughly translated 'soul'.[1] For the Budjga the *mweya*, although it develops in a temporal milieu as the individual grows, is in itself immortal. It is the 'life principle' of a man, incarnate in him and developing its personal and unique characteristics while he is alive, but surviving the death of the body. During the lifetime of an individual it is to some extent under the tutelage of the spirits of his patrilineage, and in particular of that of the *sekuru*, the paternal grandfather. If the latter did not happen to be dead at the time of the person's birth, it is usually thought that his paternal grandfather undertakes this special interest. It is sometimes maintained that a woman's special tutelage comes from the paternal grandfather, but others assert that this would be incongruous for a woman and that the sister of this *sekuru*[2] (or if there is none, any half or classificatory sister of the *sekuru*) provides it. It is, however, not the perpetutation of the *mweya* in the post-mortem existence of the individual that is important to Budjga thought, but rather its transformation into a *mudzimu*, whereby it takes its place in the spiritual hierarchy of the ancestors.

The concept of the *mudzimu* (pl. *midzimu*, or *vadzimu*)[3] is basic to Budjga religious thought. Following common practice, we translate the word here as 'spirit'. The departed ancestors, who continue to exist in the spirit world, are *midzimu*, and live in a collective society of these *midzimu*. To attain to this status and society is conceived to be the ultimate good of man's metaphysical existence, and as it is—as we shall show—in a sense a projection and culmination of human society, temporal ends are often subordinated to the attainment of this *summum bonum* in the spirit world.

---

[1] The Shona words *mwoyo* and *unhu* are at times used to indicate 'personality', but only with reference to the manifestations of the personality, and not with regard to the life principle of its existence.

[2] Called *ambuya* or *vasamukadzi*.

[3] *Midzimu* is the general term, indicating a collective unity, while *vadzimu* is more personal and is used by individuals to refer particularly to those lineage spirits who are remembered by name. The Shona words *mweya* and *mudzimu* bear a close etymological relationship to words used to denote similar concepts in a large number of Bantu languages. Willoughby cites instances of this relationship from places as far apart as Fernando Po, Bechuanaland, Congo and Uganda (Willoughby, 1928, pp. 10–11). The word *mudzimu* belongs to a class of Shona nouns which denote 'objects which are light, move, change, grow, produce or, in general, which contain some principle of life and production, a notion intimately connected with that of "power of growing up" like a tree'. (Torrend, 1921, p. 74.)

An individual's *mudzimu*, although it is conceived to have begun its existence at the time of his birth,[1] is held to be both a part of, and yet separate from, his corporeal existence. It is not incarnate within him, but is, as it were, a separate 'shadow' existence beside him.[2] This concept is not the object of precise definition or speculation on the part of the Budjga, for to them the idea of the development of the *mudzimu* is more important than the question of its locus. Furthermore, during the lifetime of the individual it is not his own *mudzimu* that is the active agent of the ancestral spirit world but rather that of the tutelary spirit, the *sekuru*[3] (or its female counterpart). During the lifetime of the individual, therefore, there is no conscious attempt to develop the *mudzimu* as distinct from the fulfilment of the normal biological and social life cycle. It is in the fulfilment of the latter, and particularly in the creation of progeny, that a man fulfils the conditions necessary for a satisfactory existence in the post-mortem world of the *midzimu*. The bearing of children is of especial importance, since one of the requisites of a happy existence in the spirit world is the existence of descendants on earth who can perform the appropriate ceremonies for the benefit of the *midzimu* from time to time, and through whom it can perpetuate its contacts with Budjga society.[4] These

[1] Some informants hold that the first cry of a newly-born child is evidence that the nascent *mudzimu* is present.

[2] In this I differ from what is otherwise an excellent treatment of this subject by Holleman (1953, pp. 27–9). Holleman implies that the *mudzimu* is incarnate within a person during his lifetime, that its maturation is linked to physical maturation, and that it 'comes out' (*kubuda*) of the body at death. In the place of this analysis I have offered the one given above, for the following reasons:

(a) Holleman's treatment is not corroborated by a general consensus of the various informants whom I have questioned on this subject, some of whom were from the Charewa area, the scene of his enquiries.

(b) The term 'come out' (*kubuda*) has in this context revelational, not spatial, connotations. On the death of a man his spirit, now freed from mortal ties, can 'come out' (*kubuda*) and reveal itself as an independent and active entity.

(c) The importance of physical maturation, which Holleman properly notes, lies not in any quasi-corporal links between the *mudzimu* and the body but rather in that it is the prerequisite of reproduction. Procreation, not simply adulthood, is necessary before the *mudzimu* can take its proper place in the spirit world, the fact emphasizing the essentially hierarchical nature of that world which will be discussed shortly.

[3] Such activity may become apparent if a person becomes ill—although illness can be attributable to many other spiritual beings as well. Holleman, 1953, p. 27.

[4] The spirit of a child that dies is conceived to be immature and of little consequence, while that of an adult without issue is often regarded as restless, seeking to 'enter' a *muzukuru* ('grandchild') among its agnatic or cognatic relatives. Holleman, 1953, p. 28.

concepts are consistent with the basically hierarchical nature of the Budjga spirit world, in which there is one single continuum, Budjga society being only its lower extremity.

Thus it is that the Budjga rites of passage, with the exception of those connected with death, are invested with very little specifically religious content; their main significance is social, for it is only in the fulfilment of social responsibilities that spiritual fulfilment is finally achieved. The ritual connected with pregnancy and childbirth is concerned mainly with avoidance and restricted sexual behaviour on the part of the mother and father, and is directed as much against the potential danger that the situation can bring to them and others as it is to the protection of the child. Magical charms are attached to the child, but these are for protection against witchcraft (*uroyi*) and not for the development of the *mudzimu*. Puberty is likewise marked by observances of avoidance, the emphasis being upon the dangers that the onset of menstruation brings to persons close to the girl, and not on any supposed change in spiritual status in the girl herself.

The Budjga perform no initiation rituals of the elaborate type found among the Nguni and other southern Bantu.[1] Circumcision is not practised.[2]

Marriage and parenthood, as we have already indicated, are of great religious importance to the individual, since they mark a change of spiritual status for him. A man who is a husband and father may pray directly to his *vadzimu* on matters of personal concern; before he has attained this status he must present his requests to them through his father.

It is therefore of interest that the rituals surrounding marriage and childbirth have little reference to this spiritual change of status and concern themselves primarily with social relationships. The marriage ceremonies and the subsequent *masungiro* ritual relate mainly to maintenance of social equilibrium between the lineages and individuals concerned. The rituals of childbirth, as has been previously mentioned, are concerned with avoidance and protection against witchcraft. The notion, then, that during the lifetime of an individual it is his proper fulfilment in society rather

---

[1] Schapera, 1937, pp. 100–4.

[2] Kuper, 1955, p. 20, states that the Barwe, Wesa and Manyika practise circumcision, but my own research has shown that this is not general among these Shona neighbours of the Budjga.

than the performance of religious ritual that prepares his *mudzimu* for a happy spirit existence is borne out by this examination of Budjga rites of passage. The transitional stages of a man's life are surrounded by ceremonies which emphasize his status in the society rather than his relationship to the *midzimu*. The success of the latter is dependent on the well-being of the former.

The one exception to this generalization concerns the ceremonies surrounding death and its aftermath. In them the religious and spiritual context is paramount. This is not surprising, for they deal with the period when the individual has left the immediate world of Budjga society and is in the most critical period of transition in the development of his spirit life.

Mortuary rituals usually include four basic elements: (1) the ceremonies following death and burial; (2) the discovery, with the help of an *nganga* (diviner), of the cause of death; (3) the ceremonies inducting the *mudzimu* into the spirit world; (4) the ceremonies to distribute the estate of the deceased. It should be noted that the procedures described here are those for a person who has been married and had children. Deceased children are accorded perfunctory burial ceremonies, while an unmarried adult is often buried with a *mupini*, an axe handle without the metal head, a symbol said to indicate incompletion and broken continuity. Alternatively, and with less subtle symbolism, the handle is said to be 'his wife'.

DEATH AND BURIAL

It is considered desirable that a person die at his own home. Away from his home the procedures described here would be difficult or impossible to perform and there would be danger that his spirit would become a wandering spirit, or *shawe*.[1]

Immediately after the death, preparations are begun for burial, and friends and relations are notified. The agnatic kin are responsible for the general management of this and the subsequent rituals, but at this stage the body of the deceased is a source of mystical danger to them. The unity of their kin group has been broken by an as yet unidentified power,[2] and until it has been

---

[1] *Infra*, pp. 50–3. Gelfand, 1959, pp. 196–9, describes the procedures followed by relatives in the case of death and burial away from home among other Shona groups.

[2] That is, the cause of the deceased's death, to be later identified by the diviner.

restored by the ritual which unites the deceased with the *vadzimu* of the family the members are vulnerable to this 'power', and to the possible wrath of the departed spirit as well. Hence the responsibility of handling the corpse falls to the affines, or preferably to an *usavira*[1] partner if the dead man had one.[2]

The body is washed, anointed with oil, dressed and placed on a reed mat inside the deceased's hut. Burial takes place soon after, usually in one or two days, as soon as the grave has been dug and the relatives have had time to assemble. Before interment friends and relatives usually pay a visit to the hut containing the corpse, to 'be seen' and leave a small token gift, the *chemo*.[3] It is considered important that all the relatives should make their appearance, otherwise the spirit of the departed would be displeased. If they are away at work it is sometimes difficult to locate and inform them, but those in charge are usually reluctant to postpone the burial until their arrival, since in the warm climate of Mtoko decomposition sets in very quickly.

Just before the corpse is taken from the hut a wooden bowl, in which has been placed some *nhope* (unfermented beer which has been specially prepared), is held up outside the door, and the *tsuri*, a small wooden flute, is blown over it, once to the east and once to the west. It is said that this is to inform the *midzimu* of the arrival of a new member. The site of the grave may be a cave in a nearby *koppie*, or more frequently an anthill near the village. The interment itself is usually a simple affair with the minimum of ceremony. A few small possessions may be buried with the body, together with a small calabash full of *nhope* and a *bikiro*, or offering of tobacco. No animal sacrifice is made, although a goat or beast (called the *fungaidzo*) may be killed for the undertakers.

The period beginning immediately after death and running

[1] *Supra*, p. 29.

[2] These people are not completely invulnerable to the mystical danger; hence they must be careful to wash their bodies after their tasks. But in their case the risk is reduced to the minimum. This mystical danger from the corpse is sometimes referred to as 'heat', and marsh grass (*nhokwe*) may be placed in the grave to 'cool' it. The association of the idea of heat with the ritual danger created by death is found elsewhere in Africa (e.g. among the Lovedu, J. D. and E. J. Krige, 1954, pp. 65, 68; and the Tswana, Pauw, 1960, p. 34) and is pervasive in Shona thought. (Its opposite, 'coolness' (*kutonhodza*) is regarded as the ritual ideal. Holleman, 1953, pp. 37–8, Powell, 1952, p. 9. The latter's translation of '*ta ku tonhodza*' as 'we have cooked you down' is surely the result of a typographical error!)

[3] The money thus collected is sometimes used to pay the diviner who is later consulted as to the cause of death. Holleman, 1953, p. 1.

through a few days after burial is one of great mystical danger, not only for the relatives of the deceased, but for the spirit of the deceased itself. During this period his *mudzimu* has become an independent and active entity, but since the proper rituals have not yet been performed to permit it to join the spiritual hierarchy it is 'outside',[1] restless and insecure. It may hover around the body and even appear as a visible shadow (*mvuri*). Should this happen it is usually taken as an indication that the *mudzimu* is displeased with some element of the proceedings, possibly the absence of a friend or relative, who is hastily sent for.[2]

A week or two after the burial the ceremony of *mharadzo* takes place. A goat is killed and the meat divided and handed out indiscriminately to all present—friends and relatives—'to show that our fellowship has been broken'. As it is held some time later, most relatives can be in attendance at this ceremony, and it provides an alternative means of ritual participation for those who could not arrive in time for the actual burial.

SECOND PROCEDURE: DETERMINATION OF THE CAUSE OF DEATH

After the burial ceremonies the *mudzimu* is thought to be wandering about, 'in the air', 'in the bush' or possibly residing in a *mutuwa* tree.[3] Several months are likely to elapse before the subsequent rituals are performed. The agnates must ascertain the cause of death, which task requires the services of a diviner. Preferably this individual should be from a good distance away, and considerable time is taken up in the necessary arrangements.

---

[1] The words 'outside' (*kunze*) and 'inside' (*mukati*) are constantly used by the Shona in their discussion of the *midzimu*. It must be remembered that, as has already been mentioned, the use of these words implies concepts of status and ritual position rather than spatial categories.

[2] It must be emphasized that the *mudzimu*, the now spiritual and indestructible ego of the man, continues to exhibit the same attributes of personality that were evident in life. Tracey, in an article (1934, pp. 39–52) that is otherwise so valuable as to demand refutation, contends that this is not so: 'Soul, in the sense of a living being, to the Mashona has both entity and human attributes. Spirit, however, has entity but no human attributes. Evidence of this may be seen in the fact that a woman may be accused of infidelity to her dead husband until secondary obsequies have been performed and he has become, so to speak, super-personal—i.e., a *mudzimu* spirit' (p. 45). What Tracey has failed to realize is that the change in status of the woman is not a result of any supposed change in the *mudzimu*, but is due to the fact that at these 'secondary obsequies' the estate of a man, including his wives, is distributed in such a way that he no longer has any claim to them.

[3] *Kirkia acuminata*.

The procedure for finding out the cause of death is known as *gata*. Most Budjga informants assert that death is attributable to malevolence—either from witchcraft or an avenging spirit.[1] In the matter of illness and death the natural and social orders are linked together, in the same way that they are in matters concerning rain and the fertility of the soil. The 'why' of any variation in the natural order of things is always interpreted in terms of human behaviour and social relationships.

In practice, however, the Budjga recognize that death may be due to natural causes, and particularly in the case of an old person the *gata* ceremony may not be performed. The ceremony and the belief behind it thus appear to be invoked only when there has been a high degree of social tension in the deceased's immediate environment, or when death occurs in a sudden or unusual way. When the *gata* procedure is followed the diviner may provide anti-witchcraft medicine, or may prescribe some compensation to be paid to members of the family of the alleged avenging spirit.

THIRD PROCEDURE: THE INDUCTION RITUAL

Even after the cause of death has been ascertained there is still likely to be some delay before the third stage, the induction ritual, and the distribution of the estate can be accomplished. The chief reason is that for the final rites a wide circle of relatives must be present, and the most convenient season for travel is when there is a lull in agricultural activity after the harvest in June. It is possible, too, that the large quantity of beer necessary for these occasions requires the storing of grain for a considerable period. There are of course exceptions to this period of long delay, and Holleman cites one case in which the final rites were held within ten days after burial. The deceased had left an unmarried son and a young widow, and it was feared that they were likely to 'burn the grave'[2] by committing illicit sexual intercourse if the ritual was postponed too long.[3]

Among the Budjga the ceremony that I have called the 'Induction Ritual' is known as *bona*.[4] The term is perhaps derived from

---

[1] *Infra*, p. 57.

[2] *Ku pisa guwa*, i.e., to violate the regulations surrounding the estate before the appropriate ceremonies have been performed.

[3] Holleman, 1953, p. 2.

[4] Which among many other Shona groups, roughly corresponds to the *kurowa guwa* ritual. Gelfand, 1959, pp. 189–93.

the verb '*ku pona*' meaning 'to live'. I have called this an Induction Ritual because it marks the transition in the status of the *mudzimu* from being 'outside' the hierarchy of the spirits to full incorporation in their ranks. Furthermore, in the family rituals (meat sacrifices, beer libations) the 'inside' spirits are mentioned and sacrificed to, while a spirit that is 'outside' is not thus propitiated.

The ritual itself, which has been fully documented for us by Holleman,[1] is the most extensive of the Budjga family rituals, and its performance can take several days. It involves the preparation of large quantities of beer, much of which is consumed by the participants and some of which is poured out in libation at the grave. In addition to the libation a goat is sacrificed at the graveside, part of the meat being set out for the spirit. These ceremonies are preceded by a night of dancing and singing at the home site to 'honour the spirit', and an expedition is made into the forest to procure a freshly-cut branch of *mutuwa* tree and bring it to the grave. This latter act is symbolic of the bringing of the spirit from the 'outside' to the grave. The sacrifices of beer and meat and their accompanying ritual are conceived to usher the *mudzimu* into the presence of his spiritual forebears well provided with food and drink. They have awaited his arrival in the anticipation of such gifts, and thus provided he can expect to be cordially and honourably received. Thus received he has attained a place 'inside' the spiritual hierarchy which is timeless, and he is 'mentioned' with the others in the prayers and sacrifices of the living.

Sometimes after the *bona* ceremony has been held the *mudzimu*, by bringing sickness on one of his descendants, may indicate his desire for a further ceremony, called '*Ku pinza mumba*' ('to bring into the house'). A small hut is built in the deceased's village, a hole dug in the floor and ceremonial beer poured into this as a libation with the words 'Now we have brought you right back into the house'. This ceremony serves as a demonstration of the *mudzimu's* ability to communicate with his descendants and their willingness to supply his wants.

FOURTH PROCEDURE: DIVISION OF THE ESTATE (*ku gadzwa kwe nhaka*)

There remains the settlement of the deceased's estate. Among the Budjga, as in most of the other Shona groups, it is imperative that

[1] Holleman, 1953, pp. 11–16.

D

the *bona* ritual, or its equivalent, be performed before the estate is settled, although this is not universally done. At this ceremony the deceased's small movable property (which has been left in his hut since death), his cattle, wives, and other assets are distributed, usually under the supervision of an executrix, the sister, real or classificatory, of the deceased. With the completion of this ceremony the deceased's temporal concerns have been ended, and henceforth his world will be that of the *midzimu*, from where he will make his presence and wishes known from time to time to his still-living descendants.

It should be emphasized that this presentation of the Budjga burial and post-mortem rites is a composite one drawn from a number of cases; there is considerable variation, as might be expected from the fact that the ceremonies are conducted by men who have no professional religious status, and whose experience in these matters is necessarily limited. The frequency with which 'atypical' features appear, and the easy informality with which these ceremonies are carried out, may be surmised from the field notes taken at one such burial: (1) When the time came for the *tsuri* to be blown, a big argument took place as to who should hold the wooden plate, the honour finally falling to one of the agnates. (2) While the corpse was being carried to the grave there was an altercation between the agnate in charge and the *varoora* ('sisters-in-law'). The latter have the task of sweeping the path before the procession; they were accused of being lazy and not doing their job properly, a charge which was stoutly denied. (3) At the grave people debated whether the blanket which had covered the body in transit should go into the grave or be kept for future use. The widow was given the decision, and she directed that it be placed in the grave. (4) This having been decided, a further long discussion ensued as to whether it should be placed underneath or on top of the corpse. (5) The placing of stones over the corpse then became an item for disagreement. (6) When the time came to put the *bikiro* by the head of the corpse it was discovered that no tobacco had been provided; this finally had to be borrowed from a non-related onlooker, who produced a grubby handful from the pocket of his ragged trousers. (7) There was strong disagreement over whether the deceased's knobkerrie should be buried with him or hung on a nearby tree, settled only when the *samukadzi* summarily took it from the grave and hung it on a limb. When someone objected that it would be stolen he retorted cryptically, 'If anyone takes it, that's his own lookout.' (8) The responsibility for 'paying' the *varoora* was also the subject of violent discussion, which was only settled after lengthy argument.

There was difference of opinion not only on procedure, but also in response to questions as to 'why' things were done as they were. Yet these uncertainties caused no consternation; at the end of the ceremony there was general satisfaction that everyone had 'done his best'. Participation and intention seemed more important than understanding or precise procedure.

THE *midzimu*

We turn now to consideration of the hierarchy of the *midzimu*, and their relationships with Budjga society, relationships which are basic to Budjga religion. The unitary nature of this hierarchy, which encompasses both the dead and the living, has been emphasized. The patrilineage is both an organic and a spiritual unity, and the living lineages form only the lowest strata of a multi-tiered structure. Thus to the individual Budjga, while his contemporary generation is of the greatest importance to him because of his social relationships with it, the concept of being a representative of a much larger spiritual group makes for the religious context in which these relationships are interpreted. To this spiritual group he has direct access particularly through the spirit of his grandfather. He thus has access to a spiritual power more senior and sympathetically inclined than that of the actual parents' generation, even if the parents are dead.[1]

In the spiritual hierarchy departed ancestors are ranked in the same relative positions that they held in life. Those whose names are remembered (usually for two or three generations back) are 'mentioned' by name during the prayers and rituals. Beyond these generations reference is made to the departed spirits collectively, as Holleman quotes: 'and you, So-and-so—i.e. the representative of the generation farthest back whose name is remembered—will share with the other old ones whose names we no longer know'.[2] This does not imply that they are thought to have lost their

---

[1] Holleman, 1953, p. 27, has noted the close correlation between this and the relations between the living grandparents and grandchildren, which are much more intimate and cordial than between parents and children.

[2] Holleman, 1953, p. 29.

individual identities, as Tracey[1] has suggested; only that they are beyond the memories of the present generation. As these generations get farther and farther away they come closer to the *midzimu* of the founders of the lineages and clans, and eventually to Mwari (God) himself. These generations, both in belief and ritual practice, serve as intermediaries to the higher powers and to God.

It will be useful at this point to indicate the significant grades in this hierarchy of spirits. They are, in the order that we shall discuss them: (1) The spirit of the grandfather (*sekuru* or *tateguru*). It is with this spirit, as we have already mentioned, that individual Budjga, and in particular married ones, have an intimate and informal relationship. They may communicate with it in private without the formalities of ritual. (2) The family spirit (*mudzimu*), that which is the active spiritual entity at the rituals of the *chizwarwa*. (3) The spirit associated with the progenitor of the lineage or clan (*musikarudzi*). This spirit is called variously *mudzimu*, or *mhondoro*, (a 'tribal spirit'). (4) The tribal spirit, or *mhondoro*. This should be distinguished from the one just mentioned in that it is the ancient spirit of the Chief's lineage which regularly reveals itself to a recognized living medium, and hence operates primarily in a territorial and political rather than a kinship context.

Beyond the primary level of the informal relationship between an individual and the spirit of his dead grandfather is that of family worship, the corporate unit for which is the *chizwarwa*. This group has already been defined as the first and second generation of agnatic descendants of one man. It comes together for ritual purposes as occasion demands, calling on the spirit of the common *sekuru* or *teteguru* (father's father) for help and support. This spirit has a particular interest in the family, governing, guarding and punishing it. It manifests itself in possession, always in one accepted medium, or through some illness or misfortune. Should such misfortune be visited upon members of the family a ceremony (*bira*) may be held to determine its cause. It may be that the ancestor has sent the affliction because of his displeasure, or it may be that some malevolent spirit has slipped through his guard and brought trouble. In any case his goodwill and help are needed. After consultation with the diviner a ritual is held at which a specified offering is made to the ancestral spirit. It is at these

[1] Tracey, 1934, p. 45.

rituals that he speaks through his medium. This medium is one that will drink the blood of the sacrifice, in contrast to those of the *mhondoro*, to be mentioned later. The animal sacrificed is frequently one that has been previously dedicated to the spirit.[1]

Closely connected as it is with the lineage system, the worship of the family *midzimu* is subject to the principles of segmentation common to such systems. When the *chizwarwa* has progressed in depth beyond two or three generations, a second *mudzimu*, or spirit of another grandfather, is likely to reveal itself in a medium, and when this happens the *chizwarwa* segments, new groups forming around the newly-revealed *midzimu*.

THE CLAN-SPIRIT

Unlike Shona practice that Gelfand has found elsewhere,[2] the spirit of the clan founder does not figure prominently in Budjga ritual. This is undoubtedly a reflection of the fact that Budjga clans are rarely, if ever, corporate functioning units. Hence the clan spirits are eclipsed in importance by those of the chiefly lineages, which have a political significance. Nevertheless they have their place in Budjga thought, and their presence is acknowledged in the rituals to the family *midzimu*, where they are 'mentioned'.

THE TRIBAL *mhondoro*[3]

As we have already suggested, as the hierarchy of the ancestors moves farther and farther away from the living generation it becomes more closely related with the founding ancestors of the tribe, and when the *mudzimu* of one of these individuals reveals itself through the possession of a medium such a spirit is regarded as *mhondoro*, a 'tribal spirit'. The term *mhondoro* has no plural form in Shona, and it can be used to mean 'lion'. These spirits are sometimes called 'lion spirits' in the literature, since to the Shona they are often understood to roam about in the form of maneless lions. The term is also applied to the clan spirits just described, but as they are not prominent this usage is not often encountered.

[1] A large amount of illustrative material on this subject is to be found in Gelfand, 1959, pp. 74–98.

[2] i.e. Gelfand, 1959, pp. 75 ff. Gelfand's accounts do not demonstrate how his distinction between the family and the clan *midzimu* is effective in ritual.

[3] Known among some tribes as *gombwe*. Gelfand, 1956, p. 19. They are also associated with the *majukwa* spirits. Bullock, 1927, pp. 2, 148.

Among the Budjga the *mhondoro* is conceived as the spirit of a member of the chief's lineage:

In everyday life, however, the term *mhondoro* primarily refers to an ancient spirit of the *Chief's lineage* who is regularly revealing himself through a recognized living medium, man or woman, and for this reason is consulted and honoured by the people as the principal spiritual power in the country.[1]

This statement must be qualified, however, by the recognition that there are usually more than one *mhondoro* in a Budjga chiefdom, and that some *mhondoro* are recognized even though they have no medium currently in operation. In the Nyamkowo chiefdom there are four acknowledged *mhondoro*, Zimbiru, Benhura, Chikowa and Nyakasanhu. Of these Zimbiru and Nyakasanhu are active. The medium of Benhura died four years ago, and this *mhondoro* has not revealed itself yet to a new one, while the medium of Chikowa, though alive, has not been possessed in recent years.

These *mhondoro* (and their mediums) are ranked according to their genealogical seniority as it appears in Budjga traditional history; Zimbiru is the senior *mhondoro* of Nyamkowo, and he is usually approached only through the other *mhondoro* of the chiefdom.

It should be noted at this point that there is some indication of a rank hierarchy between the different tribal *mhondoro*. Some are regarded as being more powerful than others.[2] There is some confusion as to whether the highest *mhondoro*, who are conceived to have trans-tribal influence and power, are really the spirits of tribal ancestors or have never had an origin in mortal existence. Some Shona assert that they are emanations of Mwari, and are closely associated with the Rozvi and their development of the Mwari cult. The present state of research on Shona religion, the general lack of precise theological categories in Shona thought, and the resultant obscurity do not permit us to do more than recognize that there has been an attempt, particularly in Rozvi times, to connect the upper layers of the Shona spiritual hierarchy with Mwari.[3]

---

[1] Holleman, 1953, p. 29.

[2] A list of some of these is given by Gelfand, 1959, p. 40.

[3] Garbett, in his study of spirit mediumship among the Korekore, suggests that the trans-tribal connections in the *mhondoro* system may have been derived from the Monomotapa period of Shona history. Garbett, 1963, p. 2.

No such hierarchy exists today among the Shona, but the Budjga do recognize a relationship, however vague, between their *mhondoro* and those of other Shona tribes. It is said in Budjga that should any crisis prove to be beyond the capacity of their senior *mhondoro*—Nohureka, Zvimbiru and Nyakutanda— the matter would be referred to Dzivaguru, whose medium is supposed to live in Korekore country. However, no informant could give me an instance of such action in recent years.[1]

It is possible that the inter-tribal network of *mhondoro* relationships broke down when the creation of native reserves reduced mobility and eliminated the necessity for inter-tribal alliances. In Budjga such a network of *mhondoro* is conceived to exist in the Native Purchase Area, where farms are allocated to Shona from all over Rhodesia on the basis of agricultural ability. Farmers taking up residence there are expected to present a gift to the local Budjga *mhondoro*, and it is asserted that if the newcomer has any undischarged responsibilities to his home *mhondoro* the Budjga *mhondoro* will know this and require him to attend to the matter before being accepted as a resident in Budjga.

The functions of the *mhondoro* are concerned with the affairs of the tribe, its land and its chief. The provision of rain and the fertility of the soil are the principal matters on which he is approached. Epidemics, plagues of locusts, or other tribal calamities are also his concern. Finally, his approval is required before a successor to the chieftainship could accede to power.

THE *mhondoro* MEDIUMS[2]

Although most of the *mhondoro* are male, some are female; likewise the mediums they possess may be of either sex, although they are usually of the same sex as the *mhondoro*. Among the Budjga (although not among all the Shona tribes) the medium may not be a member of the ruling lineage of the chiefdom. 'The *mhondoro* seizes a stranger' is a well-known saying among them, meaning that the medium of, say, Zvimbiru, can be anyone—even from another Shona tribe—except a member of Zvimbiru's own lineage. Any person claiming to be possessed by a *mhondoro* of a chiefdom is subjected to a series of tests by the elders, designed to

---

[1] Garbett, whose research has been done in Korekore country, tells me that the name Dzivaguru is known there, but only as that of one of the lesser *mhondoro*.

[2] Called *svikiro*.

ascertain his knowledge of esoterica connected with the genealogy and exploits of the *mhondoro* concerned.

It is clear that the influence of any *mhondoro* is dependent upon the ability of its medium:

If the medium loses the power of transmission (and this has happened to a number of them) or if he dies, that particular spirit recedes into the vague unknown and loses its activity, until it 'comes out' again in another medium—which may happen soon, or late, or never. His place may then be taken by another ancestral spirit who wants to find a medium.[1]

One of the most famous of the Shona *mhondoro* is Chaminuka, who united several Shona groups in resistance to the Ndebele and the legends of his life and death have made of him a symbol which is effective politically among the Shona even today.

The medium has an assistant called *nechombo* or *muzukuru*, who acts as an intermediary between him and the people. He is approached through this assistant who also translates his messages.

Possession of the medium by the *mhondoro* is ritually induced; this is done only on ritual occasions. Such rituals may be performed at any time; when the tribe is faced with some crisis or calamity, or at the regular annual ceremonies held for the tribal *mhondoro*. One of these is held in April and inaugurates the eating of the new grain crop. Another, held in September, is the most important ritual event of the year, and is concerned with thanksgiving for the past season's crops, the blessing of seed and requests for good rain.

The actual rituals for both these ceremonies are similar. In each case it is the chief who is responsible for providing the necessary ingredients for the beer to be brewed and initiating the proceedings. The remaining responsibilities, however, are those of the medium and his assistant.

Vital to the ritual is the prior brewing of beer in the prescribed way. On the morning of the ceremony some of this beer is placed in the *rushanga*, a hut sacred to the *mhondoro* which is built outside the village where the medium resides. In the evening the ritual begins in the hut of the medium, when he is also given of the beer to drink. Music and dancing follow throughout the night, and in the early morning the medium is possessed with the spirit of the *mhondoro*. He then drinks of water placed in a wooden bowl to

[1] Holleman, 1953, p. 29.

which an ember has been added, to 'cool off' his spirit. He is then approached by his assistant with the various requests that the people may have. At daybreak he leads a procession of attendant followers to the *rushanga*, where further prayers are made. A return is then made to the village, where the ceremony is brought to a close.

It is worth noting that animal sacrifice does not play a part in these annual rituals, and is required by the *mhondoro* only for special rituals in case of drought or other crises, which indicate its displeasure with the people.

During possession the medium covers his head with a ritual hat and wears a black shawl. In everyday activities the medium may not wear any special habit, but he is constantly in possession of a narrow steel rod or walking-stick.

Garbett, who made a detailed study of spirit mediumship among the Korekore, has found that the mediums there derive considerable income from the gifts they receive in return for their services. This also appears to be the case in Budjga. Not only are they presented with such gifts before the big annual ceremonies, but they also receive remuneration from businessmen who present themselves before the *mhondoro* to give notice of some new enterprise and to ask for blessing and protection. In the case already mentioned of new farmers coming to the area the set fee is £1 2s 6d.

The role played by the spirit medium in local politics depends to a large extent on the character of the individual incumbent of the office. It can be an important one, since there is often less turnover in spirit mediums than in chiefs; the Budjga rules of collateral succession have the effect that chiefs commonly come to office as old men, while a medium may be installed in office when relatively young, and hold the position through the reign of several chiefs. In the boundary and succession disputes that mediums are called upon to adjudicate, it is usually apparent that they carefully assess public opinion before making a decision; they are aware that their popularity is ultimately dependent on the consonance with it of their pronouncements which, in fact, give ritual sanction to a general consensus. This does not necessarily imply that they are opportunists or charlatans. The reflection of public opinion in their decisions is largely subjective, and may or may not actually be representative. On matters of national politics they tend to be conservative, seeing the African nationalist parties as threats to the established order of which they are a part. In September 1964 the medium of Zvimbiru made a strong statement at the *rukoto* condemning nationalist activities, thus aligning himself on the side of the chiefs and headmen and against the younger men.[1]

THE HIGH GOD

The Budjga belief in a trans-tribal Supreme Being is common to all the Shona tribes, and may usefully be examined first in a Shona rather than a Budjga context. The etymological derivation and religious content of the Shona term for the high god, 'Mwari', have excited the interest of the Culture-Historians, who have tried to connect it with the religions of the Middle East or the Orient. Von Sicard maintains that the belief in Mwari originated outside Africa and is a product of the 'Great Erythraean Culture' postulated by Frobenius, having been modified in the process of time by the Rozvi among others.[2] Any contemporary examination of this element of Shona belief must consider two distinct systems of belief. One is focused in the highly organized cult which once flourished in the Matopo Hills, served by an hereditary priesthood. Posselt describes Mwari as the oracular deity of one of the Shona sub-groups, the Vakaranga. 'The natives', he says, 'do not worship Mwari as a deity; it is merely an oracle to which they appeal in times of trouble and which manifests itself through the priests at a number of temple caves.'[3] This Mwari cult, says Posselt, was esoteric and its details carefully hidden.

The other system which we must consider is that belief in Mwari which is universal among the Shona, in which he appears as the God of the Cosmos. Etymologically the word means 'begetter' or 'bearer', and Bullock says that the few abstract ideas he found connected with Mwari have the sense of eternity.[4] Mwari is not the apotheosis of an ancient progenitor, and has never had a mortal or anthropomorphic existence.

[1] Outside Budjga, Muchatera, the medium of Chaminuka (p. 46), went to arrange an interview with Sir Edgar Whitehead, former Prime Minister of Rhodesia, to ask for a convocation of all the national political leaders, who would then be instructed by him (Chaminuka) on how he wished the affairs of the country to be run. The writer was present at this interview at the request of Muchatera in the capacity of interpreter.

[2] Von Sicard, 1944, p. 180.   [3] Posselt, 127, p. 530.
[4] Bullock, 1927, p. 121.

Between these two, says Posselt, there is no connection. 'Among the various Mashona tribes', he says, 'there is reference to Mwari, the creator, but this is purely local and not connected with the Mwari cult of the Matobo.'[1] With this conclusion Bullock is in radical disagreement. In Shona thought, he says, Mwari is too far above the mortals to be interested in particular men or even tribes.[2]

In connection with this general Shona belief in Mwari, it is of significance to note some of the other names by which he is referred to:[3]

Nyadenga	'The Great One of the Sky.'
Chipindikure	'He who turns things upside down.' (The term implies power to change things completely.)
Chirazamauva	'The One Who provides for good and bad.'
Musikavanhu	'The Creator of the people.'
Dzivaguru	'The Great Pool'—the giver of rain.
Mutangakugara	(Kutanga = to begin + kugara = to exist.) 'The One who existed in the beginning.'

The use of these terms gives us an indication of the concepts embodied in the idea of Mwari. He emerges as Creator, the source of nature, life and rain. He is, possibly, the source of both good and evil. He does not exist in only one locality, and he existed before creation.

In practice Mwari appears as remote from men, not interested in individuals but in the people as a whole.[4] Ordinarily the affairs of the individual tribes are the concern of the local *mhondoro*; only in times of serious drought will they forward the matter directly to Mwari.

Mwari, as Van der Merwe has pointed out,[5] is associated with certain social regulations, and can in this sense be connected with a Shona morality. Throughout the different tribes there are holy days, called *zwisi*, which are considered sacred to him. Any work done on them is considered an affront to Mwari which must be punished. Again, incest is regarded as a sin not only against the ancestors but against Mwari. Mwari is also concerned with the well-being and honour of the ancestral spirits, and petitioners for

[1] Posselt, 1927, p. 530   [2] Bullock, 1927, p. 123; p. 525.
[3] Van der Merwe, 1959, pp. 42–6.
[4] Von Sicard, 1944, p. 135; Van der Merwe, 1959, p. 46.
[5] Van der Merwe, pp. 46–8.

rain at his shrines are admonished to maintain the rituals due to them. Breaches of these regulations would be punished by Mwari sending lightning or other calamity to the person and property of the offenders.

What has been said here of the Shona in general applies to the Budjga in particular. The names most frequently used by them for Mwari are Nyadenga and Musikavanhu. The word Dzivaguru means, for the Budjga, not Mwari but an all-powerful rain-giving *mhondoro* in Korekore country (p. 45); this lack of definition is indicative of the way that these concepts tend to fuse at this level of Budjga and Shona thought.

It has already been pointed out[1] that there has long been a priesthood of Mwari attached to certain cave shrines in the Matopo Hills, and that it was by taking these over that the Rozvi were able to establish their spiritual as well as political dominance. When the Ndebele over-ran the country they came under the influence of the Mwari cult, and some authorities assert that Lobengula himself became an active member.[2] Today some of the central Shona tribes still send delegations to the Matopo shrines in case of extreme drought, but the Budjga to my knowledge have not done so in recent years.[3] They all, however, regard Mwari as the ultimate source of rain. Thus there is no apparent conflict between the two systems. On the one hand there is the elaborate indirect approach to Mwari through the medium, the tribal *mhondoro*, and possibly yet another *mhondoro*. On the other hand there is the direct approach by the tribe to the priests of Mwari at one of his shrines. Yet the Mwari of the shrines constantly exhorts obedience and honour to the ancestors, and the *mhondoro* of the ancestors in turn exalt Mwari as their ultimate source of power.

THE *shawe* CULTS[4]

The Budjga share with other Shona a belief in *mashawe*. In the *shawe* cults possession is the central act towards which all attendant ritual is directed. Their importance in Shona culture has been variously evaluated, but it is certainly great, even though I am not prepared to say with Burbridge that 'this Shawe cult bulks larger in Mashona worship than any other'.[5]

---

[1] *Supra*, p. 45.   [2] Blake-Thompson and Summers, 1956, p. 54.
[3] A very old informant at Mtoko, however, related to me how he himself made a pilgrimage to Mwari in the Matopos for personal reasons.
[4] pl. *mashawe*.   [5] Burbridge, 1938, p. 23.

The *mashawe* can be animal spirits, or the wandering spirits of men or women who have not been accorded the proper ritual at death. In most, though not all, they are persons who have died away from their own homes or tribal areas. Because of their failure to be properly inducted into the world of the *midzimu*, the *mashawe* desire to be realized and express themselves in some alien personality. Homeless and restless, they wander about looking for some human host. The choice is evidently capricious, and no special pattern is followed, save that the individual is of a different totem.[1] Once entrenched within the human host, the *shawe* begins to crave recognition, the opportunity to express itself, and, perhaps, some ritual beads, clothes or food. To indicate his presence, he brings sickness upon his host, which is then diagnosed by a diviner as *shawe* possession.

It sometimes happens that more than one *shawe* will possess the same person. This may be dangerous to him since the demands upon him may be too great for him to fulfil, and death may result.

Should the human host desire to be rid of the *shawe*, certain ceremonies can be performed by the diviners. Exorcism is not, however, the usual means of dealing with the *shawe* possession. The possessed is usually established in his new role, and attends all the *shawe* dances in his neighbourhood at which his *shawe* will manifest itself in possession.

The *mashawe* usually bring to those whom they possess the skills of the art or trade which they practised as human beings; some are skilled in therapy, others successful hunters, warriors, diviners, musicians and so forth. On the other hand, some are useless or anti-social; should they have been thieves, the possessed are thought to show the same characteristics.

The medium for his part has a number of responsibilities towards his *shawe*, and must provide for its desires. All *mashawe* have certain wants in common: music, singing, dancing, cloth, beer and ornaments. But different ones have their own peculiar tastes and fancies. The colour of the cloth and beads, the beat of the drum, the type of food: all these depend on the type of *shawe* that possesses a person. Thus the members of different *shawe* groups are distinguished by the character of the spirit personality (or

---

[1] If the medium of a *shawe* dies, there is a pre-disposition for him to pick another of the same family.

personalities) believed to possess them. These groups meet from time to time for all-night dances, 'playing to the *mashawe*'.

The history of the *shawe* cults is obscure, but there is some evidence that they are comparatively recent. Hugo divides *shawe* groups into three classes: those of the 'pre-Madzwiti period',[1] roughly from 1730(?) to 1830: the 'Madzwiti', from 1830 to 1895, and the 'post-Madzwiti', from 1895 to the present.[2] These groupings refer to the date of origin, for they all exist today. If these postulated periods of development are correct, this preoccupation with 'foreign' *mashawe* may indicate some correlation between the growth of the movement and the increasing intrusion of alien cultures into Shona society.

The cult of *shawe* possession is, we might say, a layman's cult; that is, it is open to all those chosen by *mashawe*, and membership in it does not usually confer professional status on its adherents. Possession by certain types of *shawe*, however, gives the right of admission into the medical or divining fraternity. Persons so admitted become *nganga*, professionals who play an important role in Shona religion.

When one compares accounts of the *mashawe* written in the 1930s and the facts observed in Budjga today it appears that the cult activities are now: (*a*) more clandestine and exclusively nocturnal than previously, (*b*) less orientated toward controlled group activity and more toward individual behaviour and (*c*) more often associated with sorcery and other anti-social behaviour.

Beattie[3] has described a similar situation in Bunyoro, and has suggested that the proliferation of similar cults there has been the result of the introduction, through colonization, of factors considered inimical and dangerous by the Nyoro—the military and political domination of the Europeans, the power of western medicine, the advent of a cash economy, etc.—and the fact that the possession cults enable the Nyoro to deal with these forces by personalizing them. This analysis seems to be valid for the Budjga, particularly when we consider the rise of the *shawe* cults in their historical context, and the association of many of the *mashawe* with either Nguni or European characteristics.

---

[1] *Madzwiti* is the Shona term applied to the Nguni invaders, both Ngoni and Ndebele.

[2] Hugo, 1935, pp. 53–5.   [3] Beattie, 1961, pp. 11–38.

It is also important to note that most Budjga who are possessed by *shawe* are women, an indication that identification with the cult is one of the few socially recognized ways by which a Budjga woman can achieve prestige, or attain at least partial escape from what may be an intolerable domestic situation for her.

It is significant that the advent of Christianity in Budjga has not led to a decline in *shawe* possession; on the contrary, it will be shown in later chapters that two Christian groups, the Methodists and the Vapostori, encourage a belief in the *mashawe* and utilize this as a means of recruitment.

THE BUDJGA DIVINER (*nganga*)[1]

In the Budjga diviner, or *nganga*, we have a religious professional who owes his position neither to his status in the ancestral *midzimu* hierarchy, his associations with Mwari or *shawe* cults, nor his medical ability as a herbalist alone, but to a combination of all these different elements. He weaves the different threads of Budjga religious thought that we have just described into one functioning role.

This variety in the *nganga's* sources of authority is readily seen in the mode of entry into the profession. We have already mentioned that possession by a 'healing' *shawe* provides one qualification, followed of course by a period of apprenticeship.[2] Alternatively, an individual may acquire the necessary ability through the assistance of his father's *mudzimu*, or inherit it from some agnatic ancestor.[3] He may be an apprentice of the older *nganga* while he is yet alive and assume his position at his death, or sometimes the *mudzimu* of the *nganga* reveals itself after his death to an agnatic descendant—real or classificatory—through dreams. It is through these dreams that the novice is instructed in his new art.

The services that a *nganga* performs are numerous and diverse. He may be called upon for the diagnosis and treatment of unexplained or mysterious diseases, to provide preventive magic

[1] The word 'diviner' is used as a term of convenience, not precision, in this text since the functions of the *nganga* include other things besides divination.

[2] Once in a family, a 'healing' *shawe* may select to stay with it through succeeding generations, and be inherited down the agnatic line.

[3] I speak in the masculine gender, although it is possible for women to become diviners. Their status is similar to that of male diviners, although the taboos applying to them and their activities are slightly different. They are known as *nyahana* as well as *nganga*.

against witchcraft, or predict events in the future. Some are thought to have the power to force such evil doers as thieves to redress the crimes that they have done. They are called in to interpret dreams, to determine the authenticity of claims to spirit possession, and above all to determine causes of death. In the days before witchcraft and witch-accusation were made illegal by the European Government, they were called in to identify witches, and they may still make veiled accusations of this type as one form of diagnosis.

Nganga have two main diagnostic techniques. Most of them have a large range of divining paraphernalia, basic to which are four *hakata* (bones) which are thrown and interpreted according to standardized procedures.[1] The other standard technique is that of spirit possession, when the *nganga* is possessed by the *mudzimu* or *shawe* that inspires him.

For preventive magic the *nganga* himself supplies the necessary charms and ingredients. In cases of disease he may prescribe sacrifice and ceremonies directed towards the *midzimu*, in effect referring the case to the ancestral medium, the *svikiro*. Alternatively he may refer the patient to a herbalist (*chiremba*) for medical treatment.

Thus it becomes evident that the potential conflict between the mediums of the ancestral spirits and the *nganga*, brought about by the close duplication both in their spheres of operation and their sources of power, is avoided by a system of informal relationships, in which each acknowledges dependence on the other's functions. Another safeguard against conflict is that a diviner rarely practises his art in his own home area,[2] and certainly never among his own kin group.[3]

There is no doubt that the *nganga* are consummate psychologists

[1] Gelfand, 1956, pp. 130–53, has given a full account of these techniques. Tracey (1963, pp. 105–7) asserts that the word *hakata* is derived from the Arabic 'haqat', meaning 'she tells the truth' or 'truth is told'.

[2] Barwe diviners in Mozambique have a great reputation in Budjga and, especially in cases of witchcraft accusation, can with impunity practise, thus enhancing this reputation. The idea that foreign diviners are more powerful is not unique, cf. Evans-Pritchard, 1937, p. 201.

[3] One informant said to me in this context, 'midzimu inokanda mvuri', 'the ancestors cast a shadow' over a diviner with regard to his own relatives, so that he cannot practise with them. Gelfand (1956, pp. 98–9) reports a *nganga* who was also a medium for a *mhondoro*. This is very unusual, but does not contradict in essence what I have said, for this particular *nganga* claimed to draw his power from an alien *shawe*, and not from his ancestral *mudzimu*.

in their dealings with the people they serve. They operate on the basis of the values and norms of traditional Budjga society, and their pronouncements and judgements reinforce these. At the same time their wide range of activities and their multiple sources of power make their position extremely flexible, and within it they act to some extent as entrepreneurs who determine their own roles. Operating within the general framework of the Budjga magico-religious system, where distinctions are not carefully drawn, this social manœuvrability enables them readily to adapt their roles in the face of social change, and makes them important agents in the process of Budjga adaptation.

It should be clear from this discussion that the analytical distinction often made between religion on the one hand and magic, divination and witchcraft on the other is not sharply drawn by the Budjga themselves. The same illness may be attributed to ancestral wrath over some ritual omission and to an enemy's witchcraft, and both diagnoses are made by the *nganga*. One cannot therefore discuss Budjga religion without including witchcraft, divination and magic in the analysis, and for this reason these subjects are treated concurrently in this study.[1]

WITCHCRAFT AND SORCERY

The Budjga belief in sorcery and witchcraft has etymological and formal parallels to similar beliefs among many Bantu peoples. Their generic term for this category of phenomena is *uroyi*, a word which is cognate with similar words used by many different tribes.[2] There are conceived to be two kinds of witch, those who become so by securing the requisite charms and spells from evil *nganga*, and those who are possessed by the *mudzimu* of an ancestor who was also a witch (*muroyi*), or perhaps by a malignant *shawe*. Murder, anthropophagy, the infliction of illness, the destruction of crops, the causing of snakes or animals to bite people and the causing of sterility are all actions attributed to witches. Most witches are women, although this is not always the case. The idea

---

[1] Pauw (1960, pp. 12–13, 146–9, 212) has analysed the significance of the magico-religious continuum among the Tswana for the impact of Christianity upon their society. The main points of his argument are valid for the Shona, and underline the important role that the *nganga* plays in the process of change.

[2] i.e. Lozi, Lunda (Turner, 1964, p. 319), Luvale (White, 1961, p. 60), Lovedu (Krige, 1954, p. 73), Tswana (Schapera, 1953, p. 65), *et al.*

E

of witchcraft as a substance in the body, as with the Azande,[1] is known to some Budjga, but there is considerable confusion on this point.

One should, however, be careful not to seek too close a parallel to the Azande model, with its rigid dichotomy between sorcery and witchcraft. Budjga do not attribute most deaths and illnesses to witchcraft as the Azande do; witchcraft is only one of several possible causes considered of these misfortunes—the *mashawe* and avenging spirits, *ngozi*, are ideologically just as important. Budjga witchcraft belief has not therefore been elaborated as much as that of the Azande. Thus the Budjga have only the one word, *uroyi*, to cover a wide variety of mystically harmful techniques.

Paradoxically, it is among the Christian Vapostori and not among the traditional religionists that witchcraft beliefs and their social contexts are most easily observed at the present time. The Witchcraft Suppression Ordinance brought in by the Government in 1899, which made the practice of witchcraft, or accusations of witchcraft, liable to a fine of £100 or three years' imprisonment, drove rituals of witchcraft detection underground, and it is very difficult for the investigator to find specific cases handled by *nganga* in Budjga. As has been mentioned, many Budjga patronize Barwe *nganga* across the border in Mozambique, since they can operate with impunity from Rhodesian law. The Vapostori, however, make witchcraft accusations quite openly, claiming that the Government is reluctant to prosecute them because 'they know that we work with God'. There is possibly some truth in this assertion, in that the Government may be reluctant to interfere in what are considered the judgements of a religious organization, particularly since the only sanction exercised by the Vapostori on witchcraft is expulsion from the Movement.

The theory that witchcraft renders intelligible unfortunate and apparently capricious events and that it reinforces approved social behaviour by negative example seems applicable to Budjga. Certainly in Budjga the belief serves to keep competitive action at a minimum and tends to prevent the ostentatious display of wealth, since the wealthier members of the society know they are open to accusations of witchcraft or sorcery.

Formerly witchcraft was punishable by death or banishment. At present, if villagers become convinced that one of their number

[1] Evans-Pritchard, 1937, p. 21.

is a witch, oblique requests may be made for the witch to leave, and if this fails to bring any result a stretcher may be placed at her door during the night, a hint that failure to leave voluntarily will result in the offender being removed either dead or injured. Further recalcitrance could lead to the accused having her hut burned down. The Budjga Vapostori have a different technique for dealing with witchcraft, emphasizing reform rather than removal, to be discussed later.

It should be noted that the Budjga do not consider witches to be inevitably malignant and active. Many of them, once their confidence is won, will name as witches members of their village with whom they live in harmony and accord. As one informant said, 'The mere fact that a person is a witch does not make her dangerous to you. It is only when and if you, by repeated mis-conduct towards that person, give her just cause to be angry with you, that she will cause you harm.' In the context of this state-ment, therefore, witchcraft is not so much a mechanism for the explanation of misfortune as a sanction against unacceptable social behaviour. The witch here does not act out of capricious malevolence, but only after provocation.

ngozi

Sudden or sustained misfortune to an individual or family group is sometimes diagnosed as a manifestation of an *ngozi*, an avenging spirit. The *ngozi* is the *mudzimu* of a murdered person, or one who has died with a grievance, often the spirit of a suicide.[1] This spirit can bring sudden retribution on those who have wronged it in life, and the procedures for placating it can involve a long and expensive process for the offender and/or his family. This process includes one of the few instances in Budjga society where res-titution is not made simply by the payment of cattle or other property, but requires a long public period of public penance, known as 'Ku tiza botso'.

THE PATTERN OF TRADITIONAL BUDJGA RITUAL

Of the pattern of traditional Budjga ritual one can safely say, as Turner does of the Lunda,[2] that no two performances are exactly

---

[1] Thus, because of the power believed to rest in the *ngozi*, revenge is one of the principal reasons for suicide in Budjga society.

[2] Turner, 1962, p. 3.

alike. This is not surprising, particularly in regard to those connected with the family *mudzimu*, where each performance involves
different actors, none of whom are religious professionals. The
rituals directed towards the tribal *mhondoro* and those conducted
by *nganga* are more uniform, since they are led by individuals who
acquire a long-standing familiarity with them, but even these
show considerable diversity.

This diversity does not, however, greatly disturb the Budjga
traditionalists, for to them the precise details of a prescribed ritual
are not as important as the sense of participation and co-operation.
Family rituals in particular are a progression of consultations at
which a consensus of opinion is sought; if this is done the result is
general satisfaction: everyone has done his best and each feels
a close identification with the group that has performed the
ritual.

Group participation, then, is seen as the dominant element in
these Budjga rituals. There are no credal statements, no set
prayers, no protracted speeches. The Budjga have few myths.
Theirs is an existential religion; it is to be experienced, not
explained. Budjga ritual therefore does not seek to articulate
statements of ideology nor to analyse them. Instead it acts them
out, dramatizes them, and in so doing gives each member of the
ritual group an opportunity to take part. The provision of music,
dancing, food, drink, and even the conduct of the ceremonies are
all shared responsibilities.

The idea of participation is not restricted to humans; it is
extended to the *midzimu* as well. The ancestral spirits are not asked
to keep their distance but are thought of as honoured guests; the
apotropaic motif is completely absent. Ritual possession is taken as
welcome evidence of their presence.[1]

---

[1] Once, when during a *rukoto* ceremony the sacralized beer had been presented
to a number of *mhondoro*, each named in the prayer, it was immediately ladled out
to the participants and observers present. I asked the medium whether the
mhondoro would not be angry that we had drunk the beer designated for them. He
smiled and replied, 'We are not like the Catholics, we do not believe that this beer
is actually drunk by the *mhondoro*. (He was evidently referring to his own understanding of the doctrine of transubstantiation.) But the *mhondoro* are here, and they
do drink it in a spiritual way. If, for instance, in the evening your wife places many
appetizing foods on the table in preparation for breakfast and you dream that
night of eating them, does that mean that when you wake in the morning they
will not be there? But did you not really eat them in your dream as well? Just so,
the *mhondoro* drink as we would in a dream, and they are glad that we drink with
them here in a different way.'

SUMMARY

The main strands of Budjga belief-ritual can be analytically presented as follows:

(1) An abstract, metaphysical conception of man and spirit.

(2) A belief in the continued existence of the personality after death.

(3) A system of ancestor worship directly linked to the lineage system.

(4) A vaguely defined belief in a remote High God.

(5) The conception of a set of reciprocal relationships between the High God and man, mediated through the ancestors.

(6) A system of worship and ritual, with an emphasis on spontaneous rather than prescribed actions.

(7) A well-developed system of beliefs and ritual involving possession as a means of revelation.

(8) A semi-independent possession cult, with groupings on a non-lineage, non-political basis, providing wide scope for innovation.

(9) Religious leadership separate from the political leadership, with a loosely organized set of officiants.

(10) A magico-religious professional group of 'diviners', incorporating and integrating many of the diverse strands of the religious system.

(11) A belief in witchcraft as an expression of anti-social behaviour, and in magic as its control.

(12) An idea that spiritual well-being depends on social well-being.

(13) Spiritual sanctions for social behaviour.

It is obvious that these concepts have much in common with those of Christianity. Their very affinity to certain Christian concepts makes them at the same time vulnerable to Christianity and viable in the face of it. Because of this, the juxtaposition of the two religious systems has not resulted in, nor necessitated, a categorical rejection of either in its totality. The inference is therefore that the elements we have delineated here as the components of Traditional Budjga Religion may be, to a greater or lesser degree, detectable in other Budjga religious systems. What value this inference may have will become evident in the following chapters.

4

Budjga Protestantism (Methodism)

A number of different religious denominations are represented in Budjga by groups which are organized and meet, at least irregularly, for worship and instruction. These are:

	Government-approved sites[1]
Methodist Episcopal	4
Roman Catholic	2
Johanne Maranke Vapostori	–
Johanne Masowe Vapostori	–
Independent African Church (Mushakata)	I
Watchtower	–
Kruger Vapostori	–
Anglican	–
Seventh-Day Adventist	2
Salvation Army	–
Apostolic Church of Pentecost of Canada	4

Of these only the first three are important to this study, numerically or in terms of influence. The Government-approved church sites listed above have little real significance as an index of either size or influence. Such sites may be granted to any religious organization in any of the township areas of the Reserve.[2] Since the Roman Catholic and Methodist Churches construct church buildings and conduct religious services on their school sites, they need separate church sites only in special circumstances,[3] while the Johanne Maranke Vapostori not only do not have church buildings but have a definite doctrine against doing so.

[1] Figures supplied by the District Commissioner's Office, Mtoko.

[2] Not all church sites are in the township areas. Official policy has been that such sites be granted only in township areas, but exceptions have been made.

[3] With the possibility in mind that the Government may in future take over rural education, pressure is being brought upon these denominations to establish church sites (as distinct from school sites) adjacent to their schools and thus separate their religious and educational activities.

As regards the Apostolic Church of Pentecost of Canada, the four sites mentioned are an indication only of the activity of a European missionary living in Salisbury, who since 1963 has been attempting to establish his denomination in Budjga. To date this Church has no significant following there. The Johanne Masowe Vapostori are members of the independent African church of Johanne Masowe, the Shona prophet who led a group of his followers to Korsten, Port Elizabeth, and there established an economically independent religious community which thrived until it was expelled by the South African Government.[1] There are only a few adherents of this group in Budjga, and it is doubtful if they hold regular services anywhere in the Reserve today. The Kruger Vapostori are followers of the Apostolic Movement introduced into Southern Rhodesia in the 1920s by European missionaries.[2] They too are few in number in Budjga, and are important to this study only because they have provided some of the early converts to the Johanne Maranke Vapostori Movement.

The Independent African Church, better known as Mushakata,[3] is a group which split off from the Methodist Episcopal Church in 1950 on issues of leadership and church policy. The split originated in Salisbury, and the Movement did not reach Budjga until 1961, when it was introduced by an evangelist named Musona. There is now one congregation in Budjga near Mtoko Centre, with about 40 adherents.

The Watchtower Movement in Budjga is divided into two groups. One, calling itself the Watchtower Church, was started at Mtoko Centre in 1934 by a worker at the local hotel, a man from Nyasaland called Jiya, and is still led by him. The other, calling

---

[1] cf. Sundkler, 1961, pp. 307–8. A large Masowe community of the Korsten type now exists on the outskirts of Lusaka, Zambia. Johanne Masowe was in his youth associated with the Methodist Episcopal Church discussed in this chapter, and started his Movement at about the same time as Johanne Maranke started his; the parallels and contrasts between the two movements offer an interesting field of enquiry.

[2] For a discussion of this development in Shona religious history see Ranger, 1964, pp. 52–74.

[3] *Mushakata* is the name of a well-known type of shade tree found in Mashonaland; the group took this name from its first meeting place. The Mushakata Church has a doctrine and policy identical to that of the Methodist Church and uses its hymn book and discipline. It, however, emphasizes its independence from the missionaries and other Europeans: 'We don't sing "God save the Queen" like the Methodist Europeans do, for we are Africans.'

itself the Watchtower Bible Society or Jehovah's Witness, has a Budjga leader.[1] Both of these groups have congregations only at Mtoko Centre, and neither is very large—ten or fifteen adherents for each being a fair estimate.

The one active Seventh-Day Adventist congregation is located in Mtoko Centre, as are those of the Anglican Church and Salvation Army. The membership of these groups is very small and drawn largely from non-Budjga who now live at Mtoko, either in Government employment or business or at the Mtemwa leper settlement nearby. The few adherents of these denominations living in Budjga outside Mtoko Centre usually associate themselves with local Methodist congregations.

As has already been stated, the Christian groups significant for this study are the Johanne Maranke Vapostori (hereafter referred to simply as 'Vapostori'), the Catholics and the Methodists. The first group is important because of its membership and rapid growth, and the last two because of their size and involvement in education. Active membership in these three groups in Budjga is estimated as: Methodist 3992, Catholic 1680, Vapostori 1800; all the other groups together totalling perhaps 270.[2] Reference to Table 8 will also indicate that between them the Roman Catholic and Methodist Churches are responsible for all the primary and secondary education in Budjga. We now turn to an examination of the formal aspects of these three organizations, leaving the analysis of their interaction with one another, with Budjga Traditional Religion, and with their society for the final chapters.

THE DEVELOPMENT OF METHODISM IN BUDJGA

Christianity was first introduced into Budjga in 1911 by a medical missionary of the Methodist Episcopal Church,[3] Dr Samuel Gurney. This Church was first established in Rhodesia at Old Umtali, 200 miles south of Budjga, and for twenty years con-

[1] The use of these names has little connection with the usage of the international Watchtower Movement, and is primarily indicative of factionalism in the Movement in Mtoko itself. The Watchtower Movement in Southern Rhodesia, unlike that in Northern Rhodesia, has never been a strong religious force. Worsley is obviously in error when he quotes figures crediting the Movement with 3,022,422 members in Southern Rhodesia, a figure approximating the total African population of the country at that time! (Worsley, 1957, p. 234.)

[2] Table 6 gives a detailed break-down of membership figures for each group and indicates the methods used to arrive at these figures.

[3] Now known officially as 'The Methodist Conference'.

centrated its efforts near Umtali. In 1910 Dr Gurney gained admittance for his Church at Mrewa, 40 miles south of Mtoko, and having been appointed Deputy District Surgeon of the area by the Government, he soon acquired the lease of an old police camp adjacent to the Mtoko District headquarters for a mission site. For several years this mission was staffed only with Shona evangelists from Old Umtali, but in 1922 a bachelor missionary from the Channel Islands, the Rev. Wilfred Bourgaize, was posted there and remained there with few interruptions until his retirement in 1956.[1] The Mtoko mission was a small one, only 56 acres in extent, and Bourgaize was the only missionary during much of this time. Although considered mildly eccentric even by his colleagues, Bourgaize was hard-working and generally well liked,[2] and over the years he built up a network of village schools and churches throughout Budjga. In this task he was assisted by an ordained Shona pastor from Old Umtali, the Rev. Samuel Chieza, together with a number of evangelists. Since for many years the village schools that Bourgaize had founded, and even the mission at Mtoko, went only through the first three to five years of school, many Budjga boys and girls were sent to the Nyadiri Mission of the same Church in an adjacent district. Here there was a large mission establishment offering advanced education (through Standard VI), teacher training, medical facilities and agricultural instruction. Some of the students were sent back to Budjga as 'pastor-teachers', to teach in the village schools during the week and preach in the churches at the weekends.

Most of the early Methodist evangelization of Budjga was therefore carried out by Budjga themselves and not by missionaries. Bourgaize himself did little preaching, considering it his main task to establish a school system and church organization.

Methodism offered the Budjga a system of belief roughly consistent with that expressed in the Articles of Religion of the Anglican faith. It included a universal God—called 'Mwari'[3]—a body of moral regulations governing conduct and man's accountability to God for them, a conception of personal immortality linked with reward or punishment for men's actions, and a belief

[1] *Journals of the Rhodesia Annual Conference*: 1907, p. 18; 1910, pp. 49–50, 53; 1912, p. 64; 1913, p. 40; 1914, p. 30; 1915, p. 58. Also James, 1935, pp. 65–6.

[2] Today one of the two streets of Mtoko to be dignified with a title bears his name, and it is not unusual to encounter the given name 'Bukesi' among Budjga men and boys.　　[3] *Supra*, pp. 48–50.

that God communicates with man through the Bible. This last was held to be particularly important, and special efforts were made to make adherents literate and provide them with copies of the New Testament.[1]

One aspect of Methodism which did not stem from its Anglican origins was the emphasis on a subjective 'experience' of salvation effected by the Holy Spirit. In the Shona context this came to mean that conversion to Christianity implied not only commitment to the creed and discipline of the Methodist organization, but also the conception of a direct encounter between the individual and God. Various subjective states, usually ecstatic, were associated with the initiation of this experience. In 1918 at Old Umtali a 'revival' marked by numerous manifestations of this kind of experience swept through the mission and made a profound impression on the African leaders of the Church.[2]

The most distinctive prohibitions imposed by the Methodists upon their members concerned marriage, beer drinking and the use of tobacco. Smoking and the drinking of beer were prohibited; marriage was a state to be sanctified by Christian rites, premarital sexual relations were condemned and marriage itself was to be monogamous.

At many points this system was congruent with existing Budjga thought. The idea concerning a High God, the post-mortem existence of the individual, communication between God and man, subjective spiritual experience, and premarital chastity were, if not exactly parallel, at least compatible with little modification. At other points Methodist belief clashed directly with Budjga belief and practice; the Budjga were polygamous, the use of tobacco and beer was important to them not only socially but ritually, while their belief in the *mhondoro* and the *midzimu* as protectors of the land and lineage segments was unacceptable to the Methodists.

The Methodist emphasis on a subjective personal experience of conversion meant that the Church did not attempt mass conversions or baptisms; rather at public services and in the classroom an attempt was made to lay the Methodist Gospel before the Budjga in such a way that they would accept it individually.

[1] Translated into Shona and printed by the British and Foreign Bible Society.

[2] One Budjga, telling me how he used to attend church without the benefit of this experience, expressed in typical Budjga idiom his concept of the difference: 'Ndaienda ku fadzwa, zwanga zwasati zwapinda mu ropa', 'I used to attend to be entertained, it (the Gospel) had not yet entered the blood'.

Conversion seems in fact to have taken place for a variety of reasons: a wish for the subjective experience, an appreciation of Methodist moral values, an awareness of practical advantages (i.e. the attainment of education, etc.), the acceptance of the Bible and its Methodist interpretation as a superior mode of divine revelation, a desire for the prestige and status conferred by the Church, the attraction of the corporate life of the Church and, in the case of children, pressure from their Methodist elders. Membership in the church was not conferred immediately upon profession of faith, but was preceded by a probationary period of instruction lasting anywhere from one to two years. Infant baptism of children of members was, however, permitted.

In 1956 the Methodist Church opened a new mission station on a 100-acre site at Nyamuzuwe in the centre of the Mtoko Reserve, and it subsequently developed a secondary school there, the only one at present in Budjga. The number of missionary personnel was increased in order to staff this school, while the Mtoko property was retained primarily as an administrative centre for the Church. In 1964 the Church had seven missionaries[1] stationed in Budjga, all of them at Nyamuzuwe. Of these six were involved in educational work at the secondary school and only one, the District Superintendent,[2] had much direct contact with the village churches.

In the same year the Church had four ordained pastors serving 41 congregations in Budjga, which were listed as having 3992 full or probationary members. The Church had 29 schools supervised by two Budjga Methodist school managers and enrolling 6795 children.[3] Two of these schools had clinics attached to them, supervised by doctors and nurses from the Methodist hospital at Nyadiri, to which many other Budjga go for medical treatment.

THE LOCAL CHURCH

The local congregation, or church, is the basic unit of group organization in Budjga Methodism. There are forty-one of these in Budjga, fairly evenly distributed throughout the Reserve. The size of these congregations varies considerably from place to place; it may consist of anywhere between 20 and 150 full members, with an approximately equal number of probationers. In theory

[1] This figure includes missionary wives.   [2] *Infra*, p. 69.
[3] *Methodist Conference Journal*, 1954, Appendix.

each congregation is organized into a rather elaborate set of committees and boards on a pattern evolved in Europe and America, dealing with membership, evangelism, finance, social service, education and ministerial relations.[1] In practice Budjga congregations are far too small to carry this elaborate organization, and local church leadership is provided by a few individuals who direct all activities without differentiation.

The most important of these individuals are the stewards, who are usually men but may be women. Small congregations may have only one steward, although most have two or three. The stewards are responsible for collecting and dispensing the funds of the group, and see that the church buildings are maintained in good repair. They are regarded, in the absence of the pastor, as the local representatives of church authority. Together with the local head teacher, the leader of the women's organization[2] and the leader of the men's organization (if any), the stewards form a leadership core which directs local church activities and acts as a liaison between the congregation and the Methodist hierarchy.

It is from this core that most of the ritual leadership for the group is drawn. The stewards are usually Local Preachers, an office which, according to the Church Discipline,[3] implies a certain level of training in preaching and church leadership, but which in practice in Budjga is usually granted to any local member in good standing who has the disposition and ability to preach and lead public services. Since the pastor is only infrequently in attendance at the worship services of any given local congregation, it is these people who usually lead them.

While, as we have just pointed out, local Budjga congregations are not organized into committees according to the ideal of the Methodist Discipline, they are sub-divided more significantly in other ways. There is the important distinction in membership between those who are full members and those who are probationers or beginners. It is from the full members that the congregation chooses its leaders, and this status carries with it other privileges and responsibilities. The duty to provide financial support weighs much more heavily on the full member than on

[1] *Doctrines and Disciplines of the Methodist Church.* Africa Central Conference Edition, 1956, pp. 66–90. This book is the definitive authority on policy and procedure for the Methodist in Africa.   [2] *Infra,* pp. 70–1.

[3] *Doctrines and Disciplines of the Methodist Church.* Africa Central Conference Edition, 1956, pp. 100–2.

the probationer. On the other hand, only a full member is entitled to receive communion, or to join the men's or women's societies.

Each congregation usually consists of from 40 to 50 per cent full members and 50 to 60 per cent probationary members. Many of those in the second group are school children, some are adults who have recently been converted, while others are adults who in effect are permanently relegated to this category, as a type of second class membership. The rules of the Church prohibit the granting of membership to polygamists or their junior wives, and the ideal is held out that at conversion a polygamist should return all his wives except the first to their homes. Yet most Budjga Methodists acknowledge the complete impracticability of such an arrangement, and assert at the same time that anyone—polygamists included—can genuinely repent and become a Christian. When such persons do present themselves before the congregation for membership, they are accepted as probationers, a procedure which, if questioned, is justified by the fiction that they are expected to rectify their domestic situation some time in the future, even though all concerned know that this will actually never happen.

A parallel situation often arises when a Methodist girl consents to a *matorwa* marriage.[1] This results in demotion to probationer status, and full membership is only restored when a church marriage is performed. But frequently the husband has no desire or intention to go through with such a marriage, and the woman may remain a probationer for many years, if not for life.

The local congregation has within it groups organized on the basis of age and sex: there is a women's society, a church youth group and, sometimes, a men's group as well. A church member does not automatically belong to one of these groups. Membership in the men's and women's organizations is a sign of special religious interest, conferred by these groups only on full members who enjoy a good reputation.

THE CIRCUIT

Each congregation is part of a circuit, of which there are four in Budjga. Each circuit is made up of between 9 and 14 congregations, which together form the unit for which a pastor is responsible. The pastor has his residence in the village of one of the larger

[1] *Supra*, p. 29.

churches and may tend to devote more of his time to this particular congregation, but he is responsible to all the congregations
on his circuit and they are all in turn responsible for his
maintenance.

At the time of this study three of the pastors on the four Budjga
circuits were from Budjga and the fourth from the neighbouring
reserve of Uzumba. All had had eight years of primary education
and three years of ministerial training in the Methodist theological
school at Old Umtali. In addition two also held teaching certifi-
cates, representing the completion of two-year teacher training
courses. Generally held in high regard by the communities in
which they serve, these pastors nevertheless come in for considerable criticism, particularly from congregations some distance from
their homes who[1] complain that they rarely see their pastor, and
are paying a man for services which they do not receive. The fact
that the pastors' salaries average about £25 per month, a figure
considerably higher than most reserve incomes, adds to this
irritation, particularly as the salaries are set, not by the circuits, but
by the Conference.

The ecclesiastical ideal of Methodism strives for a compromise
between the episcopal and congregational forms of church
government and seeks to balance the authority of the ministry
with that of the laity. Thus the local congregation has considerable
autonomy in its own affairs; it passes on the suitability of any
candidate for church membership, it has the power to suspend or
discipline any member and elects its own local leadership. It can
also influence (but not control) the appointment of a minister or
district superintendent through representations to the Bishop. On
the other hand the minister's responsibility tends to be directed
towards the central administration of the Church, since he owes
his appointment to the Bishop.[2] Conflict between the two sources
of authority sometimes arises at this point, since the ministers are
appointed by the Bishop but are paid by their circuits.

Disputes of this kind are aired at the 'Quarterly Conference',
a biannual meeting of delegates from each congregation on a

---

[1] Which can be up to eighteen miles away, a two- or three-hour ride by bicycle,
the usual mode of transport.

[2] The district superintendent, as the local representative of the Bishop, is the
person to whom the pastors are directly responsible. His recommendations to the
Bishop concerning pastoral appointments are generally followed.

circuit.[1] Presided over by the district superintendent, this meeting hears the complaints of members against their pastor, settles discipline cases and discusses financial matters. Held over a week-end, this meeting is also an occasion for considerable ritual ceremony; members are received, baptisms performed[2] and communion services held.

The four circuits in Budjga are joined with eight others in adjoining districts to make up the Mtoko-Nyadiri District under a District Superintendent. He presides over the Quarterly Conferences, mediates in disputes between the pastor and his people, co-ordinates the programmes of the circuits and dispenses mission funds collected overseas to help in church building projects and circuit budgets. His contact with the people is primarily administrative. During the period of this study the District Superintendent was a Swedish missionary. No resentment on the issue of missionary authority was apparent, and on the contrary, people expressed satisfaction with the District leadership that they had been given.[3] Since April 1965, when this missionary went on leave, a Budjga pastor has been the District Superintendent.

The District is part of the Rhodesia Annual Conference, presided over by the Bishop, who is the chief executive officer of the Church in Rhodesia. This is the legislative organ of the Church. Its voting membership is made up of all ordained ministers plus one lay delegate from each circuit, to give approximately equal lay and ministerial representation.

FINANCE

Of the different Budjga churches the Methodists have by far the largest financial programme. Each full member is expected to give a quarterly offering of 2s, and in addition to this to support incidental building and benevolent projects. In 1963 total contributions for church building, local church expenses, pastors' salaries and housing amounted to £1219 17s 11d, an average of

[1] As the name implies, this was originally designed to be held four times a year, but in practice only the 'first' and 'last' quarterly conferences of the church year are actually held.

[2] Usually by sprinkling, although immersion baptism is permitted by the Methodists for those who desire it.

[3] Such approval of missionary activity is not automatic. The Mission Board requires a vote of confidence from a missionary's local Quarterly Conference on his character and ability once each four years, and in some cases missionaries failing to get this support have not been returned to the field.

14s 7d per full member. Expenditure on pastors' salaries and ambitious church building projects in Budjga made necessary a subsidy from Methodism overseas of something more than an equal amount.

THE WOMEN'S ORGANIZATION

A three-week average of church attendances in several villages, recorded in my field notes, produces the following figures:

	Men	Women	Children
Methodist	7	41	43
Roman Catholic	6	9	57
Vapostori	12	10	5

These figures conform to my general impression of the average composition of the congregations of these denominations throughout Budjga. As regards Methodists, for whom there are more detailed enrolment figures than for the other two groups, they closely parallel the ratio of women to men in the full membership of the Church.[1] Leaving explanation for a later chapter,[2] we shall only note here that the Methodist Church is, at least numerically, a 'women's church', and that the overwhelming preponderance of women is reflected in the strength of its women's organization, the 'Rukwadzano Rwe Wadzimai'.[3] This powerful group is highly organized from the local to the Conference level. It stages two annual conventions, one for the northern section of the Conference and one for the southern, each drawing 4000–5000 people for a four-day camp. It leads an existence in some ways independent of the Church proper; all its leaders are women, and the pastors are tolerated only as advisors. The dues collected from its members give the Conference Executive of the Rukwadzano a revenue of about £1500 per year, which is distributed for benevolent causes. Pastors and other Church workers (including missionaries) may submit their requests to this Executive, but are not allowed to sit in on its deliberations. As the only women's group with this degree of organization in the

[1] In the Mtoko West Circuit (excluding figures for Nyamuzuwe Secondary School, which is attached to this circuit) there are 53 male full members and 268 female full members, a ratio of approximately 5 women to 1 man, paralleling the 6/1 ratio approximated by the attendance figures.

[2] *Infra*, pp. 122–3.

[3] Literally, 'The Fellowship of Women'.

Reserves of eastern Rhodesia, the Rukwadzano tends to provide leadership for women's activities outside the church as well.[1]

Each local congregation has its chapter of the Rukwadzano, which meets once a week on Friday mornings. On this day members in good standing wear their uniforms of blue and red, and they are frequently encountered on the paths and roads of the Reserve, either going to or returning from their meetings. Great emphasis is placed on the uniform; it is considered an indication that the wearer is living according to the standards of the Organization, and a woman who has some reason—even privately—to believe that she is not doing so is expected to abstain from wearing it until her conscience is clear.[2]

THE PATTERN OF METHODIST RITUAL

The group activities of the congregation play a very prominent role in the life of active Methodists, and the church group is the most important unit in Budjga Protestantism. Some family groups at times act as worship units and have prayers at home, but the number of these is small, especially since few families consist entirely of Methodists.[3] The most important service of the week, which attempts to draw together the entire congregation, is the Sunday worship service, but in addition to this service other gatherings of a typical church week include:

Sunday morning:	A Sunday School hour for infants and school children.
Sunday afternoon:	A youth programme conducted by the Youth Group.
Wednesday morning:	Training classes for probationers and women.
Friday morning:	Rukwadzano meeting.

Thirty of the forty-one Budjga Methodist congregations now worship in church buildings, ranging from small mud-walled

[1] In 1959, when I was Superintendent of Schools in Uzumba, adjacent to Budjga, the Government on two occasions attempted to organize women's clubs in that Reserve. It was only when the District Commissioner enlisted the aid of the Rukwadzano leaders that a women's club programme was successfully launched.

[2] So closely identified is the uniform with the idealization of church membership that often when I have asked whether a woman is a member of the Church the answer has been simply, 'Ehe, anopfeka', 'Yes, she dresses', i.e. 'Yes, she wears the uniform, she is a *real* Christian'.

[3] *Infra*, pp. 121-2.

F

thatched structures to modern burnt brick buildings with cor-
rugated iron roofs. The others usually worship in a classroom of
the local school.

Some of the most important Protestant Mission Churches to
enter Zululand were, says Dr Sundkler, '. . . in principle and
practice antiritualistic. Theirs was a Church without an altar. The
preacher's pulpit and the teacher's desk were all that was needed'.[1]
If by 'antiritualistic' we mean that teaching and preaching are
emphasized rather than liturgy and symbolism we can apply this
statement to Budjga Methodism. Sunday services follow a set
pattern laid out in the Methodist Hymnal, including hymns,
prayers, Scripture reading, announcements and a sermon, but the
only really 'liturgical' elements in this procedure are the joint
repetition of the Apostles' Creed and the Lord's Prayer and the
benediction pronounced by the leader at the end.

The sermon is the main feature of the service, and may last
forty or fifty minutes. Biblical themes predominate, and the
approach is usually moralistic. Great prestige is attached to homi-
letic finesse and the appropriate use of illustrations from life;
preaching is an exercise which gives obvious satisfaction to many
members, and there is no lack of Local Preachers to volunteer for
the leadership of any service.

The hymns that are sung come from the Methodist hymn book,
the *Ngoma* ('Drum'), which was produced under the editorship of
an early missionary of the Church in 1928. While most of the
tunes are Western in origin they were adapted with the principles
of Shona rhythm in mind, and have proved very popular over the
years.[2] Most hymns have three or four verses, which embody the
logical progression of some theme.

Thus the emphasis in the prescribed pattern of Methodist
services is upon verbal symbolization, upon teaching and cognition
of the items of ideology. This is supported by the ministers, both
because it is what they have been taught in their theological
training and because it underlines their own position as teachers
and leaders of their congregations. But while the attitude of the
pastors is backed by the official ritual of the Church, another

---

[1] Sundkler, 1960, p. 180.

[2] Since its first edition in 1928 the *Ngoma* has proved its popularity by running
through several printings, which now exceed a total of 90,000 copies. At four
shillings a copy this hymn-book continues to have a steady sale throughout
Budjga. It has been given two major revisions since its first publication.

emphasis can be detected among the laity, especially at services where ministers are not present. This is an interest in the emotive and communal aspects of ritual, whereby the religion of the participants is expressed either by informal 'testimony', by repetitive-hymn singing or by the use of non-verbal symbols. In services where the minister is absent (which, as we have pointed out, happens quite often) the number of men and women who between them take a lead is usually quite large—six or eight persons may be involved in preaching, giving testimony, leading in prayer, etc.

This tendency on the part of some Budjga Methodists to develop a different mode of ritual expression is particularly clear in two activities, singing and *shawe* exorcism:

1. Wabvuwi singing. The Wabvuwi ('Fishermen') are the members of the men's organization of the Church. Numerically smaller than the Rukwadzano, they are similar to the latter in organization and hold a similar position in the structure of the local church. The Wabvuwi have developed a style of singing to express their Christian faith which is a radical departure from the homophonic hymnology of the *Ngoma* and which, while receiving no formal approval from the Church authorities, has proved to be increasingly popular in Budjga. Taking the general theme and perhaps the melodic outline of an Ngoma hymn, the Wabvuwi develop the song in a typical African manner, with a leader and chorus. The leader will begin with an introduction (different leaders develop their own particular style) indicating the type of rhythm to be followed, and the chorus joins in with a recurring ground bass. The harmonic motif supplied by this is similar to that used on the *mbira* and other African musical instruments, and it is sung in an instrumental manner, while the leader is left with the responsibility of giving his version of the text.

While there are only a few basic themes for these Wabvuwi songs, the variations on these are numerous since the development is left to individual performers. The following version is a good example of the idiomatic and repetitive nature of the Wabvuwi texts:

Pamberi masoja	Forward, oh soldiers
Izwai mambo wangu	Hear my King
Pamberi masoja	Forward, oh soldiers

Ndakaizwa ndiri kumunda, vakomana	I heard it when I was in the field, boys[1]
Nagwindiri ndakasiya	And at the sound of it I left (my work)
Pamberi masoja	Forward, oh soldiers
Kuzi baba wangu pfene vakomana	It is said my father, baboon, boys[2]
Zwakaitwa ndiri kumunda masoja	It took place when I was in the field, oh soldiers
Pakasungwa ngeutare vakomana	It has been bound with iron, boys[3]
Pakasungwa ngeutare	It has been bound with iron
Taramba unodza woye masoja	We spurn him who turns back, oh soldiers
Pamberi masoja	Forward, oh soldiers
Izwai mambo	Hear the King
Kuzi tiri masoja	It is said we are soldiers
Uyai muone masoja	Come and see, oh soldiers
Ndazwa izwi remujana	I hear the voice of the leader
Izwai mambo wangu	Hear my King
Toita izwo munoda tenzi wangu, mambo.[4]	We will do your will, my Lord, oh King.

This is an exhortation to Christians to be steadfast in their faith and to spread the Gospel throughout the land. As the song is sung women in the audience will frequently rise to their feet one after the other and execute a few dancing steps in time to the rhythm. Women of the Rukwadzano will, on occasion, sing these songs as well.

2. Shawe exorcism. As has already been mentioned, the Rukwadzano organization holds annual camp meetings, at which large numbers of Methodists camp for three or four days in some

[1] i.e. only an extremely important task would take a man from his work in the fields.

[2] '*Pfene*', 'baboon', is an honorific reference to the singer's *mutupo*, or totem. This usage can be applied to any totem, and does not mean that the speaker's totem is actually *pfene*. The whole phrase is by way of being a solemn oath, and could be loosely translated, 'I *really* mean it, boys'.

[3] A reference to a game in which children form a ring with interlocked arms and one of them inside the ring tries to break out by rushing against the circle. Each time he bounces back unsuccessfully the cry is, 'It is bound with iron'. The inference is that the singers are firmly united in a common purpose.

[4] The Shona text reproduced here was recorded by Mr Robert Kauffman and published in an article appearing in the *Journal of the African Music Society*, Vol. II, No. 3, pp. 31–5. The translation is my own, and differs slightly from that of Mr Kauffman.

convenient spot and attend an almost constant round of services. The Wabvuwi organization and the circuits also stage similar, though smaller, meetings from time to time. During the day and early evening pastors are invited to preach and conduct services, which are similar to those held on Sundays, with perhaps less formality and more evangelistic fervour in the preaching, and including exhortations to non-Christians in attendance to commit themselves publicly to Christ by kneeling at a makeshift altar in front of the rostrum. But however emotional these services may become, they are always under the control of the ministers, and they conform generally to the approved pattern.

It is only late at night during these camps that rituals of *shawe* exorcism directed by laymen are performed, usually in the absence of the pastors. A circle of standing participants, with no identifiable leadership, will form and start to sing Wabvuwi songs, with a trance-like repetition of a few of the phrases. Eventually two or three persons (usually girls or women, but at times men) will either be led or push themselves into the middle of the circle, and seat themselves in a small clearing hastily made for them. These are people possessed by *mashawe* or *ngozi* spirits, and are presenting themselves for exorcism. The rhythmic singing will continue, increasing in volume and intensity. This is said to irritate the *shawe* and make it reveal itself. Eventually the subject will stiffen in all limbs, perhaps become violent, attempt to escape or otherwise exhibit the motor activity of *shawe* possession. The singers have been expecting this, and immediately seize the subject, holding her down in spite of her struggles, a task which may call for several strong assistants. At this point a few of the group will emerge as leaders. They will place their hands on the subject's head, pray, sing, quote Scripture, place a Bible on her head and command the *shawe* in the name of Christ to leave its victim. Sometimes paraphernalia associated with the *shawe* cults which the person has attached to her body, either around the waist or wrists, is cut away.

In several of the performances that the writer has personally witnessed, the result has been almost instantaneous. The subject has become relaxed and conscious of her surroundings, stood up and testified to her deliverance. In other cases, where no response seems forthcoming, she is often sent off with some Rukwadzano women (or Wabvuwi men, in the case of a man) to be questioned at leisure about her troubles.

The ministers tend to frown on these activities, saying that many cases are spurious and that 'they make the people sleepy the next day so that they do not listen to our sermons . . .'. Perhaps fearing scepticism, they also tend to hide these performances from the missionaries, and few of the Methodist missionaries know about or have witnessed any, although they are quite common. Those who participate in these ceremonies justify them on the grounds that they closely parallel the New Testament records of demon exorcism, and therefore cannot be objected to. Whether or not this is so, the parallels with traditional Budjga methods of exorcism are obvious, and it is a paradoxical fact that the one place in Budjga where an observer can expect without question to witness *shawe* possession is at these Methodist meetings. The fact that they are rarely attended by pastors or missionaries strengthens the impression already made by an examination of the different types of services and music found in Budjga Methodism, that two basic modes of ritual activity exist side by side in this Church today.

The one Methodist ritual with high liturgical content is the communion service. Since only ordained pastors of the Church are permitted to administer the communion, it is seldom celebrated in the local churches. Most members partake of communion perhaps four times a year—at the two Quarterly Conferences, at one of the big camp meetings and perhaps on some other special occasion. These services are conducted with great solemnity, and much attention is paid to the spiritual state of the participants. Often a church member will abstain 'because I do not feel good in my heart'.

Christmas and Easter call for special services at the local church, and the congregation usually holds a Christmas feast, a social occasion attracting many non-members, especially young people. Weddings are also the occasion of considerable activity. Banns are called on three Sundays before the marriage, which is usually scheduled for a Saturday. Church weddings usually involve considerable expense on clothes, food and drink for the reception (often held in a classroom adjoining the church), and the rental of vehicles to transport the bridal party. Part of this expense is made up by donations from guests. They present their gifts of money at the reception to a treasurer appointed for this purpose, who announces the gift to general acclamation. There are usually two receptions, one at the church immediately after the wedding, and one at the home of the groom, which may be held the next day.

A Church wedding is usually directed and controlled by the women of Rukwadzano. In many places it is their custom to determine by examination whether or not the bride is a virgin before the wedding, and, if not, to refuse her the privilege of wearing a white veil during the ceremony.[1] This practice has been strongly opposed by the missionaries and some of the younger Budjga Methodists, but the women of the Rukwadzano seek to retain it, maintaining that it inhibits pre-marital sexual intercourse.

METHODISM AND EDUCATION

Mention has already been made[2] of the close association between the churches and rural education. This has been characteristic of Methodism in Budjga, but the connection has slowly changed through the years. At first the Church was under no restrictions from the Government; it could start a village school anywhere it wished, and this Bourgaize did, sending out pastor-teachers to any village that made provision to house and care for them. As the school developed, a local committee would be formed, consisting entirely of church adherents. Bourgaize as District Superintendent was also the supervisor of the teachers and schools. Thus the school was very much a part of the Church, and to many Budjga it *was* the Church. The Church often levied a 'church fee' on every school child, deriving thereby a sizeable income for its budget.

Since the school system has been increasingly subsidized by the Government the situation has changed. Most school committee members are not now church members, although frequently the chairman is one.[3] By Government regulation, no church fees may

[1] Examination of the bride was also a practice in traditional Budjga society, but it is infrequent among non-Christian Budjga today.

[2] *Supra*, pp. 9–11.

[3] Most school committees consist of from eight to twelve members, elected by a general meeting of all parents. The Methodist Church in Budjga stipulates that the chairman of such a committee shall be a Methodist, but in practice this regulation is often ignored. The school committee has become an important local group, since it is responsible for providing and maintaining adequate school buildings, and levies taxes on the parents for this purpose. It also has the power to admit or refuse admission to the school, the principal sanction used to compel parents to pay building fees. Since the school committee also lets building contracts it is a potent economic force in the community.

now be collected from school children, nor may school children be compelled to attend religious services. The vast expansion of the educational system has forced the Church to appoint to its schools many teachers who are only nominal Christians, and the Church Superintendent is no longer the manager of the schools.

There are still, however, close ties between the Church and the school programme. The school managers are appointed and supported by the Church, and are Methodists with an interest in it. These managers have (within limits) the power to appoint and dismiss teachers, and Quarterly Conferences which are dissatisfied with the behaviour of a teacher often bring pressure to bear on the manager to remove him. The Church is also in a position to request the non-Christian section of a community to support church activities, and frequently a school committee has voluntarily decided to assist the building programme of the local church as a return for services. As a member of one such committee said, 'The Church is the mother, the school is the child. The Church has brought us the school, now we must help to build the Church a house.'

The head teacher of a school is a key figure in the programme of the local church. If this man is an enthusiastic church member he is in a strong position to develop the programme of the Church in his community; the number of school children on the probationary rolls of the local church will be high, and it is likely that he will take the lead in all local Church matters. If, on the other hand, he has little interest in church activities, the number of school children enrolled as probationers will be low, and tension may arise between him, his staff and the local church members.

METHODISM AND YOUTH

The observer soon becomes aware of a difference in attitude of Methodists towards Christianity that can be roughly equated with age. To understand this it is necessary to recapitulate a little history and to understand that the period 1940–1948 made a break in the continuity of missionary activity. Most of the missionaries sent to Rhodesia before this time, while concerned with the educational and economic development of the Shona, conceived of the Gospel primarily in terms of the conversion of the individual, of a commitment which enabled a person to face his environment and circumstances with a new attitude and reinforced spiritual resources. Between 1940 and 1949 few new missionaries arrived and those who came afterwards represented a new generation with a different approach, one which laid emphasis on the 'social gospel', with its belief that Christianity can and should change the individual's circumstances and environment. The emphasis was shifted from evangelism to education, from church community to society as a whole.

This difference was reflected in the Budjga Methodist Church. Most of the ministers and older church members are products of the earlier period, while many of the teachers and younger members have been brought up in the more recent stage of church development. The older generation complains bitterly about what it considers the lax morals of the younger generation, says that the young people have a superficial religion and are interested only in politics and money, and (with some justification) that they do not support the Church financially. The younger members retort that the religion of the older generation is 'emotional' and 'unsophisticated', that they are inattentive to the vital problems of the day, and that they deny the youth the opportunity to participate in the leadership of the Church.

In some cases this rift becomes quite obvious, almost to the point where there are two congregations on the same site. The Sunday morning worship service is attended only by the older church members and the infants in their care, while the school children, young people and teachers go to the youth meeting in the afternoon. These are extreme cases, of course, and usually the differences between the two groups are much less obtrusive. The attitude of some of the teachers spans the gap, thereby producing an interesting situation in the determination of Church policy and programme. In the local church and the Quarterly Conferences the older generation tends to have a voting preponderance and take the lead. But these bodies frequently elect teachers, because of their ability to speak English and their familiarity with parliamentary procedure, as their representatives to the District Conferences and the Annual Conference, so that the important decisions taken by these bodies (the setting of ministers' salaries, determination of over-all church educational policy, etc.) are to some extent dominated by the younger element.

5

Budjga Catholicism

THE DEVELOPMENT OF CATHOLICISM IN BUDJGA

It is entirely possible that the first Christian missionary to enter what is now Southern Rhodesia, Father Gonzalo da Silviera, passed through Budjga territory. But, as we have already noted,[1] whatever the impact of this early Catholic missionary effort was, it soon disappeared with the retreat of the Portuguese east of the Inyanga Mountain barrier. The modern history of Roman Catholicism in Budjga does not begin until 1929, when missionary priests stationed at St Benedict's Mission, 100 miles to the south, first established the All Souls' Mission. Its first site was near the Rukau Business Centre, but it was moved in 1931 to its present location away from the malarial lowland.[2] Since its inception the Mission has had five priests-in-charge, the first four being European missionary fathers while the present incumbent is a non-Budjga African priest.

Roman Catholic development in Budjga was coloured by a somewhat different approach to that of the Methodists. In the first place, for the Roman Catholics conversion involved not a subjective experience, but rather commitment to a given system of beliefs and practices, coupled with loyalty to the organization. The Catholics recognized that this type of commitment and loyalty would be difficult to inculcate in Budjga adults, and from the first their emphasis was almost entirely on children, an emphasis which still exists today and is reflected in the attendance figures at Catholic services throughout Budjga.[3] The Catholic Church did not attempt mass conversions nor baptize children indiscriminately; a child was only baptized if there was some guarantee that it would receive Catholic instruction. This meant,

---

[1] *Supra*, p. 6.

[2] Now, with malaria fairly well controlled in Budjga, the disadvantage of the second site is painfully obvious, for there is little water, a definitely restricting factor in any plans for future growth. Correspondence regarding the change of this site is found in the Government Archives File S 138/17/1921–1931.

[3] *Supra*, p. 70.

in effect, that it must be near a Catholic school, for few Budjga parents could be relied upon to give their children this type of guidance. Thus the establishment of a village school system throughout Budjga was vital to Catholic expansion there.[1]

Unfortunately for the Catholics, the Methodists had already established a sizeable village school system, with centres in some of the most populous areas. An Educational Department regulation prohibited the establishment of a school within three miles of one already approved, so that the Catholics were forced to look elsewhere. Furthermore, the Methodists were not happy to see Roman Catholic encroachment in 'their' area, and a considerable rivalry developed between the two Churches in a race to develop schools in the more desirable locations still open. In this contest the Methodists had the advantage of a prior establishment in Budjga and the generally good reputation that it bore, while the Catholics could offer a Church membership without rigid disciplinary restrictions on such issues as smoking and beer drinking.[2]

By 1964 most available school sites in Budjga had been occupied and the situation was stabilized; the Catholic Church had eleven schools, with a total of 2990 children.[3] Most of the larger schools in this system were in the eastern part of the Reserve, in the Chimoyo and Nyakuchena chiefdoms near All Souls' Mission.

Another difference between the Methodist and Roman Catholic approaches was that the Methodists, as has been described,[4] developed local congregations with a degree of autonomy in local affairs which produced a certain amount of local ritual leadership, while the Catholics created no such local organization. Parents and children were expected to meet weekly for prayers, and on occasion the priest would visit the school to celebrate Mass, but villagers held no offices in the Church, nor were they expected to provide ritual leadership. As a result the Mission at All Souls' was much more a ritual centre for the Catholics than the Mission at

---

[1] The close identification of Christianity and education in the minds of many Budjga parents is well illustrated by the testimony of one Catholic teacher, who told me how, when he was a child in a Catholic school, his non-Christian parents made no objection to his being baptized, for, he said, 'My parents made no difference between being baptized and education. They thought baptism was some kind of educational promotion'.

[2] This was not always a convincing argument to the village elders. They were happy enough to escape condemnation for drinking beer themselves. 'But,' they said, 'perhaps it is good for our children to be taught not to drink.'

[3] See Appendix, Table 8.   [4] *Supra*, pp. 65–7.

Mtoko was for the Methodists. In fact religious services (apart from school prayers) were, and are, rarely held in the Roman Catholic villages within ten miles of All Souls'; instead villagers and school children from these places are expected to attend Mass at the Mission at least once a month. Roman Catholic village centres farther away are visited once a month by a priest from All Souls' and Mass is celebrated on these occasions.

At All Souls' itself there is a continual round of services. In 1945 an attractive and imposing church, the largest in Budjga today, was built on the Mission with the aid of volunteer Italian prisoner-of-war labour. At present a large staff is in residence, consisting of two African priests, one African brother, ten African sisters and four European sisters. The two priests are involved in the administration of the Mission and the school system, while the sisters teach in the Mission primary school and staff the Mission clinic.[1]

It is difficult to gauge the numerical strength of Roman Catholicism in Budjga today. The records of the Mission show 11,141 baptisms since it started, but no indication is given as to deaths, transfers out of Budjga or defection. A run-down of attendance at monthly Mass at all the places in Budjga where this is held yields a figure of 840. A figure twice this size, 1680, may indicate roughly the active adherents of Catholicism in the Reserve.[2]

DOCTRINE AND DISCIPLINE

Roman Catholic doctrine is too well known to require elaboration here, but it will be useful to note some of the special emphases that it has been given in Budjga, particularly those that stand in contrast to the beliefs and practice of the other Christian groups and are therefore noted as identifying characteristics by many Budjga.

(a) Existence after death. Speaking of the Budjga belief in the *midzimu*, one of the Roman Catholic priests hazarded the guess that the practices surrounding it might 'be baptized into the Faith'. Whatever his superiors might think of this position, certainly Roman Catholic doctrine concerning post-mortem existence is more easily compatible with Budjga traditional belief

---

[1] A Spanish priest, Father Rubio, did pastoral work in Budjga from 1956 to 1959 with considerable success, but was later transferred elsewhere.

[2] Table 6 indicates the details and criteria used to arrive at this figure.

than is, say, that of the Methodists. The Catholic veneration of the Saints, and the belief that they are intercessors for the supplicant before higher Spiritual Powers, have parallels in Budjga traditional belief which makes them easy for a convert to accept. Moreover, while Methodists do not pray for their dead (contending that the fate of the soul is decided by an individual's acts while he is still alive), the Roman Catholic practice of praying for souls in Purgatory[1] reflects a belief that the well-being of the dead is dependent to some extent upon the actions of their living friends and relatives, a parallel to Budjga Traditional Religion not found in Methodism.

The cult of the dead thus plays a more important part in Budjga Catholicism than in Budjga Methodism. This emphasis also seems to be used by Catholics as an incentive to membership. Speaking of his conversion one Catholic teacher said, 'I learned that if you did good without being baptized you were just wasting your time. But if you were baptized and then did good, it would be counted for you in the next life.'

(b) Importance of ritual participation. While Methodists have emphasized the importance of a subjective religious experience, the Catholics have stressed attendance at prescribed ceremonies as a necessary element in Christian life. Adult Catholics throughout the Reserve are expected to attend Mass once a month, and required to do so once a year. Participation in Mass may be preceded by confession. A number of special religious days are set out in the Church calendar, and certain dietary prohibitions apply during the Lenten season and on Fridays.[2] While not all Budjga Catholics conform to these regulations, they give an explicit direction to the conduct of ritual life not found in the more subjective Methodist approach.

Other differences between the Catholics and Methodists in doctrine and discipline are recognized by the Budjga. It has only

[1] A widely distributed booklet used by the Catholics in Budjga contains the phrase, 'Thus the Church prays for the soul of one who has died, and beseeches God to have mercy, so that he may be freed from the punishments of Purgatory'. *Ushe HwaYave*, Catholic Mission Press, Gwelo, 1961, p. 63 (translated here from the Shona). The title *Ushe HwaYave* means 'The Kingdom of God'. Catholic literature tends to use *Yawe* (Jehovah) instead of *Mwari* as a designation for God.

[2] These regulations are set forth in *Rugwaro Rwokunamata Rwavanhu VeKirike Katolike* ('The Ritual of Prayers of the People of the Catholic Church') Chishawasha Mission, 1962, p. 18, and, more fully with comment, in *Ushe HwaYawe*, pp. 89–92.

been recently that the Catholic Church has begun to encourage Bible reading among its membership with the publication of the New Testament.[1] Whereas the Methodists and Vapostori both condemn the use of tobacco and the drinking of beer, the Catholic Church does not have any such prohibitions.[2]

The Church denies communion to those who have openly broken some Church regulation, a much less severe sanction than that so often utilized by the Methodists, of expulsion from the church group. To my knowledge there has never been a case of excommunication in the history of Budjga Catholicism. Once baptized a person remains on the Church rolls[3] for the rest of his life, and is considered a Christian, even if only in a lapsed state. The steps back to active status are not as many or usually as difficult as they are in the case of Methodism; confession and the performance of any penance prescribed is usually all that is necessary.

Yet in Budjga many adults who have been baptized into the Catholic Church do leave it. There are many reasons for this, but two seem to stand out from the case histories obtained. (We are speaking here only of those who revert to Budjga Traditional Religion, not those who become Methodists or Vapostori.) Many Catholics leave the Church for what might be termed indifference; their affiliation to the Church does not profoundly affect their lives and membership does not seem significant to them. Since there is no corporate local church life the Catholic villager does not enjoy the group identification produced by membership in the other Budjga Christian groups. Secondly, there is the matter of polygamy, an issue on which the Catholic Church is just as strict as the Methodist. Catholic men who become polygamists are excluded from communion, as are Catholic women who become the wives of such men. The influence of nationalist politics will be discussed in the final chapter.

CATHOLIC CHURCH ORGANIZATION

All Souls' Mission, and all the Catholic work in the Mtoko District, falls within the jurisdiction of the Archdiocese of

[1] *Chitenderano Chitsva*, Mambo Press, Gwelo, 1966.

[2] Although it urges moderation. *Muchato Nemhuri*, Catholic Mission Press, Gwelo, 1958, p. 14.

[3] i.e., the Baptismal Register mentioned on p. 82. There are no other membership records.

Salisbury, one of the five Roman Catholic dioceses in Southern Rhodesia. While for the Methodists and Vapostori the local congregation is the basic unit of church organization, in the Roman Catholic hierarchy it is the Mission at All Souls' which provides the centre for ritual activities in Budjga and the link between Budjga Catholics and the universal Church. As we have already indicated, the one Catholic church building in Budjga is located at the Mission, a large and attractive structure. It is at this centre that Catholic school children from all over Budjga present themselves for confirmation by the Bishop, and to it that most practising Budjga Catholics go at least once a year to attend Mass. All Souls' is also the centre of the Catholic school system in the Mtoko District, and the residence of all the priests, brothers and sisters who serve the Church there.

The two priests in residence at All Souls' are both Africans directly under the Archdiocese and not members of an order or society. Father Simon Tsuro, the priest-in-charge, was the first Shona priest to be ordained by his Church in Southern Rhodesia. Both he and his colleague, who has responsibility for the Mission's schools, provide a leadership of great organizational ability and technical finesse, reflecting the very thorough training that they have received. In each case this involved, after two years of secondary school,[1] eight years of seminary training. This is far superior to the training of any Budjga Methodist pastor.

The priest responsible for the village schools attempts, in addition to supervising the educational programme, to visit the more distant stations at least once a month to celebrate Mass. There is a small Roman Catholic congregation at Mtoko Centre, unattached to any school, and this congregation assembles once a month at the District Commissioner's Office, where permission has been granted to hold services.

The one brother at All Souls' is a member of the Congregation of Peter Claver.[2] Members of this congregation undergo a novitiate of two years at Musami Mission near Mrewa, and are then sent out to serve on various missions, usually in maintenance or agricultural work. Of the fourteen sisters who live at All Souls', the four Europeans are Dominicans from Germany; the ten African

---

[1] Called the 'Junior Certificate' in the Rhodesian educational system.
[2] A Roman Catholic priest, later canonized, who worked in South America among slaves shipped there from Africa.

nuns are members of the Little Children of Our Blessed Lady, the only African congregation of sisters in the Salisbury Archdiocese. Candidates for this Order must have passed Standard VI, after which they pass through a six-year novitiate at Makumbe Mission, near Salisbury. The sisters are engaged in teaching at the Mission, supervising the girls' boarding establishment and managing the Mission's small clinic.

Parents often object to the candidacy of their children for either the priesthood or the sisterhood, and sometimes prevent them from entering these professions. In the case of girls sisterhood means the loss of *rovora* payments and is frequently resisted strenuously by parents. Girls find the sisterhood attractive for ideological reasons, or because it can provide the training required for a teacher, something their parents may not be able to provide. The security of a life free from financial worry is also an attraction to some.

The one layman who plays an important part in the Catholic organization in Budjga is the local school head teacher. As with the Methodists this person holds a key position in the programme of the Church in any locality. If he is a strong supporter of the Church, attendance at services held at his school will be good; if not, religious activity at his school will rapidly decline. A dramatic example of this was given at the Karonga School, where a change of teachers took place during 1964. In February I attended a Sunday service at this school conducted by the head teacher, an active and enthusiastic Catholic layman. In attendance were 13 adults, including four of the five teachers at the school, and 114 school children (out of a total enrolment of 191). In September of the same year a new head teacher was appointed, also a Roman Catholic, but one with far less interest in the Church. In November I was present at a service similar to the one just mentioned, but this time there were only 16 school children present and no adults. At the time when it was held the head teacher and two of the assistant teachers were on the grounds of the school in their houses, but they apparently had no interest in attending the meeting and had obviously not urged any of the parents to do so. The service was led by one of the older school boys.

This would indicate that the success of the local Catholic religious programme is even more heavily dependent upon the activity of head teachers than in the Methodist system, for in the latter, even if the head teacher is indifferent to the church programme, there is usually a core of local laymen both willing and empowered to carry it on. In the instance that I have just given, neither the teachers nor the parents who absented themselves from the service had ceased to be Catholics; they simply did not attach the importance to 'school prayers' that the former head teacher had. If the priest had been in attendance to administer Mass, there would no doubt have been a good turn-out of adults and teachers.

Local school committees similar to those in the Methodist system[1] have been organized to carry out building projects and regulate parent-teacher relationships. As with the Methodists, membership of the Catholic Church has little bearing on the composition of the Committee, and frequently there are few, if any, Catholics in it. The chairman of the largest Catholic reserve school, Bwanya, is a member of the Vapostori.

The Catholics have no lay organizations comparable with the Rukwadzano and Wabvuwi of the Methodist Church. There is a Catholic Laymen's Association organized at a diocesan level. Its annual meetings are attended primarily by Catholic teachers and other professional people; it serves as a forum for discussion, but does not provide the ritual leadership found in the Wabvuwi. There are also Catholic women's organizations which have some similarities to the Rukwadzano: members wear uniforms, are supposed to be organized into local chapters, meet weekly and conform to certain standards of service and devotion. But these organizations do not have the same autonomy as the Rukwadzano has, and there are only a few active local groups.

The Catholics raise less money locally in Budjga for their church programme than any of the other Christian groups. Collections are taken at each Mass, and for the period 14 June to 20 November 1964 totalled £5 2s 3d for the whole of Budjga.[2] The balance necessary to run the Church programme during this period had to be supplied from diocesan funds. Just before the field work for this study ended, in December 1964, it was proposed that every parent having children in a Roman Catholic school should be required to give £2 10s towards the expenses of the Mission at All Souls'. It is doubtful that this programme will succeed, since political agitation has made the Government

---

[1] *Supra*, p. 77.
[2] A figure supplied from the officiating priest's notebook.

G

hesitant to endorse any action that links Church and school in this way. Ten years ago such procedure would have been common-place for both Methodists and Catholics, but today the churches cannot expect financial support from their schools; this is a fiscal fact that both denominations must now accept.

CATHOLIC RITUAL

Budjga Catholics are familiar with two basic types of religious service, the local prayer service, or 'Chinamato', and the less frequent but more important Mass, held either in the local school or at the Mission. The first type of service consists primarily of the singing of two or three hymns and the repetition of a set series of prayers, read from a Shona prayerbook. The leader may give a brief homily on some subject, but there is little extemporaneity in the service as a whole.

The Mass, with its wealth of symbolism and visual detail, is a ritual to which Budjga Catholics attach great importance. Visual and aural detail are especially in evidence in the celebrations of Mass in the Church at the Mission. The use of holy water, bells, incense, candles and ornate priestly vestments are all component parts of the service. The use of signs and symbols[1] is also evident in the Mass, and in some of the other special Catholic rituals. The baptismal service, for instance, takes place in a chapel decorated with pictures depicting the various ritual objects used. Among these are: *Mafuta*—'Oil on the chest, softening the heart'. *Mvura*—'The waters of baptism'. *Krisima*—'Oil on the head, softening the thoughts'. *Mucheka*—A white cloth on the head. 'The head should be as pure as a white cloth.' *Mwenje*—The candle given to the baptismal candidate. 'The heart should burn like a candle.'

Whether or not they are to be considered as signs or symbols, the important thing to note here is that these objects and acts have, for Budjga Catholics, a ritual efficacy, and participation in ceremonies involving them is conceived to impart both spiritual

---

[1] I am using these words in terms of the distinction made between them by Jung and quoted by Turner (1961, p. 1), i.e. that 'a sign is an analogous or abbreviated expression of a *known* thing. But a symbol is always the best possible expression of a relatively *unknown* fact, a fact, however, which is none the less recognized or postulated as existing'. As Turner points out, the same item may be both a symbol and a sign in a society, and depending upon an individual's understanding of it, may tend to become more of a sign as his esoteric knowledge makes the item an object of cognition rather than emotion.

and material wellbeing. Provided that there is no spiritual impediment in the recipient, the connection is seen as a necessary, causal one.[1]

This attitude seems to be implicit rather than explicit, and in Budjga it is by no means confined to Catholics. It is found, as we shall see, among the Vapostori, and perhaps in the thinking of some Methodists as well. But Catholicism, with such rituals as Extreme Unction, give this concept a more concrete basis.

Shona and Latin are the two languages used in Catholic services. The use of Latin is important, since the ability to use a few Latin phrases seems to be, for at least some Budjga Catholics, a symbol of religious prestige.

CATHOLICISM IN BUDJGA SOCIETY

The sense of membership in a religious organization which is transtribal in scope, nationally influential and claims to be unique, is of great importance to those Budjga who take their Catholicism seriously. The Catholic Church, like the other two major Christian groups in Budjga, has created its own religious sub-society. By this I imply an association in which membership produces a consciousness of religious alignment, of in-group and out-group relationships, an alignment which may be operative in a variety of religious, social, economic and other contexts. For the Methodists and Vapostori the principal (although not the only) agent producing this consciousness of religious alignment is the local congregation. It is to this group that the individual must answer for his actions, and from it that he receives the guidance and aid which are the exclusive prerogatives of membership. The Budjga Catholic has no such group; this type of identification is provided for him instead by membership in the Church at large, with the wide range of identifying symbols that this entails.

An example of the way the Catholic Church creates a new relationship based primarily on Catholic membership is the elaboration of the godparent relationship into a quasi-kinship link. When an infant is baptized the parents are asked to select a

---

[1] Pauw has noted the importance of this attitude in connection with the Roman Catholic doctrine of the sacraments, and sees in it an element which he defines as magical, since a given result is conceived necessarily to follow the ritual action when properly performed. This is, he considers, one of the reasons for Roman Catholic success among the Tlhaping Tswana. Pauw, 1960, p. 223.

godmother or godfather, according to the sex of the child.[1] In the case of a girl child, an adolescent girl is usually chosen to act as godmother, selected (often with the priest's advice) for her good character and Christian devotion. One such girl, selected by a Catholic teacher and his wife to be the godmother of their infant daughter, was chosen, they told me, 'because she respects both her parents and other people. She does not go about with boys and she is humble. She works in the field with her parents instead of going to work at the hotels as other girls do.'

The girl chosen must be present at the baptism, and indeed becomes the central adult subject of the ceremony, more important than the parents, who may in fact not even be present. She it is who holds the infant during the ritual, and who takes the vows to give the child proper Christian guidance. For her part in the ceremony the godmother is presented with small gifts of money, considered a token of the relationship now established between her and the child.

Ideally the godmother exercises close supervision over the child's development, and her role becomes especially important when the child has grown to adolescence and the possibility of marriage arises. The godmother should be consulted before a partner is chosen, and has authority to forbid a match which she considers unwise. At the wedding of a godchild she is given a prominent place.

I have heard a Catholic priest in Budjga give a short sermon on this subject, urging godparents in his congregation to fulfil their responsibilities, and godchildren to be obedient to their 'parents in the spirit'. This 'kinship of the spirit',[2] as it is called, gives to Catholic Budjga an alignment which parallels, and sometimes supplants, kinship relations. The intimate relationship between godmother and god-daughter is that which in traditional Budjga society exists between a girl and her *tete* (father's sister), and when a child is brought into a godchild relationship the result is to diminish the importance of kinship and emphasize Catholic affiliation in this sphere. This is of course especially important when the parents and relatives of the child are only nominal Christians, since then the priest by his selection of a godmother

---

[1] Both a godmother and a godfather may be chosen for the child, but usually in practice only one godparent is chosen.
[2] 'Ukama hwe mweya.'

moves the child into an area of Christian influence which would not otherwise be provided by the kin group.

In the economic sphere membership loyalties apparently influence to some extent the trading patterns of Catholics, the sentiment being that members should support Catholic businessmen. Catholic traders tend to establish their stores near communities with Catholic schools, and a successful Catholic store-owner at the Mtoko Centre confirmed that a large share of his business came from fellow-Catholics. Conversely, critics of some store-owners say 'They are Catholics only because they know that by being so they will get the order for school uniforms from the local Catholic school'.

Each of the three Christian groups in Budjga claims moral and theological superiority over the others, but the Catholic Church does this more explicitly than the other two. Its claim to exclusiveness appears not only in statements by its members but also in its literature.[1] Its position as the senior representative of Christianity, which is not contested by the other Budjga Churches, is an argument that many Budjga find to be of great significance. Insistence that adherents should marry only Roman Catholics, or at least that the marriage should take place under Catholic auspices and with the promise that any children shall be raised in the Church, evokes resentment from the other Christian groups, but contributes to the cohesion of the Catholic community. While no detailed figures are available, it is apparent from marriage registrations at Mtoko that Roman Catholic marriages are on the increase in the Reserve, while Protestant marriages have shown no significant change over the past ten years.[2]

[1] Emmanuel Marudzi, *Chechi Imwe Chete Yechokwadi* ('The One True Church'), Catholic Mission Press, Gwelo, n.d., pp. 30–3.
[2] See Table 9.

6

The Budjga Vapostori

HISTORY

The Budjga Vapostori are a branch of the Apostles of Johanne
Maranke, more properly called the Vapostori we Johanne, for
so free has their development been from any direct European
influence that the English word 'Apostle' is not used by them. In
a general discussion of Shona religion it is necessary to use the
qualifying 'we Johanne', since, as we have already mentioned,[1]
there are at least four major groups that use the rubric 'Apostolic',
but since the Johanne group is the only one of these with significant representation in Budjga, they are referred to throughout
this study simply as Vapostori.

The Movement was founded in 1932 in the Maranke Reserve,
near Umtali in eastern Southern Rhodesia. The founder, Mucha-
baya Ngomberume, was a Methodist layman of visionary
temperament who took the name 'Johanne' when he launched it.
Most of its early converts were Methodists, but it later attracted
adherents from the ranks of Traditional Religionists and various
Christian denominations. It has grown rapidly, especially since the
Second World War, and now has perhaps 50,000 adherents in
Southern Rhodesia alone. It has also spread to Northern Rhodesia,
Bechuanaland, Mozambique and the Congo.

Space does not permit a detailed account here of the history of
the Movement outside Budjga, nor a discussion of its religious and
cultural antecedents. Although it has had no direct connection
with any other religious organization, it can be said that the
Methodist Church was its ecclesiastical matrix, and the Vapostori
frequently refer to this church as the 'Mother Church'. They use
Methodist hymns and have taken over the Methodist insistence on
the reading of the Bible and reliance upon it as the authoritative
revelation of God, and given it an emphasis beyond that which it
finds in Methodism. Yet it is an interesting fact that several items
of Vapostori terminology and practice have more affinity with
Roman Catholic than Methodist usage. The word for a local

[1] *Supra*, p. 60.

congregation is *kireke*, a word used by Catholics but not by Methodists. *Jehovah* is the word for God, paralleling Catholic usage rather than the Methodist *Mwari*. The insistence on participation in a eucharistic service once a year, preceded by confession, and the use of colourful ritual vestments are practices closer to Catholic than Methodist tradition, but whether the connection is historical or incidental is not clear.

From the inception of his Movement Johanne rested his authority upon four credentials: his revelations,[1] his claim to foretell events much in the manner of a spirit medium, his claim to be able to heal diseases and his charismatic personality. Secure in his authority, Johanne collected around him a nucleus of men who assisted in evangelism and administration. As the Movement grew larger, Johanne instituted the Pasca,[2] or Passover, a meeting held in July and lasting two weeks, at which an annual service of communion is held. By insisting that each member should participate in this annual ritual, and by holding it near his home in Maranke, Johanne made the Pasca a unifying factor for the Movement at a time when it was expanding. It was an act of ritual merit to attend, and even those adherents who lived outside Maranke made the annual pilgrimage. Only Johanne himself was authorized to conduct the communion service at the Pasca, and thus he added a further important leadership credential to those already mentioned, that of being the exclusive High Priest of the Organization.

As areas farther away from Maranke were evangelized, it became impossible to insist that all the adherents come to Maranke for the annual Pasca, and others had to be organized, but Johanne kept a tight control of these by insisting that he must be present at each, at least to preside over the communion service. An itinerary was arranged whereby he travelled from one to another, attending to his high priestly duties, giving advice on local problems and settling disputes. The network of Pascas continued to grow, until finally it became impossible for Johanne to attend them all, and he had to delegate the supervision of a large number to his eldest son, Abel. When Johanne died in 1963, control of the Movement

---

[1] Recorded in a mimeographed booklet under the title *Humbowo Hutswa We Vapostori*, 'The New Witness of the Apostles'. This 22-page booklet contains a record of Johanne's visions which he dictated a few years before his death.

[2] Also known as the Penta (= Pentecost).

passed quickly to Abel, who has so far continued to provide effective leadership.

The Vapostori Movement first reached Budjga in 1938. A man from the Charewa Chieftainship named Machinga, an active Methodist layman, came under the influence of Vapostori preaching while visiting a neighbouring reserve and was baptized into the Movement. He took the name of Koronia (Cornelius) and brought the faith back to Budjga. Together with his son-in-law, Jonas Campa, he started an evangelism campaign in 1938.[1] The first *penta* organized in Budjga was held at Mudze; it was later moved to Nyatsine, both places being in the Mtoko Chiefdom.[2] Koronia, still living but now rather senile, continues to be associated with the Nyatsine Penta, and is honoured as being *muridzi wacho*, 'its owner', even though effective leadership is now in other hands. As the Movement spread, two other *pentas* were eventually established, one at Makosa in the Makosa Chiefdom and one at Muswaire in the Nyamkowo Chiefdom. The rate of growth in the Movement paralleled that elsewhere, with large increases after the Second World War. There are perhaps 1800 adult active adherents of the Movement in Budjga at the present time.[3]

ORGANIZATION

As with the Methodist Church, the basic unit of organization for the Vapostori is the local congregation, which meets regularly every week and is known as the *kireke*. A *kireke* usually has from 20 to 40 adult members, all of whom live within a two or three-mile radius of the group's regular place of meeting. The site is usually on a *ruware*[4] or under some large shade tree, often in a

[1] The Vapostori are usually vague about historical details, but the year of the entrance of the Movement into Budjga can be fixed with confidence on the testimony of a reliable witness, Andrew Chifodya, a messenger at the District Commissioner's Office in Mtoko. Chifodya remembers the event very well, since he was at the time a neighbour of Machinga, and at the time of Machinga's conversion received from him a gift of all his pigs, since the Vaspostori do not keep or eat swine.

[2] Nyatsine is a place name, which gives its name to the annual *penta* which meets there and thus to the organizational unit based on this meeting. Vaspostori may say that they 'belong' to the Nyatsine Penta, meaning thereby that they are members of a local congregation which is connected administratively with the annual meeting at Nyatsine.

[3] For details concerning the computation of this figure, see Table 6.

[4] A flat rock outcropping, see p. 20.

grazing area some distance from the village 'lines'. No attempt is made to acquire title to the site, and sometimes the meeting place has to be changed because it is ploughed under or villagers complain of the noise of the services. Nor is any structure erected for worship, for it is a cardinal item of Vapostori doctrine that this should take place out of doors, and Acts 7.48–9[1] is often quoted as a justification for this belief and as a condemnation of the Methodist practice of building churches.

The membership of the *kireke* is divided into ordinary members and office-holders, a division which divides the congregation approximately in half. There are four principal offices: *Vababatidzi* (baptizers), *Vavangeri* (evangelists), *Vaprophiti* (prophets), and *Varapi* (healers). Vapostori are reluctant to rank these offices, maintaining that 'they are all equal, only their functions are different', but when pressed they usually grade them in the order given. Each office is internally ranked into junior and senior members, so that there are junior baptizers and senior baptizers, etc. Men may hold any one of the four offices, but women may aspire only to those of prophet or healer.

Men are fairly evenly distributed among the four offices, with perhaps a slight preponderance of evangelists, while fewer hold that of healer than any other. With few exceptions, no man or woman may hold more than one office. Each office-holder wears a badge indicating office and rank.

In addition to the four principal offices just mentioned there are two others, those of *hakrios*[2] (singer) and *mutongi* (judge). The *mahakrios* (pl.) are usually women but may be men, and are supposed to provide the lead in congregational singing. In practice this office seems to have little significance; people lead out in singing whether or not they are *mahakrios*. Most *mahakrios* are younger members of the congregation, and this is one office which may be held in conjunction with another.

The *mutongi* office can also be held jointly with another, but is far more important. The *vatongi* (pl.) are older men who, on account of their experience and seniority, are given the responsibility of judging cases brought to them by the prophets, and give

[1] 'Howbeit the Most High dwelleth not in temples made with hands; as saith the prophet, "Heaven is my throne and earth is my footstool: what house will ye build me? saith the Lord."'
[2] For comment on the derivation of this word, see p. 99.

advice to those who voluntarily confess to sins of temper or breaches of Vapostori discipline.

Evangelists have the task of spreading the Vapostori gospel, of providing most of the preaching at services (although holders of other offices may be called upon to preach as well) and arranging for and conducting all meetings. Baptizers are, as their name implies, charged with the duty of baptizing converts, and are the only members authorized to perform this task. More will be said of the healers and prophets shortly.

Each office is conceived to be conferred upon the holder as a gift of the Spirit. In practice a variety of factors seem to be involved in the association of any member with an office; the person concerned may have dreams which are interpreted by the elders as an indication by the Spirit that he or she has been called to be a prophet, healer, etc., or one of the prophets of the *kireke* may reveal that such and such a person has been designated for an office. In each case the *vatongi* make a final judgement as to the authenticity of the claim.

Leadership of the *kireke* is vested in a small core of men led (usually) by its founder or his successor, after whom the *kireke* has been named. This man is the *muridzi* ('owner') of the *kireke*, much as a village headman who establishes a kraal is considered its *muridzi*, 'ownership' in this case implying not personal possession but trusteeship and the authority that goes with it. Vapostori say that each *kireke* is governed by a group of four men, the senior representatives of each of the four major offices, with the founder (who would naturally be one of these) as its leader. In actual fact the leadership of a Vapostori *kireke* depends less on any fixed principle of selection than on the careful evaluation by the *kireke* of the leadership capabilities of its members. Thus the effective leadership core of a *kireke* may include two or three evangelists and no healers, or in some other way reflect the recognition of ability.

One contrast between Methodists and Vapostori which emerges very clearly is that in the *kireke*, once a man has established himself as a leader (i.e. is accepted as one of the *vakuru*, 'elders') his position is far more secure than that of his counterpart in the Methodist organization. There is no vote of the Quarterly Conference hanging over his head and threatening to replace him, and his apostasy would have to be very blatant indeed to provoke the *kireke* to depose him. Often when asking informants to list the leaders of a *kireke* for me they have named men who at the time were not active members, a fact which they readily admitted.[1] Yet their position in the *kireke* was, as it were, reserved for them, to be taken up upon their return.[2] Seniority in the group is extremely important, and the principle that it confers authority on the basis of this factor is rarely evaded in the local congregation. Younger members of the *kireke* are careful to give deference on this basis. One of my best Vapostori informants, a man of about 38 years of age named Sampson Josi, was among the most active members of his *kireke*, apparently well liked by everyone and constantly called upon to perform a variety of services for the congregation. In a Methodist congregation a man of his ability and energy would no doubt have been given a position of considerable prominence, but he constantly referred to himself as one of the 'children' of the *kireke*, and was at some pains to demonstrate that he had no ambitions for a position of authority in the group. If indeed he did have such ambitions, his attitude at the time was the best way of ensuring that they would eventually be realized, for his decorous behaviour had obviously won him the respect of the rest of the *kireke*. The Vapostori say, as the Swazi do, 'No man should push himself forward',[3] and one is reminded by their practice of what the Kriges have to say concerning the Lovedu search for power: '. . . such power is sought . . . in normality, equanimity, and maturity'.[4] This maturity is achieved only by the passage of time, application to the task of conforming to the norms of the group and progress up the hierarchical ladder. Once achieved it is a lasting possession which cannot be taken away, only discarded by the individual himself. Vapostori leaders, even when old and senile, never lose their titular authority, even though their position may be an emeritus one.

Thus Vapostori leadership may be said to be built upon a combination of three criteria: (*a*) Seniority within the ranks of the group. (*b*) Office, ostensibly bestowed as a gift of the Spirit but in effect conferred by the elders as an indication of their estimate of the individual's ability, and therefore being in the nature of an

[1] *Akamira*, 'he stands', is the phrase often used, implying a temporary drawing aside of the individual from the progress of the Movement.
[2] A case of this type is described in detail later, pp. 140.
[3] Kuper, 1947, p. 160.   [4] Krige, 1943, p. 288.

explicitly recognized achieved status. (c) Reputation, based on maturity and achievement in the realm of group norms, being thus in the nature of an implicitly recognized achieved status. The way these three criteria are utilized and balanced in the selection of leadership personnel varies from *kireke* to *kireke* and depends upon local circumstances.[1]

Consistently with the qualities just mentioned, leadership is exercised unobtrusively and without ostentation. The leaders often delegate the actual conduct of services to junior members of the *kireke*, and important decisions regarding who is to preach, what special meetings are to be held or what assistance is to be rendered to a member in distress are made in informal meetings which are called as the need arises. Leadership is more obvious in the *dare*[2] meetings held before services, when members air their complaints and confess their faults. After several of the elders have spoken on some problem the leader will sum up the case and give a judgement which usually reflects general opinion.

The *kireke* is not divided into sub-groups like the Methodist congregation. There is no women's group and no youth group. The older men dominate the congregation, and neither the youth nor the women exercise much initiative in local ceremonies.

A group of *kireke* within the same general area may meet from time to time for a weekend of services known as a *sabata*. The *sabata* has, however, little administrative significance. It has no continuing name, since its venue changes from time to time, and its composition may change as well, depending on where it is held. It is therefore primarily a ritual occasion. Of far greater organizational significance are the Budjga *pentas*, which have already been mentioned. At these annual meetings these infrequent disputes between *kireke* leaders and their congregations which cannot be settled at the local level are heard and judgement given, while the joint participation of the *kirekes* in the large and impressive services involved gives the Movement a cohesiveness which would otherwise be impossible with its loosely-knit administrative structure. Joint responsibility for the financial requirements of the camp, and the convivial atmosphere of camping together for several days, create bonds of friendship and a cross-fertilization of

---

[1] Succession to leadership along kinship lines, as found at the top of the hierarchy in the case of Abel, does not appear as a discernible principle in the local group.   [2] *Infra*, p. 101.

ideas vital to the Movement, and the size of the *penta* gives the individual Mupostori a sense of identification with a large and powerful organization.

Control of the *penta* is vested in a group of twelve officials who are called *liebumah*.[1] This group is more rigidly organized than the leadership of the *kireke*; three of the *liebumah* are baptizers, three are prophets, three are healers and three evangelists. The leader of the group is the *muridzi* ('owner') of the *penta*, and is either the man who founded it or his successor. The three office-bearers in each category are ranked; for example, among the three prophet *liebumah* there are a senior, an intermediate and a junior member, and the same ranking procedure is followed for holders of the other offices. The distinction in function between offices is further emphasized, to a degree not found in the local *kireke*, by residential segregation at the camp site; in addition to the segregation of the sexes, in the male areas adherents are allotted sleeping and eating space on the basis of office, the prophets together, healers together, etc. Each group meets separately to discuss the detail of their various tasks.

The organization required to run a *penta* is considerable. Enclosures for the services and encampments for Abel and other important visitors must be erected before the camp begins, camp guards must be organized to police the area during the meeting and concessions arranged with merchants who wish to set up stalls for the sale of meat and vegetables. Finance is also involved, since the *penta* is expected to provide for Abel's travelling expenses, and *upfu* (maize meal) is purchased in quantity to be distributed free to those who come to camp.[2]

The financial arrangements are handled by the *liebumah* when they meet at the *Sangano re Masaki* ('Meeting of the Sacks') some

[1] This is the spelling of the word as it is embroidered on the garments of these office bearers, but the word is pronounced 'rabahumah'. The reason for the discrepancy between spelling and pronunciation is obscure, as is the origin of the word itself. Neither this word nor the Vapostori word for singer (*hakrios*, p. 95) has any obvious Shona or Bantu derivation. *Hakrios* bears a phonetic resemblance to the Greek ἄκρις ('hilltop') or possibly ἀκρία ('goddess of the citadel'), and *rabahumah* brings to mind the Hebrew words *rabbah* ('great', 'important') and *'ummah* ('people', 'fellowship'), but any connection between these words and Vapostori usage is purely speculative. It is not known what literature was available to Johanne besides the Bible, which he had in both English and Shona versions.

[2] The extensive nature of these operations can be deduced from the fact that at the 1964 Maranke Penta over four hundred 200lb. bags of maize meal were distributed to campers, and 67 cattle were slaughtered.

days beforehand. The *liebumah* call upon the *kireke* leaders to provide the necessary funds. The expenses of the 1964 *penta* at Nyatsine included, for example: (1) the purchase of tea, sugar and a goat for the use of Abel and his party; (2) money for burlap sacking to surround the main worship area in the camp; and (3) money to give Abel for his travel. In this case they gave him £20, which was more than his expenses. 'We try to give him something extra', was the explanation, 'as a man who does not plough. But he does not set an amount, or ask us for money. We give him what we want.'[1]

Apart from this there is very little financial activity among the Budjga Vapostori. Since there are no building projects building funds are not necessary, and since there is no paid ministry there is no need for collections for this purpose. About the only finance that a *kireke* is likely to be involved in is a benevolent fund that may be raised to help some unfortunate member who is indigent. I was shown the notebook of the treasurer of one *kireke*; it contained a record of contributions ranging from £4 10s to 10s which members of the congregation had made to help a lame man of the community. The man had shown some desire to join the *kireke* as a result, but his interest had subsequently diminished. In spite of this the *kireke* had continued to help him.

VAPOSTORI DOCTRINE AND RITUAL

The Vapostori are Sabbatarian, polygamous, lay great emphasis on spiritual healing, possession by the Holy Spirit, and in other ways generally resemble many of the groups categorized by Sundkler as 'Zionist'.[2] Vapostori dogma has little theology, but a great deal of moralistic teaching. Johanne states his manifesto thus: 'Go to all nations, teach people and cause them to repent, baptizing them and instructing them that men should cease to commit adultery and steal, to be angry for nothing or to covet the possessions of others, that they should honour their parents and love one another, and that they should be steadfast in seeking after God with all their heart. . . . Those who keep these things I will save so that they may ascend to my heaven.'[3] As has already been stated,

---

[1] Neither Abel nor his father Johanne before him has lived ostentatiously. Abel's homestead in Bocha is similar to that of many mildly successful businessmen in the Reserve. He drives a Land Rover, an expensive vehicle but one well suited to his work.   [2] Sundkler, 1961, pp. 54–9.

[3] *Humbowo Hutswa*, Chapter 12, verses 2 and 3.

Vapostori place a premium on Biblical knowledge, and a large Bible (Shona or English) under the arm is as much a badge of membership as their pointed beards or flowing robes. Favourite texts are drawn from both the Old and New Testaments, but two themes predominate: (a) Texts which are quoted to prove the validity of the Vapostori Gospel and indicate the signs that endorse true faith, such as Mark 16.17.[1] (b) Texts quoted to instruct the faithful how to live a Christian life, either by the avoidance of certain taboos or by the right kind of disposition. Considerable attention is given to God and his promised heaven, but little to the soteriological aspects of the Christian faith, and the cross does not appear in Vapostori symbolism. Yet in spite of this weak Christology no 'black Christ' dogma of messianism has yet developed concerning the founder of the Movement. Johanne frequently referred to himself simply as[6] nhumwa ('the messenger') and no movement to elevate him to divine status is yet apparent, although it is perhaps too soon to tell what may take place in the future.

The Vapostori sabbath begins at sundown on Friday and ends at sundown on Saturday. Family prayers are held at sunrise on Saturday, preferably on some small hill or koppie near the village. In the early afternoon adherents gather at the site of the local kireke. Before the service is held the leaders of the kireke gather under a convenient nearby tree for a dare, an informal court. Members of the congregation appear voluntarily before them to confess their sins of the week: anger with their children, arguments with a neighbour, disagreements with a wife or husband.

As members gather they greet each other with a kiss and remove their shoes, for they are now on holy ground. Both men and women wear white robes, and the men affect beards and carry staves. Those who are office-holders will have the emblems of their office embroidered on the front of their garments. The congregation is seated on the open ground in a circle, bisected by an aisle perhaps six feet wide, the women and girls on one side and the men and boys on the other.

---

[1] 'And these signs will accompany those who believe: in my name they will cast out demons; they will speak in tongues; they will pick up serpents, and if they drink any deadly thing, it will not hurt them; they will lay their hands on the sick, and they will recover.' This is perhaps the favourite text of Zionist-type churches, and Baeta has found it to be widely used in what he terms 'spiritual' churches in Ghana. Baeta, 1962, p. 137.

Before a member can enter the holy place and take his seat he must pass through the 'gates', where pairs of prophets pray over him and discern by the aid of the Spirit whether there is any sin in him. If some sin has not been confessed at the *dare*, it is supposed to be detected at this point and the member returned to the *dare* for further counselling.

The pattern of worship is uniform. The service is always started with the singing of the hymn 'Kwese kwese' taken from the Methodist hymnal, but sung by the Vapostori at an extremely slow tempo and with an antiphonal effect. A prayer is said congregationally, the members kneeling and facing the east, and then the Lord's Prayer is repeated. Preaching then follows by about four different men, each one expounding for about ten minutes a variety of texts drawn from both Old and New Testaments. Each preacher is accompanied by a Bible reader, who reads pre-selected verses from time to time on a signal from the preacher to illustrate and punctuate the message. A short prayer follows the sermons, during which all kneel and voice their petitions simultaneously. The service closes with announcements, perhaps an hour and a half after its commencement.

After the service those who are sick seek out the healers in the congregation and are prayed over and anointed with holy water. Each healer has his (or her) own bottle of holy water, obtained from a running stream and blessed in advance. Some also have specially carved 'healing sticks', which are rubbed on the body at points of pain.

Special rituals in which the local *kireke* is occasionally involved include services for baptism, which takes place as soon as convenient after an individual's conversion and is done by immersion in running water, and burial ceremonies. Vapostori take complete charge of burial responsibilities when a member dies, even if the deceased's family are not members of the Movement. They prepare the body for burial, dig the grave, convey the body there and conduct a service at the graveside. No traditional rituals are observed or permitted.[1] The Vapostori preference is to bury their members near each other, in what come to be in effect Vapostori

---

[1] This contrasts with many Methodist and Roman Catholic burials, where traditional rites are performed in addition to those of the churches. In the case of Roman Catholics, after Extreme Unction has been administered by the priest the burial itself is often carried out in the traditional way, described on pages 35–7. Speaking of this practice one priest at All Souls' said to me, 'I don't really mind at

graveyards. A grave about 4ft. by 6 ft. by 6ft. is dug, at the bottom of which a sarcophagus-shaped depression is carved out and lined with stones. The corpse, bound in Vapostori garments, is laid in this depression, stretched out straight, with the head to the west and facing the east, 'Because they want to pray'.[1]

Since Vapostori from all the *kirekes* within six or eight miles are mobilized for the funeral of any member, they tend to be large and impressive affairs, and the Vapostori have a reputation throughout Budjga of 'taking good care of their dead'.

At the *pentas* the pattern of the general public services follows that which has been described for those at the local *kireke*. But in addition to these services the *penta* includes a number of special rituals held only at this time of the year. Among these are exorcism ceremonies, held late at night by impromptu groups very much along the lines of those already described for the Methodists (pp. 74–6). The most important special ceremonies, however, are all connected with the communion service, which is the final, climacterical event of the *penta*.

Some four or five days before this final service the ritual of *mushecho* is carried out. The adolescent girls of the camp are taken into the bush by some of the old women and examined to determine whether they are virgins. The girls are then conducted back to the camp and seated in two groups, those who have 'passed' to be congratulated by their friends and those who have 'failed' to be jeered at by the crowd and scolded by their parents.[2] The virgins are then selected to help in the preparation of the

all. After all, does it hurt the person? If he has been in the hands of God, is the *tsuri* (p. 36) going to keep God away?' In Methodist burial a service is frequently held at the grave, but traditional rites may be held both before and after this.

[1] This emphasis on the positioning of the corpse is not exactly consistent with the oft-repeated Vapostori assertion that the body means nothing and that it is the soul that is important. When I pointed this out to a leader at one Vapostori funeral he replied, 'No, it is the soul that is important, it leaves the body at death.' 'Then', I said, pointing to the corpse which had just been placed in the grave, 'has the soul of this *mbuya* (grandmother) now gone to God?' 'Well', he said, 'It may still be finding its way there, for it has to be through many gates, just as at our services, and must be judged at each of these before it can reach God.'

The Vapostori technique of burying their dead differs from the traditional method of digging a 'shelf' on the side of the grave on which the corpse is placed, with legs bent and bound. It is now, however, being adopted by non-Vapostori in Budjga.

[2] Each girl found to be a virgin is given an undamaged tree leaf as token of the fact, while those found to have lost their virginity are given leaves with holes punched in them.

H

unleavened bread and fruit juice 'wine' that is used in the communion service.

On the last Saturday evening of the camp a confession service is held. A long line of firewood is laid out and then fired, and each participant in the camp is supposed to run around the fire at least once, shouting aloud as he does so all the sins that he (or she) has committed during the year since the preceding *penta*. In the press and noise of the moment it is difficult to distinguish what any one individual is saying. Occasionally a firewalking ceremony is held in the coals of the confession fire, 'to show the purity of the saints who walk on them, and to show unbelievers the power of God'.[1]

After having confessed the participants begin to line up at the 'gates', in order to pass by the prophets and enter the enclosure reserved for participants in the communion service. The following diagram indicates a typical layout of the communion area:

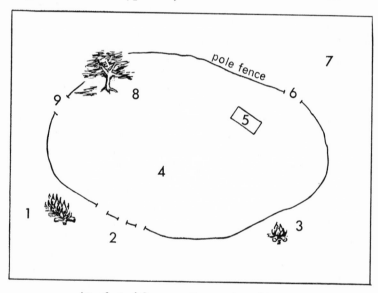

1 'Confession' fire	5 Communion table
2 'Gates'	6 Abel's entrance
3 'Judgement' fire	7 Abel's encampment
4 Pasca enclosure	8 Tree for staves and shawls
	9 Exit

[1] I have not personally observed one of these firewalking performances, but my wife was able to witness one and observe it in some detail.

Each participant is required to pass through one of these gates, stopping before each pair of prophets who shout, gesticulate and speak in tongues, discerning whether or not the person has any sin in his life.

Since a large number of people are involved, and the procedure is more deliberate than in the weekly *kireke* meetings, this ritual lasts throughout the night, with long lines of people waiting their turn at each gate. Once a person has successfully entered the enclosure he hangs his staff (or in the case of a woman her shawl) on the limb of a convenient tree within the stockade to signify that he has legitimized his presence there, and then is allowed to leave by an exit gate to await the morning service.

Those whom the prophets detain are led to the judgement fire, where the judges wait to hear the charges made by the prophet and the defence of the accused. Many charges and confessions deal with arguments between husbands and wives or sexual peccadilloes, and are settled by counsel from the judges on the spot. Witchcraft accusations are also made at this time, and are handled as special cases.

On Sunday morning, after the witchcraft cases have been dealt with, those who have successfully passed through the gates enter the enclosure once again for a footwashing ceremony,[1] and then, after a brief allocution by Abel, file by the communion table to receive both unleavened bread and the fruit juice 'wine' that is served. Once this has been received they are free to pack and leave, their ritual responsibilities discharged.

THE VAPOSTORI AND WITCHCRAFT

Mention has just been made of those who are accused of witchcraft at the judgement fire. They are taken to a separate enclosure and guarded by a pair of prophets throughout the night; early the next morning their cases are heard individually and judgement given. If the accused admits the charge and promises in the presence of her *kireke* leader to produce and destroy the witchcraft objects[2] she is permitted to remain and take part in the communion service, but if she refuses to confess she is banished from the camp.

---

[1] In accordance with John 13.3–17. Footwashing is a practice carried out by some of the South African Zionist groups. Sundkler, 1961, p. 50.

[2] 'Nhumbi dze uroyi.' These are said to be parts of all kinds of unclean animals, kept in a calabash. Some speak of a *shawe* of witchcraft, which lives in this calabash. The feminine gender is used because although men are sometimes accused of witchcraft, by far the greatest number so charged are women.

Any examination of the place of witchcraft in the Movement must hinge on an understanding of the accuser as much as the accused. What has already been said about Vapostori ritual is sufficient to indicate the extremely important part played by the prophet. Since it falls to the prophets to indicate the will of the Spirit concerning the conferment of office they constitute, in effect, a nominating committee at the local *kireke* level. Since they stand at the gates and pass judgement on each person as he passes before them they are in a position to cast suspicion on anyone.[1] Some prophets gain a reputation for being very perceptive, or perhaps even vindictive, and are avoided whenever possible. I have seen members at a *penta* carefully examine the prophet personnel at each gate and avoid the lines which they feel will be subjected to careful scrutiny. Yet the power that these functions give the prophets is carefully balanced; no prophet should be influenced by venal motives, and if this is suspected he (or she) is likely to be denounced as a 'false prophet'. Judges on occasion rebuke the prophets for having come to inadequate or incorrect conclusions, or else call in other prophets to give their views. Actually very few accusations are made at local services; most people are 'caught' at the gates in the large *penta* meetings, and these by prophets from other *kirekes*. Witchcraft cases, which are handled with special care, are usually dealt with by visiting prophets. This is done, the Vapostori say, because 'a prophet is without honour in his own country', but implicit in their practice is the idea that a stranger can be more impartial in such a situation. It is also possible that such a person, perhaps living in another District and more difficult to trace, is less liable to witchcraft accusation charges under the Witchcraft Ordinance. The apparent immunity of the Vapostori to charges under this Ordinance has already been mentioned.[2]

It is difficult, therefore, to account for the selection of those accused by local tension in the manner of Professor Marwick's

[1] They can achieve the same effect during the course of a service. If the Spirit objects to something that is happening the prophets become possessed, speak in tongues and run around the group in circles. Such action is infectious, and on several occasions I have seen them make such a disturbance while someone was preaching that he was forced to abandon the attempt and sit down. 'The Spirit is angry', people have explained to me. 'The preacher has something wrong in his life, and God will not permit him to speak in this holy place.'

[2] *Supra*, p. 56.

analysis of the Cewa.[1] Selection seems to be directed rather by physical and psychological characteristics; when a woman is first brought to the judgement fire the prophet may make some vague and cryptic accusation, but if during the interview she reveals herself as short-tempered and unmannerly, poorly dressed and groomed, smelly or unwashed, it becomes more specific. In other words, the witchcraft diagnosis is actually made during the judgement fire session, when the personality of the individual is revealed, rather than at the 'gates'. This is consistent with the Vapostori view that it is the passions of hatred and jealousy, which they consider to be characteristic of an undisciplined personality, that result in witchcraft. As one informant said, 'Hatred and jealousy are the things that lead a person to witchcraft. For when a person thinks strongly on these things, the *shawe* appears that personifies them. Then this *shawe* goes to live in that person's calabash.' What this informant was expressing was the idea that these undesirable passions, if allowed to become too strong, may exert an influence on a person which he cannot control. What were at first only evil thoughts have taken on an external and independent existence, and by acting upon the individual from whom they sprang have made him a witch.

A large number of the accused confess. Apart from the possibility that some may actually have been attempting to practise witchcraft,[2] a large proportion of these have probably at some time or another obtained from a *nganga* some protective charm, and are easily convinced that possession of this magical object actually implies witchcraft. For others the intense psychological pressures produced by repeated accusations throughout a long night against a background of hypnotic singing may induce within the individual the conviction that the charge is actually true.

There are those who steadfastly maintain their innocence in the face of heavy pressure. Occasionally such a person is banished from the camp as an unrepentant reprobate, but more often a rationalization of the charge and its denial is made. In one such case the prophet insisted that he 'smelt blood' on the woman, who likewise persisted in denying any involvement in witchcraft.

[1] Marwick, 1952, pp. 120–30.
[2] As previously noted (p. 56), the Budjga do not distinguish between witchcraft and sorcery.

After considerable discussion between judge, prophets, the leader of the woman's *kireke* and the woman herself, it was finally decided that what had happened was that the woman's husband (who was not a Mupostori and was not present at the *penta*) had purchased 'blood medicine' from a *nganga* and, without the woman's knowledge, had sprinkled it on the grain in his granary so that his crops would grow well. The woman had taken some of this grain for cooking use, and had thus innocently ingested some of the 'blood medicine', which had been detected by the prophet. In this way both the integrity of the prophet's diagnosis and the woman's innocence were maintained without damage to either.

In view of the fact that very few accusations can be traced to local tensions, and that very few actually result in the expulsion of the accused person, the belief in witchcraft cannot be said to function for the Vapostori in the 'obstetric'[1] sense. The belief and the rituals associated with it are important to them more for their ideological significance than as a means of manipulating social relationships. In addition to reinforcing the Vapostori teaching that anti-social attitudes may develop into anti-social actions, they serve as an explanation of inexplicable misfortune in a world supposedly controlled by a loving God. For many Budjga the answer to this problem lies in some carelessly neglected responsibility to the ancestors and their resultant wrath; for the Vapostori it is found rather in the careless neglect of someone in their midst to control his or her emotions.

VAPOSTORI SANCTIONS ON BEHAVIOUR

The following sanctions are utilized by the Vapostori to enforce approved standards of behaviour upon their members: (*a*) Denial of the use of the uniform. A member who is living at variance with some important Vapostori precept is expected not to wear his garments while in this condition. He may, and frequently does, attend services, but the absence of his garments is mute testimony to his lack of harmony with the group. This practice is similar to that of the Methodist Rukwadzano. (*b*) Ridicule. Occasionally, as we have described in the *musecho*

---

[1] The term used by Dr Mary Douglas to describe the view that witchcraft serves to maintain the balance of structural forces in small-scale societies by removing persons and dissolving relations that have become dangerous or redundant. Douglas, 1963, p. 141.

ceremony, ridicule is used to enforce conformity to the group norms. (c) Denunciation by the prophets, which goes hand in hand with the judgement given at the *dare* of the *kireke*. Since the possibility of this sanction faces the member every week, it is probably the most persistent and powerful of them all. Denunciation by the prophets which is not met by appropriate expiation may result in the denial of communion privileges, and is thus similar to the main Catholic sanction. (d) Expulsion. This sanction, sometimes used by Methodists, is rarely invoked by the Vapostori.

THE VAPOSTORI AND THEIR COMMUNITIES

Of all the Budjga Christian groups the Vapostori exhibit to the greatest degree the incapsulating factors that produce what Professor Mayer calls the 'totalitarian syndrome'.[1] They seek by doctrine and practice to insulate themselves from the communities in which they live, and to enforce conformity by a maximum of contact within the group. They claim to be the most faithful embodiment of Christ's religion in Budjga, and rebuke the Methodists for having 'lost the Spirit' and the Catholics for permitting the use of tobacco and alcohol. They are in active opposition to the *nganga* and the spirit mediums[2] and consider traditional religious ceremonies to be little better than excuses for ritual debauchery. The beards of the men and the dress of both sexes easily identify them, and their speech and mannerisms are punctuated with signs of Vapostori identity.[3] They practise religious endogamy, and they show more propensity to live in residential units[4] than the other groups. During harvest time Vapostori organize *nhimbe* (work parties), something which the Catholics and Methodists do not do. Frequently Vapostori also co-operate to market their produce, an alignment not found elsewhere in Budjga.[5]

Nevertheless, the Vapostori find it impossible completely to

[1] Mayer, 1964, p. 113.

[2] Garbett tells me that in Mzarabani the mediums consider the Vapostori to be their most dangerous rivals.

[3] When approaching a hut the Vapostori shout '*Rugare!*' ('Peace') rather than the customary '*Gogogo*'. This is, they say, 'So that inhabitants will know that it is a Mupostori who stands outside and not an ordinary man'.

[4] *Infra*, pp. 120–1.

[5] Vapostori show a special aptitude for market gardening and fruit growing and frequently a few Vapostori men will co-operate to organize the marketing of their produce in Salisbury.

isolate themselves from the rest of Budjga society, nor does close examination reveal that they really want to do so. They send their children to Methodist and Roman Catholic schools, and their industry has placed them in positions where they are now sometimes chosen for such positions as membership of the school committees. They are generally popular with tribal leaders, chiefs saying that they are 'easy to rule'. The extent of the Vapostori involvement in the communities of which they are a part will become evident in the next chapter, which discusses in detail one such Budjga community.

7

Religion in a Budjga Community

Much of the material which forms the basis of this study was drawn from one community in Budjga, the area in the Nyamkowo chiefdom around the Tsutskwe business centre. The reason for this focus on one comparatively small section of Budjga was twofold. In the first place no useful statistics giving data on religious affiliation for the Budjga, or for that matter any of the Shona groups, could be obtained from Government offices either at Mtoko or in Salisbury. Hence all quantitative data of this type would have to be obtained during the field work. The Budjga being 55,000 strong, it was obviously impractical to contemplate a complete religious census, and the only alternative was to select a number of representative communities and attempt to obtain from them samples which could be presumed to be representative of Budjga as a whole. Four such communities were selected, but as has already been noted in Chapter 1 political disturbances in three of these obliged me to abandon my research. But in the Tsutskwe area it was possible, after carefully establishing a satisfactory rapport, to carry out an intensive programme of research, including a comprehensive religious census of the whole population. In only two villages of the community was it impossible to obtain the necessary information because of the unwillingness of the villagers to give it.

In the second place, it was considered advisable to concentrate the research in one area, so that it would be possible to observe not only the major ritual patterns of the different religions, but also the detailed network of social relationships, so as to see whether membership of a given religious group made any significant difference in the pattern of an individual's social and economic activities and whether actual behaviour coincided with ideal patterns. Concentration on the Tsutskwe community made this kind of observation possible, and in this chapter an effort is made to demonstrate in both quantitative and descriptive terms how the

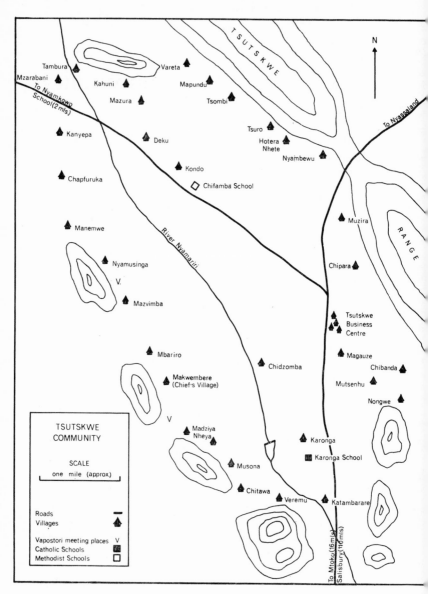

MAP 2: Tsutskwe community

different manifestations of Budjga religion co-exist side by side in a community the members of which interact with each other in a wide variety of different contexts.

An important consideration in the selection of the Tsutskwe community was the presence within this relatively small area of all four major types of Budjga religion. Only a few such areas exist in Budjga. This is not to imply that religiously heterogeneous situations are difficult to find in Budjga; such situations are found everywhere in the Reserve, but usually only three of the four religions are represented. It is easy to find a community with the Traditional Religion, the Vapostori and either a Roman Catholic or a Methodist group present, but only in a few cases are both Methodists and Roman Catholics found together in an area where the inhabitants can be said to form a 'community'. Tsutskwe is one of these areas.

In current anthropological usage the concept of community is given such a variety of definition that some comment is necessary on the use of the term. As applied here to the Tsutskwe area no single element—religious or educational discreteness, geographical contiguity or economic interaction—is the sole defining factor. Instead, a number of these elements combine in such a way as to produce a cohesion among the people of the area which sets them apart from the people of surrounding areas. The interplay of these factors can be seen from a description of the Tsutskwe community:

1. The area has a geographical cohesion. Tsutskwe is a valley encircled by hills, open (except for narrow passes between these hills) only at the north along the line of the road to Nyamakowo.[1] An inhabitant in any of the villages which ring the valley can see the whole area but little beyond it.

2. Economic activity in the valley centres in the Tsutskwe business centre. Here the women come to buy their cloth, tea, sugar and tinned foods. The men come to buy tobacco, plough-shares and bicycle parts. Here also the people sell their maize and groundnuts. All the inhabitants of the valley use the Tsutskwe township as their centre for these activities, while people from outside the area (apart from transients on the Nyasaland road) rarely trade there.

3. Politically the whole area lies in one chiefdom, Nyamakowo, and in the sub-division of that chiefdom administered by the chief

[1] See Maps 1 and 2.

himself. The chief lives in the valley and tribal court is held at his village.[1]

4. All the villages of the valley send their children to the two primary schools in the valley, and these two schools cater, with few exceptions, only for the children of these villages.

5. Religious services for adherents of all four religions in the valley are provided within the community; except for special ceremonies it is not necessary for its inhabitants to go elsewhere for their religious rituals, nor do outsiders usually attend the ceremonies held within the valley.

Most of its adult population is in at least occasional face-to-face contact, and know, or at least can recognize, each other. They identify themselves to outsiders in terms of their membership in the Tsutskwe community. If a man from one of the villages in Tsutskwe at work in Salisbury were asked where he was from, he would probably first reply 'Mtoko', identifying himself thereby as a MuBudjga; if pressed further and asked where in Budjga he would probably reply 'Ngawhe', the term used by the Budjga to refer to the Nyamakowo chiefdom. If questioned still further as to exactly where in Ngawhe, he would then be likely to reply, 'pa Tsutskwe' ('at Tsutskwe'), perhaps noting further for the in-quirer's information 'near the Tsutskwe township'. Since the Tsutskwe valley is a small area in which all the major modes of Budjga religion find objective focus, it proved to be a profitable unit for study.

The question remains how representative the Tsutskwe com-munity can be considered to be, especially since its selection for study was not random but deliberate. The work done there was part of a wider study in Budjga which involved research in a number of different communities in each of the four chiefdoms. In the light of this wider study, Tsutskwe seems to me to be atypical of Budjga as a whole in two respects: (1) As has already been mentioned, there are only a few places where Roman Catholicism and Methodism are found in the same community, and Tsutskwe is one of them. Therefore the instances found in Tsutskwe of

---

[1] The village marked as 'Makwembere' on Map 2. The chief is variously known as 'Nyamakowo' (the name of the incumbent at the time the White government occupied the area and utilized his name to designate the area), 'Chifamba' (the chief's personal name, from which was taken the name for the Methodist School in the area) and 'Makwembere', the chief's father's name, which is usually used to indicate his village.

Methodist and Roman Catholic children in the same family and of Methodist families living near a Catholic school and vice versa may not be representative of Budjga as a whole. (2) There are no outstandingly strong Methodist or Catholic congregations anywhere in Ngawhe such as can be found at several places in the other chiefdoms, and neither Chifamba nor Karonga would rate as strong stations with either of their respective denominations. One cannot find at either of these places the degree of religious activity and organization that is to be seen at, say, the Methodist community of Bondamakara or the Catholic community of Bwanya.[1] The absence of any church building at the Chifamba site is not typical of Methodism throughout the Reserve, only ten of the other forty Methodist congregations in Budjga being in a similar position. With these qualifications I feel that the Tsutskwe data can be accepted as giving a reasonably accurate representation from one area of what is true for Budjga as a whole.

THE RELIGIOUS CENSUS

The Tsutskwe community lies in a valley roughly triangular in shape, about eight miles long and four miles across at its widest point.[2] Most of the 35 villages that make up the community are situated at the base of the hills that surround the valley, and thus ring the arable land which lies in the centre. Through the valley runs a small river, the Nyamarere, which is dry most of the year, and water for domestic use is drawn from wells and springs near the various villages. The main road from Salisbury to Nyasaland runs through the valley, and the Tsutskwe business centre, consisting of four stores, a petrol pump and a grain mill, is situated on this road a little way before it crosses the Tsutskwe Pass and goes out of the Reserve to the north-east. Near the business centre is the junction of a road which branches to the north-west towards Nyamkowo School and the northern part of the Reserve. As a consequence it has become an important bus stop and staging post for people on their way to Salisbury.

The two schools of the community are located near these roads, the Roman Catholic school at Karonga being about one-and-a-half miles south of the business centre on the main Salisbury road,

[1] On the other hand, the ratio of Christians to Gentiles in Tsutskwe roughly parallels that estimated for the whole Reserve. See Table 6.
[2] Refer to Map No. 2.

and the Chifamba School of the Methodist Church being about one-and-a-half miles from the business centre on the Nyamkowo road. There are two Vapostori meeting places, one near Madziya Nheya village and one near Mazvimba village.

The first Christian institutions in the community date from the mid-1930s, when Rev. Bourgaize established a Methodist school near the site of the present Karonga School. In 1943 this school was closed, since at that time people in the valley showed little interest in education. In the late 1940s and early 1950s several young men from the valley went to the Catholic mission at All Souls' for their education and became Catholics. In 1952 the Methodist school was reopened under the name Chifamba, but at a new site. People at the old site, now disturbed because they had no school, went to All Souls' and in 1954 successfully persuaded the fathers to open a Catholic school at Karonga. The Vapostori Movement had in the meantime established itself in the valley, having been first introduced by Paul Munetsi, leader of the Munetsi *kireke*, in 1939.

A complete religious census was carried out in the community which sought to establish:

1. The number of households[1] in each village.
2. The number of married men and women in each village, and the religious affiliation of each.
3. The number of unmarried post-school-age adolescent boys and girls or young people in each village, and the religious affiliation of each.
4. The number of school children in each village.
5. The number of school-age children in each village not in school.
6. The number of pre-school children in each village.

No enquiry was made into the religious affiliation of school children, since the school records gave this information for the whole community.

As might be expected, it was found difficult to give precise definition to the categories of religious adherence that were set up. The wide range of religious attitudes and allegiances observable in Tsutskwe are difficult to reduce to a few categories. But a clearly

---

[1] i.e. family units or *imba*. Usually these consist of a man, his wife or wives and their unmarried children, but may on occasion consist of a widow and her unmarried children.

defined and workable quantitative survey demands this kind of reduction, and in the end the following categories were set up for the purpose of the census:

      I. Gentile[1]
      II. Methodist: 1. Active
                        2. Inactive
      III. Roman Catholic: 1. Active
                        2. Inactive
      IV. Vapostori: 1. Active
                        2. Inactive

Each category was further divided to give a breakdown in terms of males and females.

In this scheme 'active' membership in any of the Christian groups implies some kind of objective affiliation with the group concerned through baptism and/or inclusion in the church rolls (whether in full or probationary membership), supported by continued allegiance to the group through at least occasional attendance at services, and recognition by the member and his group of his active involvement. 'Inactive' membership is that of a person who has ceased to be an effective member of his religious group, either by being demoted as a disciplinary measure or by his own lack of active interest, but still considers himself to be affiliated with it, often with the intention of returning to active status 'sometime'. Inactive members are usually those who find the disciplinary and ritual restrictions of their church unpalatable, but still give uncritical assent to its doctrine. In this category are, for example, Methodists who have lost their church membership because of polygamy but still consider themselves Methodists, or people who have been baptized as Roman Catholics and who give assent to Roman Catholic belief but do not attend church or make any attempt to conform to Catholic discipline. As the census figures show, this group is a large one.

People who have formerly had some connection with a Christian Church but who declared themselves to have reverted completely to the Traditional Religion are listed in the 'Gentile' category.

---

[1] As was indicated in Chapter 3 (p. 31), the term 'Gentile' is used here as a useful designation for non-Christians instead of 'Pagan', a word many Budjga find objectionable.

The classification utilized here inevitably makes 'Gentile' somewhat of a residual category. Most of those included in this group are adherents of Budjga Traditional Religion, but it also includes numbers of Budjga, particularly of the younger generation, who are sceptical both of the Traditional Religion and of Christianity and who have no personal commitment to either.[1]

In the tabulation of the census results a sub-division was made to indicate figures from villages sending their children to the Roman Catholic school at Karonga and the Methodist school at Chifamba respectively.

The tables showing the results of the census appear in the Appendix, with explanatory notes. There is in Tsutskwe a total population of 2955,[2] of whom 1505 are adults or post-school-age adolescents.

There are 747 married adults in the Chifamba (Methodist) sub-community, differentiated by religion as follows:

	Number	%
Gentile	555	74·3
Methodist	69	9·2
Catholic	38	5·1
Vapostori	85	11·4
Totals	747	100·0

In the Karonga (Catholic) sub-community, comparative figures showed:

	Number	%
Gentile	250	64·9
Methodist	25	6·5
Catholic	62	16·1
Vapostori	48	12·5
Totals	385	100·0

[1] Discussions of the criteria and indices used in two other studies for situations of this type are found in Pauw (1960), pp. 8–10 and Firth (1961), pp. 21–6. In Tikopia, Firth used baptism as the simplest way of distinguishing Christian affiliation, but found that the development of a second generation Christianity and its attendant category of 'lapsed' Christians required the application of additional indices. Pauw used four categories for different degrees of church affiliation: (1) people with no church connections, (2) adherents (a term he applies to people who attend services but have no official connection with a church and to young people baptized in infancy), (3) members of Sunday School classes and catechumen classes and (4) communicants and full members. Pauw does not make it clear whether he includes 'lapsed' church members among 'adherents'.

[2] Excluding the population of the two villages where it proved impossible to carry out the census.

In both sub-communities the figures for religious adherence differed as between the sexes. At Chifamba 28·8 per cent of the women were Christian and 21·7 per cent of the men. On the other hand, in Karonga Christian women represented 31·9 per cent of the total, and men 38·9 per cent. Among post-school-age adolescents and unmarried young adults 33·4 per cent were Christian at Chifamba and 34·3 per cent at Karonga.[1] Composite totals for the entire 1505 adults and post-school-age adolescents of the community indicate a religious distribution as follows:

	Number	%
Gentile	1,052	69·9
Methodist	126	8·4
Catholic	173	11·5
Vapostori	154	10·2
Totals	1,505	100·0

These figures have been a surprise to Tsutskwe residents— teachers, storekeepers and headmen—to whom they were shown. In every case the impression had been that Christianity was numerically stronger than they indicate. They are consistent with the generally low church attendance in the community, but in spite of this the impression of the Tsutskwe inhabitants themselves was that nominal Christianity at least was more widespread than the 30·1 per cent indicated by this survey. One answer to this problem may lie in the thesis that many Budjga and other Shona in certain situations imply that they are in some way Christian even when they qualify under none of the objective criteria used in this census. Thus when Mrs Bell made her survey of the personnel of a Salisbury factory in 1961, a group which included Budjga men, only 20 of the 302 men from Southern Rhodesia admitted to being Gentiles, while the remaining 93·4 per cent claimed to be members of some Christian church.[2] Many of these men apparently felt it to be an advantage in urban employment to be identified, if only nominally, with a Christian Church. On the other hand in Tsutskwe, where claims to church membership are open to greater scrutiny and involve closer conformity to Christian discipline, Budjga men may not be anxious to identify

[1] Because this category is much smaller and more transient, most of the analysis given here is based on the figures for married adults. The tables on young people have therefore not been sexed or given 'active' and 'inactive' differentiation.

[2] Bell, 1961, p. 78.

I

themselves with a church in such a way as to bring upon themselves the responsibilities of membership.

RELIGIOUS AFFILIATION AND RESIDENTIAL DISTRIBUTION

Tables 3 and 4 list religion by villages. The statistics reveal little correlation between residential distribution and religious allegiance. It is true that clusters of Christians of one or other group are found in certain villages, but what is more impressive is the wide distribution of the different religious groups throughout most of the villages. Methodism is represented by at least one member in 20 of the 33 villages of the valley, Catholicism in 15 and Vapostori in 20. The number of Christian denominations represented in a given village generally increases with the size of the village, as the following table shows:

Size of villages (by households)	Gentile only	Christian denominations			Total
		1	2	3	
2–9	5	2	2	1	10
10–14		4	6		10
15–19			2		2
20–24		1	2	1	4
25 +		3	1	3	7
Totals	5	10	13	5	33

In only five of the thirty-three villages are there no Christians at all, and all of these are small, together accounting for only 64 adults. On the other hand, few villages have such a high concentration of Christians as to be categorized as 'Roman Catholic', 'Methodist' or 'Vapostori'. Only two villages, Madziya Nheya and Patambura, contain active Christian groups constituting over 50 per cent of the adult population.[1] Both these villages are controlled by headmen who are active Vapostori members, and in each case the Christian group is entirely Vapostori. Apart from these instances, where ardent Vapostori have utilized their leadership positions and kinship affiliation to recruit a large following within their villages, it appears that to date there has been little

[1] The small village of Chidzomba is predominantly Roman Catholic, but this Catholic membership is inactive. The same is true of Maruza, where the large Vapostori section is for the most part inactive. Some other villages, such as Veremu and Kanyepa, are almost equally divided between Christian and Gentile elements.

tendency in Tsutskwe for religious allegiance to be polarized along residential lines.

RELIGIOUS AFFILIATION WITHIN FAMILY UNITS

There are 516 households in the Tsutskwe community. The Christian population (30·1 per cent) is represented in 46·4 per cent of these. The following table indicates the distribution of Christian denominations by household:

No. of denomina-tions present	Households	%
0	275	53·6
1	217	41·4
2	21	4·4
3	3	·6
	516	100·0

These figures indicate that there is a degree of denominational alignment along household lines. Christians of the same household are likely to be of the same denomination. This is not, however, an invariable rule, for 24 households numbered more than one Christian denomination among their members. An extreme example is that of Chief Chifamba. He is a Traditional Religionist, as is his first wife. She has two children, both married and both Vapostori. The second wife is a Methodist, who has seven children classified as follows: one man, married, Roman Catholic; one man, married, Methodist; three women, married, Methodist; one boy, in school, Roman Catholic; one boy, in school, no church. Wife number three is a Traditional Religionist, with two Roman Catholic post-school-age adolescent daughters and three children in school, no church. Wife number four is a Traditional Religionist with one post-school-age adolescent Roman Catholic daughter, three non-church children in school and one pre-school child.

In one type of situation a definite pattern does emerge. If the husband is a member of a Christian group, in most cases the wife (or wives in the case of the Vapostori) will also belong to it. Out of 82 husbands who were active members of some Christian group 72 had wives of the same denomination. Three types of families of mixed religion were most common: (a) Husband a Traditional Religionist, wife a member of a Christian group. The children may or may not be Christian. (b) Parents Traditional Religionists, children Christians. (*c*) Parents (or mother) members of one Christian group, children members of another.

As has been suggested in previous chapters,[1] religious endogamy is encouraged by all the Christian groups, and especially by the Catholics. Contacts made at religious meetings tend to promote intra-faith marriages, but no statistical evidence on this point is at present available.

SEX AND RELIGIOUS AFFILIATION

Among the three Christian groups the Roman Catholics stand out as the only denomination with more male adult members than female (52 men to 48 women). This can be attributed to the fact that this Church has recruited almost exclusively through the school system. To date, more boys than girls have gone through the Roman Catholic educational system, hence the slight preponderance of men over women in this denomination in Tsutskwe.

The Vapostori register more female than male members (80 women to 53 men). This ratio is not, however, maintained in the attendance figures for Vapostori services, where men tend to outnumber women. In this church men take a definite lead in administrative and ritual activities. While some Vapostori women are active and influential adherents of the Movement as prophets or healers, one gets the general impression that most are passive and nominal members, in the church primarily because of their husband's interest. Since polygamy is permitted, family units may bring to the Movement several adult female members for every adult male.

An excess of female over male members is the most striking feature of Methodist membership. There are nearly twice as many adult female Methodists in Tsutskwe as there are males (61 women to 33 men), and among active membership the preponderance is even more marked (54 women to 17 men).

A description of the active and influential Methodist women's organization, Rukwadzano, has already been given.[2] In the Rukwadzano the Methodist Church presents the women of Chifamba with opportunities for self-expression and organization not otherwise open to them, a fact particularly important to married women in this virilocal society, where lineage identity frequently does not find local expression for them. Methodism,

[1] *Supra*, pp. 91, 109.   [2] *Supra*, pp. 70–1.

with its legalistic emphasis, also appeals to women, who see in it support for such ideals as the stability of marriage and pre-marital chastity at a time when they feel such standards to be threatened.

The power and authority now held by women in the Methodist Church has reached such proportions that it seems to act as a deterrent to men. Gentile husbands of Methodist women some-times accuse Methodist men of being members 'because they are interested in our wives'. Men are aware of such accusations and hesitate to join what has the appearance of being a woman's organization.[1]

Reasons which have been cited elsewhere in Africa for the numerical preponderance of women in the Christian churches, such as labour migration and the stumbling-blocks that the ideal of polygyny and the ritual responsibilities of political leadership place in the way of male membership,[2] seem to be operative in Budjga also. Other reasons which have been suggested, such as the warrior mystique and initiation ceremonies,[3] are not valid there.

VILLAGE LEADERSHIP AND RELIGIOUS AFFILIATION

Seven of the 33 village headmen are Christians, the rest are Traditional Religionists. The ratio of Christian to Traditional Religionist headmen (21 per cent) is thus not significantly different from the over-all ratio for men in the community.

Of the seven Christian headmen, three are Vapostori, one is Roman Catholic, one Methodist, one Salvation Army (who attends Methodist services at Chifamba) and one is a member of the Kruger Apostolic Faith group.[4] Apart from the two Vapostori headmen of Madziya Nheya and Patambura villages, headmen do not seem to have utilized their position to recruit for their own religious groups. The Methodist headman is a very active member of his Church, the chairman of the school committee at Chifamba and one of the stewards of the local congregation. Yet he, his wife and one daughter, are the only Christians in his rather large village of Chapfuruka.

[1] Outside Tsutskwe, in a Methodist congregation consisting entirely of women and presided over by a woman steward, it was alleged that men were afraid to join the church because 'The steward is a witch and will bewitch any man who tries to join, for she is afraid that he would take her place as leader'.
[2] Pauw, 1960, pp. 92–4.   [3] Sundkler, 1961, p. 140; Pauw, 1960, p. 93.
[4] Headman Tsuro of Tsuro village. See Table 6.

Membership in a Christian group does not noticeably affect the way in which the seven Christian headmen perform their leadership functions. Village headmanship does not usually involve ritual responsibilities of the traditional kind, except at the time of the *rukoto* ceremony in October.[1] At this time the chief requests all his headmen to collect and present to him gifts of grain to be used in the preparation of the beer required during the ceremony. Most of the Christian headmen delegate this task to Gentiles in their villages, an arrangement which is satisfactory to the chief. The two strongly Vapostori villages excuse themselves from presenting the *rukoto* gift on religious grounds, and so far this lack of co-operation has caused no discernible dissension in the community. The fact that the two headmen concerned are efficient at their work and also, as the chief says, 'easy to rule', probably mitigates any resentment that he might feel towards this lack of co-operation on their part.

AGE AND RELIGIOUS AFFILIATION

Tables 6 to 8 indicate the religious affiliation, by village, of the unmarried post-school-age adolescents and young people of the community. The following table gives a comparison of totals for the youth with those for married adults by sub-community:

| | Adults | | Youth | |
	No.	%	No.	%
Chifamba				
Gentile	555	74·3	128	66·6
Methodist	69	9·2	26	13·6
Catholic	38	5·1	26	13·6
Vapostori	85	11·4	12	8·2
Karonga				
Gentile	250	64·9	119	65·7
Methodist	25	6·5	6	3·3
Catholic	62	16·1	47	26·0
Vapostori	48	12·5	9	5·0

These figures suggest several important points: (*a*) The percentage drop in Vapostori youth at both Chifamba and Karonga confirms what will be said[2] concerning the loss of Vapostori youth to other denominations. (*b*) The preponderance of Methodist adults over youth at Karonga must be attributed to the fact

[1] *Supra*, p. 46.   [2] *Infra*, pp. 143–4.

that these adults were recruited during the days when there was a Methodist school there, and that without a school Methodism cannot recruit effectively. (c) On the other hand, Catholics have been able to attain a percentage increase in the Methodist community of Chifamba—mostly through children who have attended All Souls' Mission—and at the same time have used their school at Karonga with great effect to achieve a large percentage increase in the number of adherents among youth. This reflects the greater Catholic emphasis on recruitment during the school years, and probably indicates a trend towards increasing numerical strength for them. The Catholic stress on recruitment through education is even more clearly seen by an examination of school enrolments. The Karonga Roman Catholic school has a Standard III class of 27 children, ranging in age from 10 to 14. Of these 26 are baptized Catholics and one is a Mupostori girl. The Chifamba Methodist School has a Standard III class of 21 children, ranging in age from 11 to 14. Of these, three are Methodist members, one is a Roman Catholic, one is a Mupostori and the rest are Gentiles.

THE PATTERN OF RELIGIOUS ACTIVITY IN TSUTSKWE

In the Tsutskwe community there are four recognized ritual centres where Christian services are held: the Chifamba School (Methodist), Karonga School (Roman Catholic), a Vapostori meeting place between the Madziya Nheya and Makwembere villages and a Vapostori meeting place between the Mazvimba and Nyamuzinga villages. There are no fixed ritual centres for Traditional Religionists, since their ceremonies are held in different villages as occasion demands. None of the tribal spirit mediums live in the valley, and the annual *rukoto* ceremony for the tribe is held at the home of the medium Benhura, some six miles to the north.

Methodist services are held at the Chifamba school, started by this Church in 1952 and now having 266 students. There are 6 teachers, all men and all Methodists.[1] The religious programme of the school suffers from a lack of strong leadership. Both the head teacher and the other married man on the staff keep their families at their homes in Mtoko,[2] and are away visiting them at weekends.

---

[1] The teachers in the two schools do not appear in the religious census figures. None are native to the community.

[2] A practice which is fairly common among teachers, although looked upon with disfavour by church authorities.

The unmarried teachers show little interest in the religious programme of the church, and attend services only rarely. Thus it depends for leadership almost entirely on local people. Headman Mfawa of Chapfuruka village is the chief steward of the congregation; he and two other men are the only males in regular attendance at the Sunday worship services at present, although irregular visits from other men in the community usually keeps male attendance at these services to about six.

The women's group at Chifamba is much stronger, with an active Rukwadzano chapter led by a woman who was at one time a Roman Catholic. Attendance at the weekly Rukwadzano meetings average about 28, and anyone near the school on a Friday morning will be made aware of the group's presence by the sight of the women in their brightly coloured uniforms.

Sunday services are held in one of the school classrooms, since there is no church building. Average attendance over a six-week period worked out to 6 men, 26 women and 15 children.

The local school committee is made up of eight men. Five of these are Gentile. The chairman, Mfawa, is a Methodist (the chief steward of the local congregation), and the head teacher, also a Methodist, is another member. The eighth is Stephen Makwembere, son of the chief. This man is currently acting chief of the Nyamakope chiefdom, since his father is senile and has delegated his responsibilities to his son. Both Government and people are quite willing to accept this arrangement, since Stephen is both capable and energetic, and he is at present the most influential individual in the community. He went to a Methodist school, was baptized a Methodist and later became a polygamist. Although his name was removed from the church rolls he still considers himself a Methodist and frequently attends the local services.

Catholic ritual activity centres on the Karonga School, started by the All Souls' Mission in 1954 and now having 181 pupils and five teachers. This school is situated near the site of the first Methodist school in the area, a short-lived enterprise which was closed in the early 1940s before the present Chifamba school was opened. Apart from the daily prayers and religious instruction which are part of the programme of the school, the only religious services held are the Mass, conducted once a month by a priest from All Souls', and a Sunday prayer service of the type described on page 88. No youth or women's groups meet locally.

Like the Methodist congregation at Chifamba, the religious programme at Karonga has suffered recently through lack of leadership from the head teacher, and the decline in attendance at the
Sunday church services of this congregation has already been
described. Average attendance for a five-Sunday period before the
present head teacher came worked out to four men, five women
and 79 children. Recently only a small group of school children
have been attending these services.

The Karonga School Committee is composed of eight men,
four of whom are Traditional Religionists. Two are Roman
Catholic, one is headman Tsuro (a member of the Kruger Apostolic Faith) and the chairman, Paul Kaitano, is a former Methodist
who now occasionally attends Roman Catholic services.[1]

Vapostori services follow the pattern described in Chapter 6.
The two congregations usually meet separately for their weekly
services, but on occasion they come together for joint meetings.
Both meeting sites are near well-used footpaths, and the sight of
the white-robed Vapostori congregation is familiar to all. Average
attendances for the two *kireke* for the services attended were:
(Munetsi *Kireke*) men 11, women 12, children 4; (Mazvimba
Kireke) men 8, women 6, children 2.

Traditional Budjga Religion does not call for regular rituals in
fixed places; when a death occurs or a *bona* ceremony is called for,
the relatives concerned circulate the news by word of mouth and
the community is quickly apprised of the ceremonies to be
performed. Attendance at these is open to all, Traditional Religionists and Christians alike, and a general knowledge of the content
of these rituals is the possession of most inhabitants of the valley.
Services for propitiating family *midzimu* or *ngozi*, and the
divination procedures that often precede them, are more esoteric,
and are held without the general knowledge of the community.

More than any other type of ceremony, those connected with
death and burial draw together the people of the community,
regardless of their religious affiliation. If, for instance, a Mupostori
dies, four or five hundred people are likely to visit his village
during the ceremonies to offer their condolences. Most will not be
Vapostori, for the important fact is that a neighbour, friend or
acquaintance has died, not his church membership. When at these
services the non-Vapostori are given a good exposure to Vapostori

[1] More of this man's case history will be given on pages 137–8.

concepts and religious practices. The same holds true for similar ceremonies held by the other religious groups. Roman Catholic, Methodist, Vapostori and Traditional Religionists freely visit the ceremonies of other groups at such times.

The material presented here leads to the conclusion that the Budjga, in spite of the disparate influences that the last few decades have brought them, still find the focus of their lives in relatively small-scale communities such as Tsutskwe. In such communities the forces contributing to equilibrium, co-operation and harmony are more important than those which might tend to separate. Thus the fact that the community is heterogeneous in religion and that this heterogeneity involves lines of association leading outside the community to different centres of religious influence is recognized, but not allowed basically to affect the unity of the community. Membership of any given religious group does not appear to affect the selection of individuals for leadership positions; the fact that a man is a Christian does not prevent his becoming a village headman, while a large proportion of the membership of school committees is Gentile. Except in the two Vapostori villages the village headmen have not used their position to recruit for their own faiths, and there has been no religious polarization along residential lines. Recruitment to the various religious groups has depended upon other factors than residence.

The material further indicates that most Budjga do not put a high premium on regular ritual activity. The Christian groups hold regular weekly services which are poorly attended, while the Traditional Religionists hold ceremonies only occasionally. This is not to say that the Budjga are not 'religious'; most of them believe in the existence of supernatural beings and their influence on human society. But ritual action is not one of their preoccupations, and in the light of the Tsutskwe material the existence of different ritual centres in the community, each with its nucleus of membership, cannot be said to have any noticeably divisive effect on the community as a whole.

8

Religion in Budjga Society

Previous chapters have described the four principal modes of Budjga religion, and summarized their historical and social context. An examination has been made of one Budjga community in some detail, yielding quantitative data on the relative numerical strengths of the four types of Budjga religion for one area. The question remains how these data can be arranged in such a way as to exhibit a system; how the various religious processes relate to each other and how individual members of Budjga society resort to and identify with them.

Budjga society is a society in change. The imposition of an alien administrative and judicial system, the introduction of a cash economy, land pressure resulting from a rapidly growing population, migration to industrial areas and other factors already noted in Chapter 2[1] have generated vast alterations throughout the fabric of the society. Against the background of this situation one approach might be to see the different modes of Budjga religion as reflecting the segmentation of rural society; as polarizing agents acting reciprocally both to symbolize and stimulate the fission of old Budjga society and its alignment into new segments organized on different principles.

There are certain justifications for such an approach. The leaders and members of all the religious groups consider them to be separate and distinct religious communities, actively competing for the loyalties of the Budjga. Expressions of stereotyped criticism directed at the various religious groups are frequently encountered. The Methodists consider the Roman Catholics to be 'worldly' because of their position on tobacco and alcohol, and the Vapostori as being hopelessly compromised because of their permissiveness with regard to polygyny. The Roman Catholics have an officially exclusivist view towards the other Christian groups, considering themselves to be the only true Christian Church, and regarding

[1] Especially pages 19–23.

the other organizations as misguided and over-emotional sects.[1] The Vapostori acknowledge the historical priority of the other two Christian groups, but consider that both have lost the original message of the Christian faith, which now finds its true expression only in the Vapostori gospel. All these groups consider Budjga Traditional Religion to be, at best, an outmoded and inferior type of divine revelation and response, or, worse, as nothing but an avenue for charlatanism. The Traditional Religionists, for their part, blame the Christians for all the contemporary misfortunes of the society, asserting that their apostasy has alienated the guardian spirits and caused them to withhold their beneficent influence.

All three Christian groups, and in particular the Vapostori, exhibit the techniques of self-isolation discussed by Phillip Mayer in the South African urban context and variously referred to by him as 'incapsulation' or 'the totalitarian syndrome'.[2] In an important paper on the subject Mayer describes how a particular Christian group in East London has created for its members a discrete and relatively isolated field of interaction based on the twin rules of minimum participation outside the group and maximum participation within. The norms of the group are continually reinforced by the condemnation of values current in the wider society outside the group, while an individual's membership is continually validated by the minimization of contact with this wider society and close identification with the group itself. Elsewhere Mayer has shown how an individual's identification with a group of this type is augmented by distinctive pattern of dress, speech and behaviour.[3]

As previous chapters have already shown, all these techniques, to a greater or lesser degree, are in evidence among the Christian Budjga groups. We have seen how the Roman Catholics make it an article of doctrine not to attend the religious services of any of the other groups, and encourage their young people to contract marriages only with other Roman Catholics. If Roman Catholic young people do marry outside the Faith their marriage is only recognized by the Church if it is performed by a priest, and both parties undertake to raise the children as Catholics. The creation of quasi-kinship links at baptism through the godchild-godparent

---

[1] The term 'maseketi' ('sects') has passed into the vocabulary of Budjga Catholics as a term for non-Catholic groups.
[2] Mayer, 1963, pp. 113–26.   [3] Mayer, 1961, pp. 4, 10, 22–41.

relationship has been mentioned, as has the tendency of some Catholics to confine their trading to stores owned by Catholic businessmen.[1]

For their part Methodists tend to isolate themselves by refusing to participate in the beer drinks that are an integral part of the social and ritual life of much of the society, and their men's and women's organizations have an exclusive membership which emphasizes its select character by the use of badges and uniforms.[2] The Vapostori, like the Roman Catholics, encourage religious endogamy. As we have already noted, their distinctive dress on ritual occasions and the beards worn by their men give overt testimony to their separation from the rest of the community. They frequently organize work parties on the basis of Vapostori membership, and co-operate with each other in the marketing of produce.[3]

Other co-ordinates between economic activity, education and religious affiliation can be seen. As might be expected from the involvement of the churches in education, Christian males in Budjga have a higher average level of education than do non-Christians. It is unusual to find an adult Christian Budjga man who has not had at least a year or two of formal education, which is more than one can say of their non-Christian counterparts. All the teachers in Budjga, as far as this study was able to ascertain, were at least nominal members of one of the 'orthodox' Christian denominations, providing an instance of an entire professional group which can be correlated with a certain type of religious affiliation. In the business and trading sector of the society Christians predominate, and most of the locally owned stores and other business enterprises in Budjga are run by Christians.[4]

But having recognized these congruences, one is disappointed in the search for further evidence of a pattern displaying clear-cut polarities along religious lines in Budjga. It cannot be found in the sphere of political activity.[5] Nor, as we have seen from the Tsutskwe materials, can one find any high correlation between residential distribution and religious allegiance.[6] It is true that there are 'clusters' of Christians in certain villages, and that there is

---

[1] cf. p. 91.   [2] cf. pp. 70–1.   [3] cf. p. 109.

[4] For example, of the four stores in the Tsutskwe business centre, two are owned and operated by Methodists, one by a Roman Catholic and one by a Traditional Religionist.

[5] More will be said on this subject in Chapter 9, pp. 152–71.

[6] cf. 120–1.

a tendency for villages with Vapostori headmen to have heavy concentrations of Vapostori membership, but what is impressive in the final analysis is the wide distribution of the different groups throughout the villages surveyed.

When one goes further with the data and examines case studies, attendance records for given rituals, the results of attitudinal tests and the pattern of ritual activity in Budjga communities, what in fact appears is not polarity but rather heterodoxy, mobility and interdependence. Thus, although the four principal religious groups in Budjga stand apart from each other as belief/ritual systems, their respective memberships are linked by shared beliefs and mutual experiences. It is to the three characteristics reflecting this situation, heterodoxy, religious mobility and interdependence, that attention is now turned.

BUDJGA RELIGIOUS HETERODOXY

Dowa Nyakuna is the sub-chief of the *dunhu* in the Mtoko chiefdom where the Methodist school of Chitekwe is located. Baptized a Methodist and educated for five years in a Methodist school, since becoming a sub-chief he has ceased to be a member of the Church and now considers himself to be a Traditional Religionist, since, he says, the ritual duties of his office are inconsistent with Methodist discipline. His children are Methodists, and his wife is a member of the local Rukwadzano chapter. When questioned about his beliefs and religious practice he answers that he prays to the *midzimu* and *mhondoro*, but that he also believes in Jesus and the Holy Spirit. 'It is best', he says, 'to believe it all.' Nyakuna's heterodoxy, i.e. his willingness to accept the veracity and efficacy of beliefs outside the system of the religious group to which he claims affiliation, is typical not only of Traditional Religionists with his Christian background but also of many others who have never been associated with the Christian Church. Many, if not most, Traditional Religionists in Budjga accept the proposition that Jesus was a supernatural manifestation of God (Nyadenga), and one of the *mhondoro* mediums once suggested to me that it was perfectly proper for all the Budjga to pray to Jesus 'as long as they do not forget to pray to the *midzimu* as well'.

That this latitude in belief is not confined to the Traditional Religionists in Budjga can be seen from the following cases taken from field notes:

Case One. Vapostori Heterodoxy. (Notes on a conversation at a weekend Vapostori meeting held at Campa in December 1963. About ten men were seated around a campfire in the early evening, before the evening service.)

Comments were made on the weather and the desperate need for rain to save the crops:

'*He*[1] knows and will send it in time.'

'Yes, was not Isaac just about to be killed and then came deliverance?'

Discussion then turned to whether the chief had arranged for the *rukoto* ceremony to be held this year. One person commented that he had heard that the chief at Mtoko had done so, and that rain had fallen there. The group then started to discuss the local *mhondoro* medium, who was said to be very effective. All apparently accepted his power. One then asked the obvious question:

'Why then does Jehovah hear him and not us who are his children?'

Another answered:

'These are miracles to show the unbelieving. He will take care of us in His own good time.'

Throughout the conversation none of the group expressed any scepticism concerning the power of the *mhondoro* or his medium, even though the Vapostori are firmly opposed to sacrifices to the *mhondoro*. The conversation turned not on the validity of the belief in the *mhondoro*, but rather on the relationship between the phenomena surrounding it and their own beliefs.

Case Two. Methodist Heterodoxy. (Notes on a conversation with a young teacher, an active Methodist, from a village in the Mtoko Chiefdom. The quotation is the teacher's statement as recorded in the field notes.)

'In our village there was an old woman whom we all knew to be a witch. She was a member of our Church, and all the church members knew that she was a witch. The matter was never discussed in church, since we were not supposed to be involved in such things, but nevertheless we knew her to be a witch.'

When I asked why, if they believed this, they did not put the woman out of the church, the teacher replied,

'Well, I think everyone was a little afraid of her. And anyway, she did no harm to anyone unless they first harmed her.'

Case Three. Roman Catholic Heterodoxy. (The following account is extracted from the notes of a two-session interview captioned in my notebook 'The Case of the Dissatisfied *Mudzimu*', and dated

[1] i.e., Jehovah.

November 1964. The informants were two Roman Catholic lay brothers of All Souls' Mission who were present at the reburial session mentioned, and Rinos Nyawasha, one of the main participants in the drama and a Roman Catholic.)

About four months ago Tom Nyawasha, a Roman Catholic of advanced age living about three miles from All Souls' Mission, died and was buried near his village. Two weeks ago his daughter's daughter[1] Agnes, recently married and living with her husband in his village some ten miles away from the Mission, became violently ill. Agnes was also a Catholic. Her husband made plans to take her to hospital, but that night Agnes showed manifestations of spirit possession and her dead grandfather Tom proclaimed his presence. He wished, he said, to speak with his family. Agnes's husband, as was proper for a man in his position, sent word to Tom's agnatic kin early the next day and then delivered his wife to their village, where Tom's brother (my informant) was now the family head. That night Agnes again became possessed, and Tom, speaking through her, said, 'I want you to dig me up. The grave that you have dug for me is too narrow, and my head is twisted and uncomfortable. You must dig the grave wider and longer. And put all my clothes in the grave! Do you want to keep them all?' The next day agnates who had not been present at the evening session were informed of these events and all agreed to participate in the burial, which was set for Saturday the 14th of November. The night before the reburial Agnes, who had stayed at Tom's village, was again possessed, and this time Tom added the request that the brothers from All Souls' be in attendance at the reburial and that Christian prayers and hymns be said and sung during the ceremony. On Saturday the reburial took place as arranged, with the Catholic brothers (also my informants) and a large number of kin, both Christian and non-Christian, in attendance. My informants all assert that no decomposition of the body had taken place. That night Agnes was once again possessed, and Tom, speaking through her, expressed his satisfaction and gratitude for a job well done. Agnes subsequently went home, and Tom's *mudzimu* has, to date, made no subsequent appearances.

Leaving aside the important questions which this story raises concerning the settlement of Tom's estate and Agnes's relationship with her cognatic kin, this case is interesting as a demonstration of the eclectic nature of the beliefs of the Catholics involved. Cases could be cited to illustrate other types of Budjga heterodoxy — Catholic acceptance of items of Vapostori belief, Methodist

[1] In Budjga terminology, his *muzukuru*.

acceptance of items of Catholic belief, etc.[1]—but these three are perhaps sufficient.

Further evidence of the widespread heterodoxy can be found in the results of a survey designed to test attitudes and beliefs on a wide range of religious, ethical and political subjects. The test was administered to 250 adults in the Tsutskwe community (50 Methodists, 50 Vapostori, 50 Catholics and 100 Gentiles) and 100 Standard III school children from various schools in the Reserve. A list of the questions asked and the analysis of the replies appear in the Appendix, Tables 2 and 3. Although certain questions arise as to the size of the sample and the utility of all the questions asked,[2] the results sufficiently parallel those obtained by other techniques to be considered valid as corroborative material.

Questions Number One, Two, Three and Thirteen in particular point to the phenomenon of Budjga heterodoxy. Question Number One asked informants who they believed had the power to give and withhold rain, the tribal spirits or Mwari, the Christian God.[3] While a majority of each group answered in a manner consistent with the group's ideology, it is significant that nearly 30 per cent of the Gentiles said Mwari controlled the rains, while 34 per cent of the Methodists and 24 per cent of the Catholics indicated a belief that the *mhondoro* were responsible. Question Number Two asked informants for their opinion concerning the fate of the soul. Here again the majority in each of the Christian groups answered as might be expected, but in the Gentile group 56 per cent responded with the Christian concept that a man's spirit 'goes to heaven' after his death. Sixteen per cent of the Methodists and 22 per cent of the Catholics stated, on the other hand, that a person 'became a *mudzimu*' at death, and the Vapostori were the only Christian group that decisively rejected this idea.

Question Number Three sought to discover people's ideas about supernatural revelation. Forty-seven per cent of the Gentile

---

[1] Although these are less common. The main movement of Budjga heterodoxy is between the Christian and Traditional positions.

[2] Points which are discussed in the presentation of the questionnaire material in the Appendix.

[3] As explained in the comments which appear with the questionnaire analysis in the Appendix, the word Mwari tends in Budjga to be associated with the Christian concept of God as opposed to Nyadenga, the name for God more frequently used by the Traditionalists. Constant reference should be made to the question analysis given in the Appendix, since important qualifications are made concerning the points discussed here.

K

group accepted the Bible as a source of divine revelation, and another 23 per cent accepted ministers and priests as channels of this revelation. A small percentage of both the Methodist and Catholic groups indicated a belief in the *mhondoro* as the channel of divine revelation, and again only the Vapostori unanimously rejected this. Question Number Eleven sought to determine the extent of belief in witchcraft; it was found that 90 per cent or more in each of the adult groups believed in it, with a significant group of sceptics found only among the school children, where 25 per cent denied the existence of witches.[1]

Questions Number Five, Six and Seven dealt with disciplinary proscriptions imposed by the different Christian groups, and are especially interesting for the way in which they reveal how significant sections of each group reject the rules of conduct standard for their group and accept those of another. This is especially significant in light of the emphasis placed on these issues in preaching and public pronouncements, producing the stereotypes in Budjga of the Methodists as solid supporters of total abstinence from tobacco and alcohol, the Roman Catholics as being profligate on these same issues, and the Traditional Religionists as being almost all polygynous. But in spite of these stereotypes, 40 per cent of the adult Methodists questioned thought that beer drinking was permissible, at least in moderation, while 20 per cent of the Roman Catholics considered it to be wrong. Forty-four per cent of the Roman Catholics likewise thought smoking was wrong. In response to Question Number Eight on polygyny, only the Vapostori group was strongly in favour of it. Surprisingly, 67 per cent of the Gentile group supported the ethic of the Methodist and Roman Catholic groups and said polygyny was a sin. This figure is interesting in that it corresponds roughly to the percentage of married Gentile Budjga males who are in fact monogamous (77 per cent in the Tsutskwe community).

The results of the survey make it clear that there is considerable variety in the beliefs of members of the different religious groups.

---

[1] The implication here that belief by Christians in witchcraft is unorthodox is made in the context of the modern Shona Christian setting. The early missionary approach to witchcraft was to ridicule the belief in its existence, a position which came to be standard for the mission churches, both Catholic and Protestant. Historically the Judeo-Christian tradition furnishes many instances of belief in witchcraft, from the Old Testament records to the witch-hunting activities of the New England Puritans in more modern times.

In the first place, members of any group vary widely in their response to the same question. Secondly, it is evident that significant sections of each group hold positions at wide variance from the norm of their group. The Vapostori in general exhibit more unanimity of opinion than any of the others, the Traditionalists[1] tend to be the most eclectic, while Roman Catholics and Methodists fall somewhere in between. Thus one cannot represent the Budjga as being sharply divided into adherents of closed ideological systems, isolated from one another by differences in belief. It is true that many members of each group conform closely to the ideology of their faith, but it is also evident that there has been a constant interchange of ideas between them, and that considerable heterodoxy exists.

BUDJGA RELIGIOUS MOBILITY

That a certain amount of religious mobility would be observable in Budjga can be inferred from what has already been said, i.e. that Budjga society, once homogeneous in religious belief, now includes a significant section which adheres to Christianity, and that the Vapostori have recruited primarily from the other Christian groups. But beyond this, case histories show a large number of instances where individuals convert not only once, but several times, and that in different directions. Three examples from many cases representing every conceivable kind of change in religious affiliation will illustrate some of the factors involved:

(a) Paul Kaitano is headman of the village of this name in the Karonga sub-community of Tsutskwe. His father, headman before him, was a Traditional Religionist, and Kaitano was raised in early boyhood as such. During his adolescent years he went to Nyadiri Mission for education and became a Methodist. While at Nyadiri he was married in the Church, but when he returned to the Tsutskwe valley he took a second wife, and his active membership of the Church lapsed. He entered the Vapostori Movement in 1955, taking his four wives with him into the nearby Munetsi *kireke*. His stay with the Vapostori lasted only two years; he left them at the end of 1956 as a result of a dispute with the leader of the *kireke*. His own version of this incident is that the prophets had determined that he should be a baptizer, but the chief baptizer

---

[1] For the purposes of this analysis the Gentile group is assumed to represent Traditionalist belief.

and leader of the *kireke* (Munetsi) was afraid that because of his education he would become too powerful, and so stood in his way. Kaitano also complained that the Vapostori would not let him eat pigs and rabbits.

Subsequently Kaitano came under the influence of the Roman Catholic evangelist Father Rubio.[1] 'He told me, "You should not leave off praying because you have four wives. Who told you that you cannot go to heaven because you have four wives? It is better for you to go with two wives on each arm to church!"' As a result Kaitano and his wives began to attend Roman Catholic services, but later, when Father Rubio left All Souls' Mission and the incentive of his visits was gone, Kaitano gave up the attempt to be a Catholic and now considers himself a Traditional Religionist.

(*b*) Ruth Mpasu is a woman perhaps 35 years of age. The daughter of Chief Nyamkowo, she went at an early age to All Souls' Mission to study, and was baptized a member of the Roman Catholic Church while she was there. Subsequently she returned to the Tsutskwe valley and married a Traditional Religionist living near Chifamba School. She started to attend Methodist services at Chifamba in company with other women of her village, and in 1962 became a full member of the Methodist Church. A woman with an attractive personality and great natural ability, she was quickly accepted by the other women of the congregation, and in 1964 was elected leader of the Rukwadzano group.

(*c*) William Sibanda is a storekeeper at Mtoko. He was raised in a community with a Methodist school, and became a member of the Methodist Church in early adolescence. To get an upper primary education he went to All Souls' Mission, where he became a Roman Catholic. Asked why he changed his faith Sibanda replied, 'The Methodists gave me no place for an upper primary education, and therefore they did not deserve my loyalty.' Sibanda comes from a family of mixed religions; two of his sisters are Methodists while his brother—living elsewhere—is an Anglican.

Why do these people, and many others like them, convert from one religious group to another? The cases that have just been cited give some indication of the major factors involved. Education is obviously very important. Not only does the provision of

[1] *Supra*, p. 82.

education give the Methodists and Catholics a 'captive' audience; an ethic of reciprocal responsibility seems to have established itself: the church has an obligation to provide the children of the community with an education, while they in return have an obligation to accept membership in the church. If, as in the case of Sibanda, the church fails to meet its obligation, the child in return has no responsibility to it. In this context the church is a social service institution, owing services to the community and deserving loyalty in return.

Kaitano's case shows the importance of the Vapostori position on polygyny. The Vapostori provide the polygynist who has aligned himself with Christianity the opportunity to continue this identification, an identification denied him by his first Christian church. This case also illustrates the way in which personality conflicts and role rivalries can cause a person to leave one group for another. Kaitano's brief identification with the Catholic Church was probably the result of at least two factors. He was no doubt attracted by Father Rubio's evangelism, as well as by the possibility that was held out to him of re-identification with a Christian group, in spite of his polygyny. Much the same combination of factors, a conviction of the relevance of the Christian faith for her life and the appeal of the corporate life of the church, was operative in the case of Ruth Mpasu. She was attracted by the Methodist preaching that she heard at Chifamba, while identification with an active and respected group of women was hers if she joined the Methodists.

Other reasons for conversion from one religious group to another can be seen. Kaitano's case illustrates how the conversion of a husband is followed by a parallel change for his wife or wives. This is particularly true where the husband converts to a Christian group; as we have seen from the religious census figures, if a man belongs to one Christian group his wife (or wives) is very rarely a member of another.[1] Again, as we have seen in the case of Sub-chief Dowa Nyakuna, the assumption of tribal leadership, with heavy ritual responsibilities of the Traditional type, can lead to a conflict resulting in conversion to Traditional Religion.

The kind of mobility just described might be called 'affiliational mobility', in which an individual over the course of a lifetime changes his religious group membership one or more times.

[1] *Supra*, pp. 121–2.

Another type of religious mobility is also evident in Budjga. This is essentially temporary, and is a concomitant of the religious heterodoxy already discussed. This type of mobility is seen when an individual, *at certain times and in given circumstances*, moves out of the pattern of belief and practice standard for his religious group, and temporarily and for specific purposes aligns himself with those of another. In Budjga this most often occurs at times of sickness, but there may be other reasons. The 'Case of the Dissatisfied *Mudzimu*' is an example, in which Roman Catholic laymen initiated and participated in a Traditional religious ritual involving a dead man's estate. Some illustrations of this kind of temporary movement from the other religious groups in Budjga are:

(*a*) *Vapostori*. Paul Munetsi is the bearded and venerable leader of the Munetsi *kireke* in the Tsutskwe community. He is also the headman of Madziya Nheya village, and he proved to be a valuable informant on Vapostori matters during my first few months in the valley. A time came, however, when he was conspicuous by his absence from the weekly *kireke* services. After considerable probing, other members of the *kireke* revealed that one of his wives had been chronically ill for a long time, and that under pressure from her parents Munetsi had finally agreed to submit her to a *nganga* for treatment, and had taken her to a well-known diviner across the border in Mozambique. During the series of treatments, which lasted four months, Munetsi did not function as the leader of the *kireke* or attend its services, although he was present in the community for much of the time. The other members would shake their heads sadly when he was discussed, and speak of him as a 'backslider', but no one attempted to usurp his position. He was still their leader, although in temporary exile. The implicit assumption on everyone's part was that he would be back. In this they were right, for he eventually returned, duly confessed his sin, and returned to the fold—as its shepherd. This man's action, though explicitly and vehemently condemned by his religious group, was at the same time tacitly condoned by them.

(*b*) *Methodist*. Zebediah Kadoro was born and raised near the Methodist school at Kawazwa, and became a full member of the Methodist Church at the age of 16. Although he was later demoted to probationary status for having contracted a *matorwa* marriage,[1] he continued to take an active part in church activities, and when he resettled in Area C in 1963 he and his wife started a Methodist congregation there. The leadership of this congregation was later taken over by another newcomer, Samuel, on the ground that he was a full member of the Church and Kadoro only a probationer.

Kadoro is an industrious farmer, and during the first growing season on the new lands in 1963/4 he produced noticeably better crops than his neighbours. As a result, during the harvest of May/June 1964 covert accusations of witchcraft were made against him.[2] When his vigorous denials appeared to make no impression on public opinion, he finally suggested that the people of the community call in a Vapostori prophet of considerable local reputation, Naboth. Naboth came, consulted and prophesied, and pronounced Kadoro innocent. The verdict was accepted without question, and the Methodist congregation subsequently elected Kadoro as their chief steward to replace Samuel, whom they considered incompetent.

This is another example where temporary religious mobility took place for reasons other then illness. Kadoro utilized Vapostori techniques and personnel in a matter involving his relationship with his neighbours; his vindication by the Vapostori prophet brought him increased prestige even among his fellow Methodists.

(c) *Traditional Religion.* Mandipa Mugomo is a Traditional Religionist who was married at about the age of twenty. Shortly after her marriage she became subject to a series of epileptiform seizures. Symptoms developed which were diagnosed as *ngozi* possession. The avenging spirit was said to be that of her mother, who had died a few years before as a result of a long illness and alleged mistreatment by her husband, Mandipa's father. It had first attacked this man, who became ill and eventually died. But before he died Mandipa had been married, and this angered the *ngozi* because she had not wished Mandipa's father and his agnates to 'enjoy' the bridal payments. In possessing Mandipa the *ngozi* was demanding heavy reparations from them, to be paid to the relatives of the dead woman.

Several attempts were made by a local *nganga* to remove the

---

[1] For *matorwa* marriage, see p. 29.
[2] In this case *kutswera*, the witchcraft enabling you to take the crops of other people from their lands and place them in your own.

ngozi, culminating in a *kutandira* ceremony in which symbolic payments were made by Mandipa's kin to the *ngozi's* family, but without immediate success. While treatment by the *nganga* was going on, a Vapostori meeting was held near by, and Mandipa's husband called in one of the Vapostori prophets. The prophet confirmed the diagnosis of *ngozi* possession, but asserted that no evil-doer (i.e. *nganga*) could possibly exorcize the *ngozi*. He declared himself willing to attempt a cure, even though he claimed this to be 'the most powerful *ngozi*' he had ever encountered. Mandipa was taken to the Vapostori meeting, and an exorcism ceremony was held similar to that described for the Methodists.[1] Since this ceremony Mandipa has continued to be subject to occasional seizures, but these have not been ascribed to *ngozi* possession. This has been interpreted by the community as a triumphant vindication of the efficacy of Vapostori techniques and a defeat for the local *nganga*. The *nganga* defends himself by the argument that his procedures would eventually have been successful had it not been for the interference of the Vapostori.

How representative are these instances? It must be pointed out that the case histories of a large number of Budjga informants show no record of this kind of religious mobility. Many Budjga can speak with exclusive confidence concerning their own religious group as did one Methodist informant (the wife of a store owner at Tsutskwe) of her own: 'I was raised from a child as a Methodist. As for my life, my trust is in Christ alone. We pray and read the Bible sometimes, especially at times when we are in trouble. We have never gone outside our faith. For instance, when we are sick we have never gone to a *nganga*, no not once in our whole lives.' Others, whose personal histories have brought them in close contact with a number of different religious groups, show no inclination to deviate from the ideology and standards of the one in which they have been raised. The Roman Catholic head teacher at Karonga, for instance, had spent several years as a teacher at the Methodist school at Mtoko centre; he could speak with considerable objectivity on the merits and faults of both the Catholic and Methodist churches, but he showed no indication of being anything but a good Catholic in his personal allegiance.

Instances of the kinds of mobility that have been discussed here are discovered only through careful interviews. No statistics on

[1] *Supra*, pp 74.-6.

this type of mobility can be given, and it is impossible to state with precision just how widespread either affiliational or temporary mobility is in Budjga. The general impression produced by the field work is, however, that this kind of movement is widespread, and is a significant factor on the Budjga religious scene.

INTERDEPENDENCE IN BUDJGA RELIGION

The heterodoxy and mobility just discussed point to a further widespread characteristic of Budjga religion, interdependence. In so far as individual members of each religious group tend from time to time to utilize the ideology and techniques of other groups, these groups can be said to depend upon each other for services important to their membership. But beyond this there is a sense in which the activities of the different religious organizations tend to be complementary, making them interdependent for their continued existence, at least in their present form.

This interdependence is not symmetrical; some groups are more, some less, dependent upon others. Of the four religious groups the Traditional Religionists and the Catholics are the most independent, while the Vapostori programme depends at many points on the assumption, however unacknowledged and perhaps unrecognized, that its members must be expected to have significant contacts with other religious groups. This can be recognized in a number of features of the Vapostori programme.

There is first of all the mode of recruitment. A large number of new converts to the Vapostori Movement, even today, are adult males who have had a history of affiliation with either the Roman Catholic or Methodist Churches. Many of them are men who, after joining one of the mission churches, contract polygynous marriages. They find a welcome in the Vapostori Movement and take their wives with them. The Movement is primarily an adult and male church. Attendance figures already quoted[1] show clearly the preponderence of adults in Vapostori services. From the almost complete absence of children and the case history data available it is obvious that the large increase in numbers of recent years is not provided by the Vapostori families directly; they are losing their children to other denominations during the school years and gaining them back as adult males with families from other churches.

[1] *Supra*, pp. 70, 127.

The second dependency which can be mentioned is implicit in what has just been said. The Vapostori depend upon the other two Christian groups to educate their young and properly induct them into contemporary Budjga society. In the schools provided by these groups Vapostori children are introduced to religious systems more closely orientated to the type of life that is constantly intruding on Budjga society through the influences of education and urbanization, and reject the faith of their parents. The Vapostori are aware that this is happening, but do not seem to be much concerned; there seems to be a tacit acknowledgment that they cannot compete effectively with the mission churches for the teenager, an acknowledgment made all the easier by the confidence that they will win their children back to the Movement later on. Often Vapostori informants have said to me when I have questioned them about their children, 'During this time in school they are Roman Catholics (or Methodists), but later on I shall ask them to be Vapostori and they will come back.' The statistics already referred to seem to indicate that they are often right.

Thirdly, there is the treatment of disease, a matter of tremendous significance to the Budjga. The appeal of the Vapostori emphasis on faith healing is one of the reasons for the success of the Movement, but this emphasis has led the Vapostori to forbid any use of medicine or surgery, whether by mission doctor or Traditional diviner. Several case studies indicate that in certain circumstances many Vapostori do not accept this prohibition. There are times when the efficacy of European medicines attracts them and they go to a mission for treatment. As one Mupostori said to me: 'Certain diseases are cured by our prayers. Other diseases are cured by the church. (In this case he was referring to the mission hospital.) So if I am sick I will go to the hospital and be healed and then later I will repent and be forgiven.'

The use of the word 'church' is significant. It might be argued that what the Methodists and Catholics give the Vapostori in education and medical treatment is essentially a number of non-religious techniques. But to the Vapostori the mission churches do not represent utter apostasy, and the fact that these organizations invest the services they give with religious significance reinforces to those Vapostori who utilize them the belief that under different circumstances the Vapostori method of direct ritual action is the appropriate one. The same applies to situations where the Vapostori resort to the traditional *nganga* for medical assistance, as in the case of headman Munetsi.[1] The Traditional assumption that disease and its treatment lie within the province of ritual action underlines the relevance of Vapostori ideology on this subject in the very context in which the two groups stand in strongest opposition.

Again, it is important to note that one of the strengths of the Vapostori Movement lies in the fact that it creates roles conferring prestige. One such role, now generally accepted as prestigious by all Budjga society (and not just the Vapostori), is that of Biblical scholar. Vapostori know their Bible well, and love to exhibit their superiority in the knowledge of its less familiar details, particularly over men who have had more formal education. The following dialogue, between the writer and a group of Vapostori men seated around a camp-fire at one of their meetings, illustrates this characteristic in action:

Vapostori: 'Why do you European Christians celebrate Christmas?'

Anthropologist: 'Well, it is the time of the year when we remember the birth of Christ.'

Vapostori: 'But why do you celebrate his birth in December, of all months?'

Anthropologist: (hesitantly) 'Well, they tell us that perhaps that was the time of the year when he was born.'

Vapostori: 'Ah, but are you sure that December was *really* the month?'

Anthropologist: (By now the conversation has all the appearance of a baited trap, and the anthropologist wants to see how it is sprung.) 'No, I'm not sure. Can you help me?'

Vapostori: 'What does Luke, Chapter One, verse 26 say? Do you know it?'

Anthropologist: (reluctantly) 'No, I can't say I do.'

(Vapostori produce a Bible and force it into the anthropologist's hands, make him look up the passage and read in the firelight: 'In the sixth month the angel Gabriel was sent from God with a message for . . . Mary, etc.')

Vapostori: 'How long does it take after a woman has conceived for her to bear a child?'

[1] *Supra*, p. 140.

Anthropologist: 'About nine months.'

Vapostori: (triumphantly) 'Now our passage shows us that Mary conceived in the sixth month, i.e. June, therefore she must have borne her son, not in December, but during the following March!'

(Great satisfaction ripples around the camp-fire at this demonstration of Vapostori superiority in Biblical knowledge, and the anthropologist has no heart to suggest that the Jewish calendar might suggest a different conclusion.)

Now the need for such a prestige-conferring role is to a large extent the making of the mission churches. The value systems of these churches stressed achievement in formal education in preference to the traditional Budjga values of seniority and maturity. Budjga who could have expected prestige under the traditional system have turned to the Vapostori as a means of fulfilment. This is achieved in the instance just cited by scorning the Methodist's failure to study the Bible he claims is so important and pointing with pride to the Vapostori mastery in this field. By giving inflated importance to certain aspects of mission church teaching and achieving special proficiency in them a superiority is achieved which depends on the incompetence of the other religious groups.

Finally, there is the fact that Budjga still expect persons holding political authority to take part in traditional religious rites even when, if they are Christians, their church forbids it. The same holds true for Christians who have an *usavira*[1] relationship with a Gentile if that man dies. Vapostori in this position will hire or otherwise provide a Gentile acquaintance to perform these duties in their stead.

The dependence of the Vapostori on the other religious groups has now been discussed in some detail. Without question it is among the Vapostori that this dependence can be most clearly seen. But there is evidence to show that there is an element of similar dependence, or at least interaction, to be found in the other groups. Both Methodists and Catholics will on occasion employ Traditional Religionists so that they can contract out of ritual activities which the society demands of them. Just as the Vapostori use the mission churches as negative examples to outline their successes, so the Methodists and Roman Catholics use the lack of

[1] *Supra,* p. 29.

institutional programmes in education and health among the Traditionalists and Vapostori as an argument for their own superiority. The Traditional Religionists, for their part, excuse the ineffectiveness of their ritual techniques by the presence of Christianity. 'It used to be', they say, 'that when we prayed the rains came immediately. Now the ancestors are angry because the Christians do not properly honour them, and thus we all suffer.'

THE BUDJGA RELIGIOUS SPECTRUM

It seems clear from the evidence that has just been presented that the different modes of Budjga religious life, in spite of their formally competitive roles, complement each other when regarded in the context of the society as a whole. Budjga society, at least up to the present, has resisted fission along religious lines, and in spite of overt religious differentiation its members continue to retain the freedom to select in thought and action, from the wide range of religious alternatives that are available to them. In this perspective Budjga society is seen, not as a battlefield for conflicting religious systems, but rather as presenting a religion involving different institutional modalities which appear along a broad religious spectrum that spans this society at a time when it is subject to a variety of extraneous influences. Individual members of Budjga society whose lives are subject to a fairly integrated set of these influences tend to focus their religious experience on one of these modalities, while those more subject to disparate influences move from one to another in the course of a lifetime.

It is, therefore, my contention that the recognition of the composite nature of contemporary Budjga society is a key factor to the understanding of its religion. A process of selective adaptation has been going on; a new cultural and economic complex has appeared on the Budjga scene, and the differential reaction of individual Budjga has greatly enlarged the range of situations calling for religious solution. Given the realization that Budjga society stands at the present moment at a position intermediate between those polarities variously known to sociology as 'community' and 'contract', *Gemeinschaft* and *Gesellschaft*, that it stands midway along the road to what is called Westernization, it is not hard to see how its Traditional Religion found it difficult adequately to serve the whole range of religious needs which Budjga began to develop. Religious specificity and religious inclusiveness rarely go together. It is difficult for a religious system to be based simultaneously on agnatic kinship and on voluntary association, difficult for an inclusive religious system to create an organization rigid enough to carry out institutional programmes relating religion to current needs in education and social service.

Early in the process of Westernization the Budjga were presented, by the arrival of the Methodist and Roman Catholic Churches, with two alternative forms of religious organization. The range of alternatives was later expanded by the advent of the Vapostori. Each of these groups, in varying degree, made claims of superiority and exclusiveness, and demanded a categorical loyalty as the price of membership. Each proclaimed its relevance to all aspects of Budjga society, but in actual fact the appeal of each was necessarily restricted to certain sections. For this reason they are best seen as overlapping religious orientations, each with characteristics which appeal to significant sections of Budjga society and which constitute its 'strengths'. The same character-istics may make it difficult for any organization to win general approval, and so constitute its 'weaknesses'.

The Traditional Religion has the great advantage of being the historic religion of the people, with all the emotional and cultural associations that this implies. It forms the residual category; membership is automatic if an individual is not in another group, and there are no initiations or expulsions. In addition the Tradi-tional Religion has the advantage of a close connection with tribal leadership, and with ideas of land ownership and land fertility. On the other hand, its orientation to kin groups, to local political alignments and to agriculture is of limited utility or interest today to the many Budjga who spend much of their time away from the Reserve in towns. Organized on a tribal basis, it has been unable to give any guidance in nationalist politics, a subject of absorbing interest to many younger Budjga.

The Roman Catholic Church has its own particular points of strength. We have mentioned the parallels between its belief in ritual efficacy and that held by most Budjga. It has the ability to create and inspire loyalty to new relationships based on Church membership. Like the Methodist Church, it is so organized that it can provide the educational and social services that the Budjga now associate with religion. It also has its weaknesses. Control is so centralized that it offers little scope for ritual leadership to

Budjga laymen; adult support in the villages for the Church is correspondingly weak, and local financial support almost non-existent.

The Methodists share with the Catholics the distinction of having a church of national scope, able to provide guidance on political and social issues. But unlike the Catholics, the Methodists have a system of organization which extends considerable auto-nomy to the local level. Wide scope is given for local ritual leadership in song and worship patterns, leading to such innova-tions as Wabvuwi singing and exorcism ceremonies. Financial responsibility has been emphasized, and local financial program-mes are vigorous. Opportunities for religious participation by women are greater with this group than with any of the others, and as a result this Church has by far the most significant women's movement.

But this emphasis on women in Methodism is both a strength and a weakness, for many Budjga men regard this church as a women's organization and hesitate to give it their religious loyalties. In a similar manner Methodism's appeal to an older adult generation has resulted in a rift within its membership between the young and the old. Perhaps the greatest unresolved problem facing the Methodists is the conflict between this Church's concept of its mission and the maintenance of its disciplinary standards. On the one hand it interprets its mission in the broadest possible terms; it seeks to convert the whole of Budjga society as well as individuals in that society, and carries out a wide range of institutional programmes designed to direct and Christianize Budjga. In this sense it is, in Troeltsch's useful categorization, a 'church' and not a 'sect'.[1] At this point the Methodist Church

[1] Troeltsch distinguishes 'churches' from 'sects' in terms of their attitude towards society. The 'churches', he says, recognize the secular order and work within it, seeking to influence the institutions of the society as well as individuals. The 'sects' on the other hand are groups which tend to isolate themselves from society. 'Their attitude towards the world, the State and Society may be indifferent, tolerant or hostile since they have no desire to incorporate these forms of social life; on the contrary, they tend to avoid them . . .' (Troeltsch, 1931, p. 331). Wishlade (1965, pp. 2–3) considers that this distinction is not useful in a mission context, noting the difference between the attitude of the Church of Scotland to the colonial government in Nyasaland and its attitude towards the government in its home country. But Troeltsch's differentiation does not revolve around the attitude of a religious organization towards a given government, but rather the comprehensiveness of its involvement in the society in which it exists, a valuable distinction for the analysis of African religious movements.

shares with the Catholic Church a common sense of mission. But, unlike the Catholics, the Methodists have attempted to impose a narrow code of behaviour upon their members, one which is unacceptable in practice to a large proportion of the society. They are, moreover, handicapped in this task by a disciplinary system with an inadequate range of sanctions. As a result, when the inevitable breaches in discipline occur, local Methodist congregations are often forced either to exercise the drastic sanction of expulsion or else to overlook the situation. In either case the Church suffers; either it is not as inclusive as it claims to be, or else it is open to the charge of proclaiming standards it does not maintain.

The Vapostori Movement has the advantage of the many parallels that exist between its ideology and ritual forms and those traditional to the people, such as the belief in spirit possession as a mode of religious experience, witchcraft control and healing by ritual techniques. Its provision of a Christianity permitting polygyny, its redefinition of the roles of men and women at a time when this definition is getting blurred, and the absence of educational or economic barriers to membership, are attractions to many Budjga. It does not have the same difficulties with discipline that the Methodist Church does, since it exercises a wider range of sanctions and is more content to be a closed organization. The Movement thus approximates what Troeltsch calls a 'sect', and can provide a greater sense of group solidarity and identification than any other Budjga religious group. On the other hand, Vapostori detachment in matters of education, and the adamant refusal of its leaders to approve the use of Western medical techniques, make the Movement an object of ridicule to many Budjga, and lose the Vapostori the support of their children during the formative school years.

Thus there are in Budjga four religious orientations, each with aspects which attract certain segments of the Budjga population at the same time as they repel others, and none of them able to meet the whole range of religious needs in contemporary Budjga society. If the process of social differentiation in Budjga had produced rigidly stratified economic, political or other groupings it is possible that certain clear-cut correlations might have developed between them and these religious orientations. They might have become, in Professor Firth's phrase, 'banners for sectionalism'.[1]

[1] Firth, 1948, p. 17.

But in spite of labour migration, the introduction of a cash economy and formal education, Budjga society remains basically communal. Most members of Budjga society exist in a network of associations which involves them closely and continually with members of other religious groups, and the ideologies and ritual of each group are, at least to some extent, part of the shared experience of the whole society. Each group is therefore best understood as a modality on a religious spectrum which they must all share. No single one of them in itself represents 'Contemporary Budjga Religion'; Budjga religion is the complete religious spectrum itself, of which they are only related parts.

This view challenges the assumption that 'the religion' of a society must be an integrated, logically consistent set of beliefs expressed in a unified and organized pattern of ritual. There is such a thing as 'Contemporary Budjga Religion'. This entity is not the traditional religion of the Budjga of pre-Occupation days, nor is it Christianity; these are only the component parts of a contemporary religion which by the circumstances of its development and environment is something different from, and more than, the sum of the two.

9

Conclusion

RELIGION AND POLITICS IN BUDJGA

The observation already made that the different religious groups in Budjga have not, up to the present moment, become foci for political differentiation[1] has implications which call for further comment. Religion has, of course, played a role in Budjga local politics for a long time. The decision of church authorities to establish a school in one village and not another has inevitably had political repercussions at the village level, and the fact that the establishment of these schools implied the provision of certain services has been a factor in inter-village rivalries and on occasion led to political intrigue. But what is under consideration here is alignment in terms of national politics, an issue which in the last eight years has had wide-ranging effects in Budjga, as elsewhere in rural Southern Rhodesia.

One District Commissioner at Mtoko, in a conversation about the possible fortunes of the African nationalist movement in the District, once expressed to me his confidence that nationalist politicians would make little progress there, and added, 'Their only hope is to gain the support of the religious leaders here.' From the context of this remark it was obvious that the District Commissioner meant by 'religious leaders' the leaders of the Vapostori and Traditional Religionists, but from the policies and actions of the Government it is apparent that many officials see the leadership of the mission churches also as a possible centre of anti-government activity.

The Government is not the only group which sees the churches as possible sources of political rivalry. In speeches and conversation many nationalist leaders attack the churches as enemies of political freedom, and the assertion that Christianity is 'the religion of the

[1] *Supra*, p. 131.

white man' is commonly heard on the lips of many Budjga.[1] At a rally of the largest nationalist party[2] at Mtoko Centre in 1962 the speaker closed the meeting with an appeal to the crowd to join in a prayer to the *mhondoro* of the land to give them power to drive out the white man and restore their land to African control. The prayer was led by a member of one of the ruling Mtoko lineages, and enthusiastically supported by the crowd.

There are several political positions that a Budjga could conceivably take: he could support one of the predominantly European parties, he could advocate a slow evolution from the present political status quo or he could join one of the African political parties. But in the political context of Budjga at the time of this study there were in effect only two alternatives for a Budjga: either he could be an active and vocal supporter of the largest nationalist party or else he remained politically passive. In view of the nationalist evocation of the *mhondoro*, and their frequent depreciation of the Christian churches, it might have been expected that the Traditional Religionists would align themselves with the nationalist cause, while the Christians would take up a passive or anti-nationalist stand. To date no such clear picture has emerged, and each religious group in Budjga proves on examination to be subject to a variety of influences which have militated against this type of polarity.

Leadership among the Traditional Religionists is on the whole hostile to the nationalist movement. At the *rukoto* in September 1964 of the Nyamkowo chiefdom the mediums of Zimbiru and Nyakasanhu[3] declared that the tribal spirits were angry with the 'young politicians' for causing 'trouble in the land', and urged people to withdraw support from them and voice their complaints to the Government solely through the tribal leaders. One obvious inference is that the spirit mediums are closely aligned with the chiefs and headmen, a group which has vested interests in maintaining the status quo. This group receives much of its income

[1] Not all nationalist leaders are anti-Christian. The leader of the P.C.C., Mr Joshua Nkomo, is a Local Preacher in the Wesleyan Methodist Church. The leader of Z.A.N.U. (The Zimbabwe African National Union, cf. p. 13), the Rev. Ndabaningi Sithole, is an ordained minister of the Congregational Church. For neither of these men has politics meant a repudiation of their Christian faith.

[2] The People's Caretaker Council (P.C.C.) is the successor to the Zimbabwe African People's Union (Z.A.P.U.) and is still often referred to by this name.

[3] *Supra*, p. 44.

through subsidies or salaries from the Government, and this income, together with much of its political power, would be threatened by the ascendency of nationalist politics.

Another reason for the Traditionalist leaders' hostility to the nationalist cause lies in their suspicion that the nationalist appeal for their support is nothing but political opportunism. People active in nationalist politics are rarely active participants in Traditional rituals. Their ideas of power and authority based on party membership and activity are essentially secular, and have little in common with Traditional ideas based on a seniority resting ultimately on supernatural authentication. Thus even the diviners, who do not have the same close connection with the tribal leaders as the spirit mediums, are on the whole antagonistic to nationalist politics.[1] At the same time those Traditional Religionists who have no claim to ritual leadership are less concerned with threats from nationalist politics to the Traditional association of ritual with political leadership. They feel a strong compatibility between their religion and nationalist aims, and support the nationalist cause. The result seems to be an uneasy equilibrium between these divergent forces, so that at present Budjga Traditional Religion cannot be said to be either strongly pro- or anti-nationalist.

Of all the Budjga religious groups the Vapostori are perhaps the most unwillingly involved in a conflict not of their own making. Their own preference for non-involvement in political issues is clearly demonstrated in the results of Question Ten of the Attitudinal Questionnaire (Table 2), where 76 per cent of the Vapostori informants held that Christians should not be involved in any way in politics (as contrasted to 12 per cent of the Methodists and 10 per cent of the Catholics). In spite of this the Vapostori are subject to attack from both the Government and the nationalists. Even though they are completely clear of any suspicion of European control, the nationalists resent Vapostori failure to support their programme, and many Vapostori have had their

---

[1] A prime example of a Traditionalist leader's opposition to nationalist politics from outside Budjga is the case of Muchatera, an important medium of the great Shona *mhondoro* Chaminuka. (*Supra*, p. 48.) This man's support would be invaluable to the nationalist cause, yet in spite of the fact that he has little connection with any tribal leadership Muchatera has been implacably opposed to nationalist politics, an attitude which has led to the burning of his huts in retaliation.

huts burned as a result.[1] The Government for its part appears to be under considerable misapprehension as to Vapostori objectives, and evidently regards the group as one of the main breeding grounds for sedition.[2] One of my best Vapostori informants, G., had some of his grain huts burned down by the nationalists in June 1964 because he did not attend political meetings. He was arrested by Government security forces in September, and under emergency regulations in force was sent without trial to a detention camp in a remote corner of the country.[3]

The Roman Catholics and Methodists have both been subjected to a variety of pressures which might be expected to align them against the nationalists. Nationalists not only accuse these churches of representing the 'white man's religion', they have frequently prevented church members by intimidation from attending services. Political rallies have been scheduled on Sundays at service times, earning the disapproval of the ministers and priests. The church leaders have advised their members to 'attend the political rallies, but only after you have rendered your first allegiance to God by attending church', a compromise unacceptable to many of the politicians. Irresponsible members of the youth wing of the nationalist parties have on occasion appeared outside the homes of church members at night demanding that the daughters of the house be sent out 'to attend a youth rally', when what in fact is intended is a dance which the Christians consider inappropriate for their youth.

On the other hand, the Methodists and Catholics have both been involved in incidents scarcely calculated to promote friendly

[1] Hut burning has been a technique of political coercion in common use in Budjga, since it has disastrous consequences for the victim, requires no special equipment and can be carried out with little fear of detection. Not all hut burnings can be attributed to political motivation, since personal scores have been settled in this manner under the cover of politics.

[2] Possibly influenced in this conclusion by recent events involving the Lumpa insurrection against the Government in Northern Rhodesia, and by a long-standing conviction that 'Ethiopian' religious movements are politically suspect. This attitude is amply illustrated by correspondence found in Files S 138/148 and S 138/140 of the Government Archives in Salisbury.

[3] It might be suggested that G. had actually been involved in seditious activity and had been sent to detention camp with good cause. On enquiry at Mtoko I was informed that he had been arrested 'on information supplied to the effect that he had been involved in illegal political activity'. From the impressions gained of his attitudes and activities during the field-work period I can only conclude that the 'information' stemmed from personal antagonism and had no basis in fact. This is, of course, only an impression which I cannot at present substantiate.

relations with the Government. The leaders of both these groups in Budjga think the District Administration is fundamentally hostile to them, and Government officials have on occasion been involved in serious altercation with priests and ministers.

The effect of these divergent forces is illustrated by an incident which was precipitated, in the first instance, by the field work for this study. As was mentioned in the Preface,[1] an attempt was made in January 1964 to place research assistants in a number of Budjga communities. Two were sent to Katsukunya in the Charewa Chiefdom, and M., the head teacher of the Methodist school there, arranged for their accommodation at the school. They were regarded with suspicion by local political leaders, and had to leave. After their departure his willingness to accommodate the two men became the focus for a political attack on M. and the Methodist Church at Katsukunya. Church members were met on their way to church services by groups of youths, and forbidden to proceed to the school. Attendances dropped drastically, and towards the end of March anonymous placards threatening M.'s life were put up at the school.

But in six months the picture at Katsukunya changed completely, through a variety of circumstances both within and without the community. In July the Methodist Bishop, Ralph E. Dodge, was forced by the Government to leave the country. No reason was given, but African opinion was almost unanimous in attributing this action to the fact that he was 'too sympathetic to the Africans'. In August a new church building in the village, which has been in the process of construction for a long time, was dedicated in a ceremony carried off with considerable pomp. Several local political leaders had been invited by the District Superintendent to take part and had agreed to do so. Members of the church began to be invited to political rallies, and were asked to open and close the sessions with prayer. Attendances at church services climbed until they exceeded pre-1964 levels.

These and other similar instances show how difficult it is to generalize on the relationship between the various religious groups and Budjga politicians. The general situation seems to be that the Traditional religious leaders are hostile to nationalist politics while the rank and file of this group are not. The Vapostori, while perhaps not entirely satisfied with the treatment they receive

[1] *Supra*, pp. v, vi.

from the present Government, prefer not to be involved in any movement actively seeking its overthrow, and justify this attitude on scriptural grounds.[1] Methodist and Roman Catholic leadership tends to be discreetly pro-nationalist, while within the ranks of lay membership in both churches there is considerable divergence of opinion. Some members are anti-nationalist, and justify their position on religious grounds.[2] Others are openly pro-nationalist, and some church members have been arrested for political activity.

Recently published anthropological studies from other parts of the world have demonstrated the interplay of religion and politics.[3] Kuper's study, done at the national level in South Africa, shows how the Dutch Reformed Church there is aligned with the politics of the National Party, while most of the other Christian denominations are opposed to it. The Geertz and Jay studies have a special relevance to this enquiry, since they also deal with a rural, religiously heterogeneous society in which two religions—a semi-orthodox Javanese Islam and a syncretistic Javanese rural religion—existed side by side in equilibrium for over four hundred years until the intrusion of Western political and economic modes of association produced a situation in which political polarization took place along the lines of religious cleavage. In the heightened political activity of rural Java today religious positions, says Geertz, 'become political ones almost without alteration'.[4]

Why has this not been the case, up to the present time, in Budjga? For one thing, Budjga has not experienced the cataclysmic upheaval that affected Java with the withdrawal of European power. But beyond this, I believe the answer lies in the network of interlocking relationships along the Budjga religious spectrum which was the subject of the previous chapter and which prevents the different Budjga religious groups from acting as

---

[1] Romans 13. 1–7, which contains the passage 'Every person must submit to the supreme authorities. There is no authority but by act of God, and the existing authorities are instituted by him; consequently anyone who rebels against authority is resisting a divine institution', is frequently quoted in this connection.

[2] I heard one Methodist businessman, faced with the boycott of his bus service because he refused to contribute to party funds, tell his church group, 'In spite of all this pressure I am determined to resist and remain a Christian. Pray for me.'

[3] Boissevain, 1965; Geertz, 1960; Jay, 1963; L. Kuper, 1965. The Geertz and Jay studies are part of an integrated research project.

[4] Geertz, 1960, p. 363.

completely isolated units. In Budjga, religious units are not village units as they are in Java, and are therefore not as readily amenable to political organization. Nor do they represent discrete economic, educational or other units. Furthermore, owing to the diversity within each religious group, each includes a membership with different political ends. The Traditional Religion has an ideology which supports the idea of African political control, but also a leadership in whose interest it is to interpret this ideology only on a tribal, not national, level. The Methodist and Catholic churches have an ideology which gives rise to status aspirations that are frustrated by the continued existence of European Government, and at the same time recruits teachers and small businessmen for an educational and economic system which relies on that same Government. Only the Vapostori show a relative consistency between their political goals and their ideology of non-participation in politics, and this is a position which neither Government nor nationalist politics is apparently willing to concede them at the present time.[1]

BUDJGA RELIGION IN THE LIGHT OF SELECTED SOUTHERN AFRICAN STUDIES

Although this is not a comparative study, it will be useful in conclusion to examine this analysis of the Budjga materials in the light of data on the religion of some other African societies. For this purpose three such studies, Kuper's examination of Swazi religion,[2] Schapera's study of Christianity among the Tswana[3] and Pauw's of religion among the Tlhaping Tswana[4] are of special interest, since they all involve situations of religious heterogeneity which parallel in many ways the position in Budjga.[5]

---

[1] This is, of course, a synchronic view based on one period of field study. The discussion on religion and politics in Budjga underlines *inter alia*, the importance of replication studies in this as in other fields of anthropological investigation. An investigation, for instance, of the Katsukunya community confined to March 1964 would have led to a very different conclusion on the position of the Methodist Church in local politics from that of a similar study carried out in September of the same year.

[2] Kuper, 1964.   [3] Schapera, 1934, 1958.   [4] Pauw, 1960.

[5] Considerations of space make it impossible to bring the many other recent studies of African religion into this discussion. Such well-known works as Sundkler's *Bantu Prophets in South Africa* and Baeta's *Prophetism in Ghana* do not parallel this study in the same way that the Swazi and Tswana studies do.

In each a traditional tribal religion is found existing side by side with an immigrant Christianity, brought in the first instance by missionaries. In the Kuper and Pauw studies Christianity is represented by Protestant, Catholic and Independent groups as in Budjga, while in Bechuanaland, although each of these groups was present in the territory as a whole, each tribe tended to have only one form of Christianity alongside its traditional faith. In each case the missions are, or have been, closely involved with government in providing medical, educational and other services. In three of the societies the percentage of Christians is remarkably similar (Budjga 30.1 per cent,[1] Swazi 31.19 per cent,[2] Tswana 27 per cent).[3] Only among the Tlhaping Tswana does the percentage of Christians at 45 per cent rise significantly above this level.[4]

There are important background differences between the four studies. Christianity is much older among the Tswana than among the Swazi, and among the Budjga it is younger still.[5] The political background, both national and tribal, is somewhat different in each case. Several of the Tswana chiefs were converted to Christianity during the early stages of missionary evangelization, something which did not happen among the Swazi. Within Christian ranks, both the percentage of Independent Christians and the number of Independent groups is far higher among the Swazi and the Tlhaping Tswana than it is among the Budjga or the Tswana of Bechuanaland. It is important also to keep in mind the different dates at which these studies were made.

But in spite of these important differences, certain characteristics appear with consistent regularity in the religion of the four societies concerned:

1. In no case has Christianity arrived on the scene as an isolated system of religious ideas and moral precepts. In each society its advent was accompanied by economic and political innovations not directly connected with mission policy or activity. So close

---

[1] *Supra*, p. 119. Based on the Tsutskwe community.
[2] Kuper, 1946, p. 111.   [3] Schapera, 1958, p. 2.
[4] Pauw, 1960, p. 9.
[5] Mission work started in Swaziland at the end of the nineteenth century (Kuper, 1946, p. 107). Christianity among the Tlhaping Tswana has a history dating back to 1821, when Robert Moffat worked among them at Kuruman. Permanent mission work at Taung dates from 1842, while the beginnings of missionary activity among the Tswana date back to 1860. Chief Lentswe of the BaKxatla accepted Christianity in 1892 (Schapera, 1934, p. 48). Organized Christianity first reached Budjga in 1911. (*Supra*, p. 62.)

was the coincidence between the advent of Christianity and these other factors making for social change that it is difficult to attribute any given ritual or social change *solely* to religious factors. For example, while it is true that Christian teaching discouraged rituals directed towards the ancestors, other factors, such as the declining importance of kinship as a basis for social organization and the dispersal of what were once closely knit residential and kinship units, also tended to reduce interest in these rituals. Or again, although Church regulations have discouraged polygyny, the imposition of additional taxation upon polygynists has also contributed to its decline.

2. In each society Christianity has presented one of the first and most important new forms of social grouping at a time when political changes and personal mobility were creating the need for new forms. Church membership cut across kinship lines and offered new roles. Later the appeal that these opportunities for emancipation had for women was to contribute to the numerical preponderance of females among many of the Christian groups observed.[1]

3. In spite of the fact that everywhere Christian churches have provided new forms of social grouping, in none of the societies studied have Christians become a distinct social group, separated from other members of their communities. The results of the Tsutskwe census indicating a lack of residential or social segregation along religious lines[2] are paralleled by materials from the Swazi and Tswana. Thus Schapera says: 'But except for their special activities and obligations, Christians are not as a group socially distinct. In ordinary daily life and domestic ceremonies they associate together freely with the pagans, some of whom occasionally even go to church as a pastime or out of curiosity, and there is no obvious means of telling the two sections apart.'[3]

[1] Schapera, 1958, p. 6; Kuper, 1946, pp. 183–4; Pauw, 1960, pp. 92–4. In another study Monica Wilson points out that in the Keiskammahoek District '. . . voluntary association based on mutual belief in Christianity would appear to be the largest single group cutting across the traditional structure of the society, which is based on local, kinship and sex-age groupings'. (Wilson, 1952, p. 136.)

[2] *Supra*, pp. 120–5, 127–8.

[3] Schapera, 1958, p. 7. Writing about the early history of Christianity in South Africa and citing as examples the BaKopa and BaPedi, Eiselen said in 1934, 'Those natives who became Christians were lost to their tribe', and 'The Christian gospel was, during the nineteenth century, the most powerful agency in the disintegration of South African tribes' (Eiselen, 1934, pp. 70–1). But these statements must be

Likewise Kuper says, 'In Swaziland, however, the cleavage between Christians and pagans is not as sharp as in some other parts of Africa.'[1] Nor do kinship alignments necessarily determine religious affiliation; the Swazi materials indicate that there, as in Budjga, members of one family may belong to different faiths.[2]

4. Under the impact of Christianity and other factors inducing social change there has been a differential modification in the various items of belief and ritual in the traditional religions of each society. Some elements have been susceptible to rapid deterioration, while others have demonstrated remarkable resiliency. Correspondingly there has been a selective acceptance of the items of Christian belief and practice, and features which in both religions rest on a similar ideology often reinforce each other in spite of their apparent hostility. What Kuper says of the Swazi is applicable to all four societies: 'The co-existence of missionary and "magician" has led to a weakening of the ancestral cult, and of certain other rituals, but has reinforced belief in supernatural power. To dismiss the ancestors as "things of the Devil" does not deny their existence. Substitution of a cross for an amulet or animal-skin indicates a transference in the Freudian sense.'[3] A reinterpretation and incorporation of magical beliefs into the ritual and belief systems of the Christian churches can be traced in each society, and in every case the belief in witchcraft persists among Christians as well as Traditional Religionists.

5. Together with this lack of orthodoxy, the Christian groups in each society show a great deal of inconsistency between ideal and action, between the moral standards and actual behaviour of many of their adherents. In his analysis Pauw has detected a distinctly moralistic and legalistic trend among many of the Christian groups

taken in their historical context; the two tribes concerned were both involved in military conflict at the time when Christianity was introduced, and the refusal of Christians to participate in tribal rituals was made the excuse for military failures. Christian reaction to this hostility, combined with missionary policy, led to the establishment of separate Christian villages and tribal sections. This development does not seem to have been paralleled elsewhere, and certainly not in the societies which are under discussion here.

[1] Kuper, 1946, p. 122.

[2] 'In the same family one child may be an orthodox pagan fighting for the old worship, while another child preaches submission to a new God', Kuper, 1946, p. 110.

[3] Kuper, 1946, p. 127.

he studied, in which adherence to a particular code of behaviour—usually predominantly negative in character—is associated with salvation. He attributes this trend largely to the disintegration of traditional sanctions on behaviour, and the need for a new clear-cut set of regulations backed up by strong sanctions.[1] These observations and conclusions can, I consider, be applied with equal validity to the Budjga situation, and especially to the Methodists and Vapostori. Yet in spite of this emphasis on a moral legalism, the behaviour of many Budjga Christians is not consistent with the moral codes of their churches, and it can be said of them, as Schapera says of some Tswana Christians, 'Others maintain their allegiance, but do not always behave as they should. They have illicit love affairs, drink beer, resort to magicians, seldom go to communion, and in various ways show that they are Christians in name only.'[2]

Schapera ascribes this to the fact that many of the Tswana chiefs accepted Christianity and that large numbers of their subjects followed them into the Christian Church in mass movements that had little significance in terms of moral commitment. This factor has not been present in Budjga, but the Christian monopoly over the educational system there, giving the Methodists and Catholics a subtle means of coercion, has undoubtedly produced a mass conversion of Budjga young people with a similar lack of genuine personal commitment.

6. In one important respect the religious situation in the four societies differs sharply. Among both Swazi and Tlhaping Tswana the number of Independent churches is relatively high, Pauw listing nineteen for his area[3] and Kuper 21 for Swaziland.[4] On the other hand, in Bechuanaland the Independent groups are insignificant, and in Budjga the only numerically significant Independents are the Vapostori, who are represented in strength throughout the Reserve. The question why the Independent groups in Swaziland and among the Tlhaping Tswana should have multiplied progres-

---

[1] Pauw (1960, pp. 218–19) finds a connection between this moralism and the belief in magical ritual and doctrine, in that they both imply a direct and necessary causal relation between human action and supernatural response. He reasons therefore that a legalistic Christianity is particularly acceptable in a society in which the belif in magic is strong, a conclusion which Budjga materials would tend to support.

[2] Schapera, 1958, p. 7.

[3] Pauw, 1960, pp. 59–60.   [4] Kuper, 1946, p. 122.

sively, while in Budjga the Vapostori have remained the only significant representatives of this sector of Christianity for nearly twenty years, is a difficult one to answer. Both Pauw and Kuper stress the politically fissiparous tendencies of their respective societies, and suggest that this tendency conditioned Swazi and Tswana ideas on church unity.[1] But this affords no useful clue to the absence of Separatism in Budjga, for the same conditions of political segmentation resulting from collateral succession disputes and land pressure are present in Budjga, yet have not given rise to segmentation among the Vapostori.[2]

The major reason for the absence of Separatism in Bechuanaland seems to lie in the way tribal leaders were converted to Christianity near the outset of missionary activity, and subsequently made a given denomination the official religion of the people. When, for instance, Chief Lentswe of the BaKxatla was converted to Christianity in 1892, he gave a religious monopoly of his tribe to the Dutch Reformed Church. This monopoly, together with Lentswe's vigorous support for the missionary programme, produced a rapid and almost complete change in the religious affiliation of the BaKxatla within forty years.[3] One unified tribal religion was substituted for another, denominational competition was avoided, and a totalitarian religious climate was preserved which was inimical to any form of Christian proliferation.

Budjga exhibits some parallels to this situation. It is true that in Budjga Protestant-Catholic rivalry exists, but Budjga has not had a large number of Protestant missions active in its midst, and it is possible that this absence of interdenominational rivalry has helped to minimize the multiplication of Independent groups there.

We are left with the Swazi and Tlhaping societies for comparison, and here it must be pointed out that the Swazi are not exactly analogous to the other two, for Swazi society is far larger, and the profusion of Independent groups there may be in part attributed to the more diffuse influences that such a large population is likely to encounter. The most significant comparison with Budjga is therefore to be found with the Tlhaping Tswana at Taung. The

---

[1] Pauw, 1960, pp. 236–7; Kuper, 1946, p. 124.

[2] *Supra*, p. 24.

[3] Speaking of Lentswe's conversion Schapera says, 'The marked encouragement he gave to the new doctrines, coupled with his abolition of many of the old ceremonies, has led in forty years to a condition where little active trace remains of the old religious system.' (Schapera, 1934, p. 52.)

two societies are more nearly the same size, and in both the numerical relation of Independent Christian groups to the other churches is about the same (20·3 per cent in Taung, 24·8 per cent in Budjga).[1] But whereas the Taung Independents are distributed among 19 groups the Budjga Independents are represented by only five, and four of these are numerically insignificant, having a combined membership of only 118. There is thus a marked contrast between Budjga Independency, where one group, the Vapostori, represent over 90 per cent of all adherents in this class, and Taung Independency, where in a total membership of 2070 there are 19 groups, 10 with a membership of 100 or more.

As we have already noted, Christianity is considerably younger in Budjga, and it is possible that time will bring to it the multiplicity of Independent groups that is now found in Taung. However, the most significant reasons for Vapostori (and therefore Independent) unity in Budjga must be sought in the peculiar characteristics of the organization itself. Johanne's genius created an organization permitting considerable flexibility and autonomy at local levels while retaining over-all control through a ritual focus on himself. This ritual focus on his leadership was not obtrusive, and became concrete only once a year, when he came to the Reserve for the *Penta*. He stood, as his successor does, as an authority external to the Reserve, permitting a high degree of autonomy to local leaders and yet able to arbitrate, from a non-partisan position, any internal disputes that might arise between them. Serious disputes within the Vapostori have in fact often been solved by the tested Budjga technique of segmentation, the *kireke* or *penta* splitting and one half moving to a new location, while all concerned remain members of the Movement.

I would further suggest that the success of this way of solving internal disputes has been greatly facilitated by the absence of church property among the Vapostori. Neither Pauw nor Kuper give detailed information on the financial policies of the Independent churches they studied, but both imply that they all have some form of corporate treasury, and Pauw cites an example of a church split over financial matters in an Independent group in Taung.[2] A Vapostori group, without a congregational treasury or a church building, can divide without any dispute over property to exacerbate ill-feeling and perpetuate hostilities, and

[1] Pauw, 1960, p. 57, and Appendix, Table 6. [2] Pauw, 1960, p. 104.

a congregation, or any section of it, can move from one site to another with a minimum of inconvenience.

Thirdly, it is important to note that the Vapostori are not 'Separatists' in the strict sense of the word, i.e. they have not broken away from some other Christian group.[1] Their founder was not a secessionist religious leader, he was a young prophet who had no previous experience as a religious leader. Pauw, in discussing separatism in Taung, suggests that the Pentecostal history of many of the groups there has given them a precedent for schism, since the European Pentecostalism with which they have had connections has been prone to secession.[2] This assertion would seem to be validated by the history of some of these groups in Southern Rhodesia, which is replete with leadership disputes and schisms among both European and African adherents.[3] But although the Vapostori are Pentecostal in doctrine, they have no history linking them with these groups, and their own history gives the discontented among them no precedent for schism.

Finally, reference should be made in this connection to the high degree of religious mobility already noted for Budjga.[4] Two types of mobility have been defined, affiliational mobility, in which an individual in the course of his lifetime changes his religious group membership one or more times; and temporary mobility, where an individual moves out of the pattern of belief and practice standard for his group and temporarily, for specific purposes, aligns himself with those of another. Among reasons for the first type of mobility are personality conflicts and role rivalries, factors often related to religious schism. But the second type is perhaps more important in this context. The acceptance by Vapostori of temporary mobility on the part of their members permits divergence from the norms of the group while the privilege of membership is retained. Heterodoxy and heteropraxy do not therefore necessarily lead to expulsion, nor to the formation of groups of malcontents seeking to create new groups with revised standards.

With the important exception of the multiplicity of independent groups in Swaziland and Taung, the four studies present what

---

[1] This is one reason why they are consistently referred to in this text by the alternative (and not altogether satisfactory) term 'Independent'.

[2] Pauw, 1960, p. 236.

[3] cf. Ranger, 1964, pp. 52–74.   [4] *Supra*, pp. 137–43.

is on the whole a remarkably uniform picture of religion in four societies of southern Africa undergoing rapid social change. In each, Christianity has become an important religious factor; in each, Christianity has been represented by more than one organization, and in none has the impact of Christianity been so pervasive that the society could now be characterized as 'Christian'. The differences in the over-all assessment made by the various studies of the place of Christianity in the societies concerned can to a certain extent be attributed to different perspectives. Kuper considers that Christianity has had a disintegrative effect on Swazi society, and in her conclusion says, 'Christianity in Swaziland is embodied in a number of churches, often antagonistic to each other as well as to pagan practices. The moral unity of the human society may be proclaimed in theory, but it is denied in action. The missions instead of introducing greater co-operation in the nation have accentuated differences, and bolstered European domination.'[1] Schapera's evaluation of Christianity in Bechuanaland is different: 'Although Christianity did often cause trouble, it never seriously disturbed tribal unity, except perhaps when used to cloak the ambitions of a chief's enemies . . . Christians seldom had to choose between tribal allegiance and devotion to the gospel.'[2] On the other hand, Schapera questions whether Christianity has exerted a creative influence in Tswana society, noting its relative failure to achieve its desired goals and suggesting that it has itself been critically affected in the process: 'It is rather Christianity itself that seems to have suffered in the process of acceptance by the Tswana. As a faith it appeals, even nominally, to little more than a quarter of the people. . . .'[3]

Pauw interprets the Taung situation primarily as of a transitional process involving a change of religions in Tlhaping society, but adds that this transition is a complex process, involving a variety of religious and social interconnections which make it more than just the substitution of one religion for another: 'If one were to characterize the Phuduhutswana chiefdom from a religious point of view in a single sentence, it could be called a society in an advanced stage of transition from paganism to Christianity. . . . However, the transition . . . is a much more complex process than the mere supplanting of one religion by another . . .

[1] Kuper, 1946, p. 128.
[2] Schapera, 1958, p. 8.   [3] Ibid., p. 9.

this complexity results from the fact that the old and the new mutually influence each other in the contact situation.'[1]

As was suggested in the Preface[2] and has been illustrated in Chapters 7 and 8, this study of Budjga religion has attempted to focus on the actual choices, deviations and alterations in the behaviour and belief of individual members of the society. This focus, coupled with the discovery of a high degree of religious mobility and heterodoxy in Budjga, has led to a perspective which sees Christianity and the Traditional Religion not as polar opposites, but as constituent elements of a spectrum admitting a wide variety of religious behaviour and belief. This perspective, therefore, emphasizes the functional unity underlying the diversity which characterizes Budjga religion in its institutional forms. From this point of view Christianity can be said to have contributed to a more complex religious situation in Budjga, but it can hardly be credited with the divisive character that Kuper gives it among the Swazi.[3]

Again, this approach evaluates the present status of Christianity in Budjga primarily in terms of the extent and frequency with which it becomes a reference point for Budjga, not in terms of its deviation from Western Christian norms or its failure to achieve numerical ascendency. As in Bechuanaland, Christianity has been modified in the process of introduction into Budjga. Many of its adherents deviate from prescribed norms of belief and behaviour, particularly in times of stress and crisis.[4] Numerically, it has not

---

[1] Pauw, 1960, pp. 237–8.   [2] *Supra*, p. vi.

[3] Nor, it is suggested, would this perspective yield the same evaluation of the materials Kuper presents. Kuper speaks of friendships between Swazi of different religious groups, and gives an example of N.T., who 'was considering conversion, but was not sure whether to join the Catholics, the A.M.E., Nazarenes or Wesleyans. Preachers of all these faiths were his friends, and the multiplicity of churches did not make him doubt the value of any. "I want a church that suits me. Everyone must choose for himself, and God hears all voices, but you must not be out of tune with those with whom you are singing. You must be friends with your neighbours." ' (Kuper, 1946, pp. 111–12.) Kuper elsewhere makes a statement which indicates that the same functional unity underlying the Budjga religious groups is to be found among the Swazi: 'Between the missionary (umfundisi) and the Swazi ritual specialist (inyanga) exists a common bond: though they openly condemn and criticise each other's beliefs, *these beliefs are rooted in an unrealised and inadmissible similarity*... Both believe in a power beyond man, a Power that can be tapped by prayer and ritual.' (Kuper, 1946, p. 126, my italics.)

[4] The significance of behaviour in times of stress as an index of religious commitment has, I feel, been over-emphasized. Kuper makes the statement, '... the depth of... conversion cannot be measured, though it can to some extent

M

achieved the success that might have been expected from its close connection with education or its implicit support by Government. Judged in the light of missionary aims and objectives it must be considered a relative failure. But when we take into consideration the fact that items of Christian belief form part of the ideological framework of most Budjga today—even non-Christians—and that a significant section of the Budjga population focuses its ritual activity in the Christian groups, their provision of alternative forms of religious expression must be considered to be of profound sociological significance. In this light their diversity, and the ease with which individuals move between them, may be an indication of viability rather than failure. They thereby provide not one, but several, additional frameworks within which the Budjga can organize new associations and assimilate new values at a time when rapid social change demands this kind of innovation.

Since we have found that certain general observations concerning the contemporary religion of societies in southern Africa have widespread validity, it is interesting to note what a pioneer anthropologist in the area said nearly forty years ago on the subject of the introduction of Christianity among the Bantu. Writing in 1927, Winifred Hoernlé placed great stress on the role of ancestor worship in African societies in promoting lineage unity and maintaining kinship organization.[1] She correctly predicted the decline of the kinship group as a basis of social organization and the emergence of other forms of association. In the religious reorientation which she saw as the necessary accompaniment of this change, she suggested that the most useful contribution that Christianity could make was to provide an education for the African people which would wean them from the belief that the moral and natural orders are bound together, that the behaviour of natural phenomena reflects conditions in the social order.

be observed from behaviour in crises such as illness or accidents' (Kuper, 1946, p. 107). The implication that what an individual does at such times indicates a basic orientation or allegiance may be valid psychologically or theologically, but if, for instance, a person spends one month of the year in a diviner's village being treated for illness and the other eleven months in his own village attending church every Sunday and conforming to Christian behaviour patterns, can one set of actions be said to be *sociologically* more significant than the other? Here intensity and frequency of action must be balanced against each other; both patterns of behaviour say something about the man's religious orientation and both affect the society in which he lives.

[1] Hoernlé, 1927, pp. 84–109.

This would, she thought, remove the undesirable effects of belief in witchcraft and magic and free the African peoples from 'the enormous burden of ritual which today bears them down'.[1]

Mrs Hoernlé recognized that such an educational process would be a long and arduous task, but it was left to Professor Westermann, writing ten years later, to point out that Christianity in Africa was not always concerned in its educational programme with separating the moral and natural orders, nor 'lightening the burden of ritual' which lay on African shoulders. On the contrary, Westermann predicted that the differential response elicited by Christianity in African societies might create a situation in which education would produce the opposite effect, and that, while ancestor worship might decline, magic and witchcraft would persist.[2] The evidence from Budjga and the comparative studies mentioned here would seem to bear out Westermann's prediction.

Westermann also foresaw the coalescence of Traditional and Christian belief and ritual which is demonstrated in this study by the heterodoxy and ritual mobility of the Budjga. He saw this syncretic tendency exemplified by the Independent Churches of South and West Africa, but was not consistent in his evaluation of their place in African Christianity. At one point he writes of them sympathetically, noting that the 'Ethiopian and similar movements, with all their failures and shortcomings, show that the Christian Church has found its place in native life'.[3] Yet at another point he maintains that the missionary must be 'inexorable in trying to exterminate everything connected with the old religion, because his experience has taught him that any form of syncretism is the death of genuine Christian life'.[4]

This study has not been focused solely on the syncretic aspects of Budjga religion, nor has it attempted any judgement such as Westermann made on any of the forms of Budjga religious life. It has sought to examine all four forms of religious organization in Budjga, and has suggested that each exists as a modality on a broad

[1] Hoernlé, 1927, p. 108.
[2] 'School teaching will seldom succeed in destroying religious and magic beliefs altogether, but it will push them into the lower regions of the mind, and gradually their best features, reverence for the ancestors and gods and the moral sanctions growing out of them, will disappear, while the darker sides, fear of spirits, spells, and witches remain and enter into an unholy alliance with scientific and religious ideas learnt at school.' (Westermann, 1937, p. 23.)
[3] Westermann, 1937, p. 56.   [4] Westermann, 1937, p. 135.

religious spectrum from which individuals select the ingredients of their religious life. This approach has special relevance for anthropological studies of the modern religious movements of which the Vapostori are one example. These movements have proved amenable, in given contexts, to sociological analysis from a variety of different perspectives. Worsley, in his study of millenarianism, has shown the importance of economic determinants in the Melanesian context.[1] In the South African urban setting Mayer has demonstrated how one of these movements can be interpreted primarily in terms of organization for social control in an anomic situation,[2] while in the area from which the material for this study has been drawn Ranger has given a preliminary historical sketch of religious independency in Southern Rhodesia which emphasizes its political contexts.[3]

While all these interpretations have been useful in the analysis of such movements elsewhere, this study indicates that the Vapostori Movement cannot be understood primarily in terms of the realignment of social control, of economic activity or political expression, but only when it is first of all seen in the religious context in which it exists, as representing a sub-species of Budjga religion in reciprocal relationship with other modes of religious behaviour. The connection that it has with the other forms of Budjga religious life is not simply an historical one, it is a continuing sociological fact.

Moreover, this relationship is reciprocal, and the other types of Budjga religion sustain a continuous reaction to the Vapostori and to each other. The application of the word 'syncretistic' to the Independent groups implies that they stand at some mid-point along a continuum which stretches from the Traditional Religion at one end to the 'orthodox' churches at the other. But we have seen that at least on some points of doctrine the Vapostori are more consistently 'orthodox' in their Christian belief than members of the older denominations, while in the matter of polygyny, in ideal and practice, they are more 'traditional' than the Traditionalists. In Budjga at least, all the religious groups, from the Traditional Religionists to the mission-sponsored

---

[1] Worsley, 1947.   [2] Mayer, 1963, pp. 113–26.

[3] Ranger, 1964, pp. 52–74. Ranger candidly admits that his materials, drawn as they are from Government archives, give an unavoidable political bias to his treatment.

churches, are to some extent 'syncretistic'. In this they all reflect the process of modification and adaptation which is taking place not only in religion, but in the other institutions of Budjga society as well.

APPENDIX

TABLE I. Tsutskwe Census. Population by Village: Chifamba Sub-Community

Column	1	2	3	4	5	6	7	8	9	10	11
				Post-school-age adoles-cents &		*Total,*	*School-age children*		*Pre-school*		
		Married Adults		*young adults*		*Cols.*	*In*	*Out of*		*Total*	*Total*
Village	*House-holds*	*M*	*F*	*M*	*F*	*2–5*	*school*	*school*	*children*	*children*	*Pop.*
Kondo	18	16	24	6	3	49	28	2	38	68	117
Marumisa	29	25	35	6	8	74	29	14	50	93	167
Nyamuzinga	10	10	15	3	10	38	11	10	15	36	74
Deku	25	25	31	4	3	63	13	6	46	65	128
Patambura	12	12	21	1	2	36	11	18	31	60	96
Kanyepa	17	17	17	5	1	40	8	10	21	39	79
Mzarabani	14	14	16	3	1	34	5	13	28	46	80
Nyambeu	6	6	7	3	0	16	8	3	11	22	38
Chipara	38	35	41	9	1	86	28	28	64	120	206
Sambi	5	5	7	1	1	14	5	7	8	20	34
Mapundu	6	6	7	5	1	19	3	0	6	9	28
Tsuro	11	11	15	1	1	28	18	9	18	45	73
Chifamba	36	36	48	18	9	111	54	8	55	117	228
Muzira	10	10	12	9	6	37	12	3	14	29	66
Mbariro	12	12	12	0	1	25	6	4	8	18	43
Manemwe	12	12	17	11	4	44	6	6	25	37	81
Maruza	23	23	38	4	11	76	25	13	54	92	168
Hotera Nhete	7	5	9	3	4	21	3	4	7	14	35
Chapfuruka	21	21	24	12	8	65	5	34	30	69	134
Vareta	22	22	28	6	7	63	8	12	35	55	118
Totals	334	323	424	110	82	939	286	204	564	1054	1993

Column Two. This figure is less than the total for column One because a few households consist only of widows and their children.

Column Three. The preponderance of married women over married men (column Two) can be accounted for in part by the following factors: (*a*) Girls tend to marry sooner than boys in this polygynous society, a fact reflected in the excess of boys over girls in columns Four and Five. (*b*) A number of widows maintaining their own households are present, whereas only a few old men without wives were recorded. Several men have wives inherited on the death of brothers. These facts may indicate a higher mortality rate among men than women in the community. (*c*) It is possible that a few villages (i.e. Marumisa,

Patambura, Chifamba, Maruza) exhibit an abnormally high ratio of wives per polygynous marriage and have recruited more females by marriages than they have lost. The ratio of men to women in Chifamba (approximately three to four) is lower than that found in Karonga (approximately seven to eight).

Column Five. As has been suggested, this figure is less than that for column Four because the girls tend to marry sooner than do the boys in this category. It is possible that the discrepancy might be even larger were it not for the fact that girls tend to leave school earlier than boys and thus move from columns Seven and Eight to this category before boys do.

Column Seven. The enrolment at Chifamba School is 266. This figure is higher since a number of villages equidistant from Chifamba and Karonga Schools but included in this table (Makwembere, Chipara) send some of their children to Karonga School.

TABLE 2. Tsutskwe Census. Population by Village: Karonga Sub-Community

Column	1	2	3	4	5	6	7	8	9	10	11
				Post-school-age adolescents & young adults		Total,	School-age children		Pre-		
		Married Adults					In	Out of	school	Total	Total
Village	House-holds	M	F	M	F	Cols. 2–5	school	school	children	children	Pop.
Kaitano	24	24	29	13	11	77	19	6	40	65	142
Chidzomba	8	8	6	1	2	17	7	0	12	19	36
Veremu	8	8	8	0	0	16	4	6	6	16	32
Chitawa	8	8	7	3	2	20	0	2	7	9	29
Musona	13	13	13	7	7	40	5	0	10	15	55
Madziya Nheya	10	10	17	3	2	32	6	0	17	23	55
Magauze	10	7	8	3	2	20	1	0	7	8	28
Katambarare	29	28	31	17	18	94	22	12	31	65	159
Nongwe	8	6	9	11	12	38	4	3	12	19	57
Chibanda	4	4	6	5	4	19	1	0	10	11	30
Mutsenhu	33	32	45	17	23	117	35	12	26	73	190
Karonga	2	2	6	5	4	17	4	2	2	8	25
Tsuro	25	25	25	6	3	59	23	1	41	65	124
Totals	182	175	210	91	90	566	131	44	221	396	962

Column Five. As has been suggested for Table 1, this figure might be much less than the total for column Four because of the earlier marriage age for girls were it not for the fact that girls leave school earlier and come into this category sooner than boys.

Column Seven. Karonga School has an enrolment of 181. About twenty children from villages listed under Chifamba attend school at Karonga, as do some from Area C who live with relatives during school term.

TABLE 3. Tsutskwe Census. Religious Affiliation, Adults
(Chifamba Sub-Community)

Village	Gentile M	Gentile F	Methodist Active M	Methodist Active F	Methodist Inactive M	Methodist Inactive F	Roman Catholic Active M	Roman Catholic Active F	Roman Catholic Inactive M	Roman Catholic Inactive F	Vapostori Active M	Vapostori Active F	Vapostori Inactive M	Vapostori Inactive F
Kondo	14	16		7			2	1						
Marumisa	18	21	2	7	1		2				3	4		2
Nyamuzinga	7	11	1	2			2	2						
Deku	20	27									4	4	1	
Patambura	5	8									6	12	1	1
Kanyepa	10	6	3	7							3	3	1	1
Mzarabani	12	11	1*	4*							1	1		
Nyambeu	5	5		1*							1	1		
Chipara	29	31	1	3			4	5			1	2		
Sambi	5	7												
Mapundu	6	7												
Tsuro	11	14	1											
Chifamba	25	32		7	4	2	6	7	1					
Muzira	7	7	2	3		1	1	1						
Mbariro	11	10	1				1	1						
Manemwe	12	16	1											
Maruza	13	17	1								2	4	8	16
Hotera Nhete	5	9												
Chapfuruka	18	21	1	2	2	1								
Vareta	20	26							1	1	1	1		
Totals	253	302	11	47	6	5	18	17	2	1	22	32	11	20

* Members of the Salvation Army who attend Methodist services at Chifamba.

TABLE 4. Tsutskwe Census. Religious Affiliation, Adults
(Karonga Sub-Community)

Village	Gentile M	Gentile F	Methodist Active M	Methodist Active F	Methodist Inactive M	Methodist Inactive F	Roman Catholic Active M	Roman Catholic Active F	Roman Catholic Inactive M	Roman Catholic Inactive F	Vapostori Active M	Vapostori Active F	Vapostori Inactive M	Vapostori Inactive F
Kaitano	14	16	3	3	1		3	3	1	5	2	2		
Chidzomba	1	3			1				6	3				
Veremu	5	3				1		1	3	1				2
Chitawa	4	7			4									
Musona	6	11					1	1	6	1				
Madziya Nheya	5	6									5	11		
Magauze	5	5					1	1					1	2
Katambarare	19	22									5	5	4	4
Nongwe	6	9												

TABLE 4. Tsutskwe Census. Religious Affiliation, Adults
(Karonga Sub-Community) (contd.)

Village	Gentile		Methodist Active		Methodist Inactive		Roman Catholic Active		Roman Catholic Inactive		Vapostori Active		Vapostori Inactive	
	M	F	M	F	M	F	M	F	M	F	M	F	M	F
Chibanda	4	6												
Mutsenhu	25	36					3	4	4	5				
Karonga	2	5			1									
Tsuro	11	14	3	4	4	0	4	5			2*	1*	1*	1*
Totals	107	143	6	7	10	2	12	15	20	15	14	19	6	9

* Members of Kruger Vapostori Church.

Note on 'active' and 'inactive' categories. All the Christian denominations register large 'inactive' segments in their membership, both at Karonga and at Chifamba (Table 3). This is particularly noticeable among the Roman Catholics at Karonga (above), where there are 12 'active' male members and 20 'inactive' male members. The fact that this should be so in a sub-community with a Roman Catholic school while in the Methodist sub-community of Chifamba there are 18 'active' Catholic male members as against only 2 'inactive' members may be in part attributed to the following factors:

(*a*) As was suggested in the text (p. 119) the degree of involvement in church activities claimed may vary in direct proportion to the distance a member is from his home congregation. In the Chifamba sub-community Roman Catholics could claim to be active members and be accepted as such without their claims being subjected to close scrutiny; in the Karonga sub-community such claims would have to be supported by conformity to Catholic practice. This is, however, an argument which cannot be pushed too far. The distance from Chifamba to Karonga is not so great as to allow residents at Chifamba to assume that they can exist in complete isolation from Karonga. Furthermore the ratios of 'active' to 'inactive' male members of the Methodist Church in the two sub-communities do not follow the same pattern.

(*b*) An historical factor may be present, as in the case of the Vapostori at Maruza Village in the Chifamba sub-community (Table 3). Here a disagreement between Vapostori members of this village and the leaders of the Mazvimba *kireke* led to widespread disaffection in this village, and 24 of this village's 30 Vapostori are currently listed as 'inactive'. If, however, there has been such an event among the Catholics at Karonga it did not come to light during the field work period.

(*c*) As has been pointed out, there have been several cross-currents of Methodist and Catholic influence in the valley: a Methodist school once existed near the site of the present Catholic school, while during the late 1940s and early 1950s many young people—especially boys—went from the Chifamba area to the Catholic mission at All Souls' for their schooling. There are thus residual memberships of Methodists at Karonga and Catholics at Chifamba as a result of these cross-currents that are now semi-isolated from the organized programmes of their churches. Since the criteria used to evaluate 'active' and 'inactive' membership were to an extent the subjective judgements of informants themselves, it is possible that the difference in evaluation concerning the membership status of these groups

[contd. on p. 177]

TABLE 5. Tsutskwe Census. Religious Affiliation, Adults. Composite Totals
(Chifamba Sub-Community)

	Gentile		Christian		Methodist		Catholic		Vapostori	
	No.	%	No.	%	No.	%	No.	%	No.	%
Males	253	78·3	70	21·7	17	5·3	20	6·2	33	10·2
Females	302	71·2	122	28·8	52	12·3	18	4·1	52	12·3
Totals	555	74·3	192	25·7	69	9·2	38	5·1	85	11·4

(Karonga Sub-Community)

	Gentile		Christian		Methodist		Catholic		Vapostori	
	No.	%	No.	%	No.	%	No.	%	No.	%
Males	107	61·1	68	38·9	16	9·2	32	18·3	20	11·4
Females	143	68·1	67	31·9	9	4·3	30	14·3	28	13·3
Totals	250	64·9	135	35·1	25	6·5	62	16·1	48	12·5

TABLE 6. Tsutskwe Census. Religious Affiliation, Post-school Age. Adolescents
and Young Adults
(Chifamba Sub-Community)

Village	Gentile	Methodist	R.C.	Vapostori	Total No.
Kondo	5	4			9
Marumisa	9	2	3		14
Nyamuzinga	8	2	3		13
Deku	5	2			7
Patambura	1			2	3
Kanyepa	3			3	6
Mzarabani	3	1*			4
Nyambeu	3				3
Chipara	2	2	5	1	10
Sambi	2				2
Mapundu	4		2		6
Tsuro	1	1			2
Chifamba	12	5	10		27
Muzira	8	4	3		15
Mbariro	1				1
Manemwe	14	1			15
Maruza	8	1		6	15
Hotera Nhete	7				7
Chapfuruka	20				20
Vareta	12	1			13
Totals	128	26	26	12	192

★ Salvation Army member who attends Methodist services at Chifamba.

may reflect the different concepts of membership and orientations towards church activities discussed in Chapter 5 (p. 89). Methodists in the Karonga sub-community tend to slip into 'inactive' status since they are cut off from the activities of a local congregation which are the mainstay of Methodist membership, while the Catholics at Chifamba, not having this same dependence on local church activities, can maintain their identification with their Church on the basis of non-residential factors.

TABLE 7. Tsutskwe Census. Religious Affiliation, Post-school Age. Adolescents and Young Adults
(Karonga Sub-Community)

Village	Gentile	Methodist	R.C.	Vapostori	Total No.
Kaitano	4	6	14		24
Chidzomba	3				3
Veremu					0
Chitawa	4		1		5
Musona	7		7		14
Madziya Nheya	1		2	2	5
Magauze	4			1	5
Katambarare	29			6	35
Nongwe	23				23
Chibanda	5		4		9
Mutsenhu	28		12		40
Karonga	4		5		9
Tsuro	7		2		9
Totals	119	6	47	9	181

TABLE 8. Tsutskwe Census. Religious Affiliation, Post-school Age. Adolescents and Young Adults
(Composite Totals)

	Chifamba		Karonga		Total	
	No.	%	No.	%	No.	%
Gentile	128	66·6	119	65·7	247	66·2
Methodist	26	13·6	6	3·3	32	8·6
Catholic	26	13·6	47	26·0	73	19·6
Vapostori	12	6·2	9	5·0	21	5·6
Totals	192	100·0	181	100·0	373	100·0

	Chifamba		Karonga		Total	
	No.	%	No.	%	No.	%
Gentile	128	66·6	119	65·7	247	66·2
Christian	64	33·4	62	34·3	126	33·8
Totals	192	100·0	181	100·0	373	100·0

TABLE 9. Tsutskwe Census. Composite Totals for Religious Affiliation: Married
Adults and Adolescent Post-school Age Young People
(From Table 5 and Table 8)

	Chifamba		Karonga		Total	
	No.	%	No.	%	No.	%
Gentile	683	72·8	369	65·2	1052	69·9
Methodist	95	10·1	31	5·5	126	8·4
Catholic	64	6·8	109	19·2	173	11·5
Vapostori	97	10·3	57	10·1	154	10·2
Totals	939	100·0	566	100·0	1505	100·0

	Chifamba		Karonga		Total	
	No.	%	No.	%	No.	%
Gentile	683	72·8	369	65·2	1052	69·9
Christian	256	27·2	197	34·8	433	30·1
Totals	939	100·0	566	100·0	1505	100·0

TABLE 10. Budjga Attitudinal Survey

The questionnaire was designed to test Budgja attitudes on various items of
religious belief, attitudes towards authority, concepts of illness and its treatment,
and ideas concerning marriage, particularly on those issues in which the ideologies of the different religious groups tend to differ.

The survey employed the use of a questionnaire administered to 250 Budgja
adults and 100 Standard Three Budgja school children. Of the two hundred
and fifty adults 50 were Methodists, 50 Catholic, 50 Vapostori and 100 Gentiles.
The school children were from various Methodist and Roman Catholic Schools
in the Reserve, while the adults were all from the Tsutskwe community. The
size of the sample, particularly with regard to the adults, was restricted by the
fact that each questionnaire had to be administered individually, and this in a
political situation where such techniques were under considerable suspicion.
The adult investigation was therefore restricted to the Tsutskwe community
where a prolonged research period had made relationships easier. Most of the
adult informants were men, the women having been found to be extremely
reticent about responding to a procedure of this type.

Some of the questions posed a straightforward query, while others called for
an answer indicating the type of action the informant thought appropriate to
a hypothetical situation. 'Open ended' questions were avoided, since this would
have made the grading of a large sample difficult and the classification of the
answers almost impossible. Instead the informants were given the opportunity
of a 'multiple choice' response, in most cases involving three answers conceived
to represent the range of opinion presented by the different ideologies. The
informant was at liberty to indicate two responses to the same question if he
felt that both were applicable.

Having administered the questionnaire and reviewed the results I question the utility of some of the questions and the reliability of some of the categories of response that were provided. Comments are appended to the analysis of most question responses which indicate possible revisions that might be made for a future project of this type.

All the questions were phrased in Shona, and what appears here in this appendix is an English translation.

The responses of each informant were recorded on a separate questionnaire form. Each form recorded the age, sex, education and religious affiliation of the informant, but informants' names were not requested, in the hope that this would encourage a free response. The 100 samples obtained from the school children were read and filled in by the students themselves, and therefore contain answers made in the freedom of anonymity. The 250 adult questionnaires were read to the informants either by myself or by my assistants and their responses recorded on individual forms. It is difficult to assess the extent to which these adults may have been influenced in their responses by the personal element in this type of confrontation, but the fact that so many indicated beliefs contrary to the accepted ideology of their religious groups is perhaps an indication of candour on the part of most.

QUESTION ONE:

The rains have not fallen in the area of Chief Makuni for two years, and his people are starving. Why?

- (a) The *mhondoro* (tribal spirits) have refused to send the rains because the people have not offered the proper sacrifices.
- (b) God (Mwari) has not sent the rain.
- (c) The winds have failed to bring the rains to his area.

Responses:

	Methodist		Catholic		Vapostori		Gentile		School Children	
	No.	%	No.	%	No.	%	No.	%	No.	%
(a)	17	34	12	24	3	6	57	57	29	29
(b)	27	54	31	62	47	94	28	28	53	53
(c)	6	12	1	2	0	0	9	9	3	3
Combined			b & c	6			b & c	3	a & b	10
responses							a & c	2	b & c	2
							a & b	1	a & c	3

Comments:

1. The alternative responses supplied were designed to provide: (a) an answer representing Traditional religious ideology, (b) an answer typical of that taught in the sermons and catechisms of the Christian churches and (c) a scientific theory of causation such as is taught in the schools. 'Mwari', the word used for God in response 'b', is the name commonly used for deity by Christians, while Traditional Religionists more often use the word 'Nyadenga' (cf. pp. 49–50). Since Mwari is the ultimate power behind the *mhondoro* a (b) response here

could conceivably be orthodox for this group, but would not be typical since the emphasis in the Traditional Religion is on the activity of the *mhondoro* themselves in a situation of this kind. In the same way a (*c*) response could be an orthodox Christian answer, but in this case the issue is not important since few gave a reply in this category.

2. The Vapostori are the most uniform and orthodox Christian group on this issue, while the response of the school children roughly approximated the Methodist/Roman Catholic position.

QUESTION TWO:

If a good man dies, what happens to his soul? (*mweya*)
   (*a*) It perishes completely.
   (*b*) It becomes a family spirit (*mudzimu*).
   (*c*) It will go to heaven.

Responses:

	Methodist		Catholic		Vapostori		Gentile		School Children	
	No.	%	No.	%	No.	%	No.	%	No.	%
(*a*)	0	0	1	2	3	6	2	2	1	1
(*b*)	8	16	11	22	0	0	42	42	8	8
(*c*)	42	84	37	74	47	94	56	56	86	86
Combined responses			*b & c*	2					*b & c*	5

Comments:

1. For meanings attached to the words *mweya* and *mudzimi* see pp. 32–3.
2. The word used for 'heaven', *denga*, means 'sky', or in Shona Christian terminology 'heaven'.
3. The Gentile response here is less traditional than it was to Question One. I can offer no suitable explanation for this fact other than to suggest that Traditionalists find the political implications of belief in the *mhondoro* a support for their faith at this point, while on matters of personal immortality the Christian doctrine has proved ideologically attractive. Interviews have indicated that many Traditional Religionists have a vague belief that the soul both becomes a *mudzimu and* goes to heaven, even though informants here give no multiple responses. *Denga* is said by some to have been conceived of as a 'place for the *midzumu*' in pre-Christian times, and to convey this idea to Budjga Traditional Religionists even today.

QUESTION THREE:

God speaks to his people through:
   (*a*) The tribal spirits (*mhondoro*).
   (*b*) The Bible.
   (*c*) The priests or ministers.

Responses:

	Methodist No.	%	Catholic No.	%	Vapostori No.	%	Gentile No.	%	School Children No.	%
(a)	7	14	3	6	0	0	26	26	12	12
(b)	24	48	30	60	44	88	47	47	44	44
(c)	13	26	15	30	5	10	23	23	30	30

Combined *b&c* 6 12   *b&c* 1 2   *b&c* 1 2   *a&c* 1 1   *b&c* 14
responses   *b&c* 1 2   *b&c* 3 3

Comments:

1. This question may not have been completely relevant to the Traditional Religionists, since in their ideology God rarely has occasion to speak to people anyway; it is the revelations of the *mhondoro* themselves that are important.

2. The word *svikiro* (spirit medium for the *mhondoro*, cf. pp. 45–8) should probably have been used in response (*a*), since they are more closely associated with mediation than the *mhondoro*, who are spirit powers, not mediators.

3. Even with the qualifications just made, the Gentile acceptance of the Bible, priests and ministers as mediators of divine revelation (although not necessarily exclusively) is noteworthy.

4. Surprisingly there was no significant difference between the Roman Catholics and the Methodists on the question of the Bible vis-à-vis ministers and priests as means of revelation.

QUESTION FOUR:

Mr Ndebvu sold a donkey to Mr Mbizi. He told Mr Mbizi that the donkey was very strong but he knew that the donkey was sick. His sister's son saw this. The donkey died even before Mr Mbizi reached his home. Mr Mbizi brought the case to court. The sister's son was called to testify. What should he do?

(*a*) He should say the donkey was well.

(*b*) He should run and hide until the case was finished so that he does not have to testify.

(*c*) He should go and tell the truth that the donkey was sick, even if his uncle is put in jail as a result.

Responses:

	Methodist No.	%	Catholic No.	%	Vapostori No.	%	Gentile No.	%	School Children No.	%
(a)	1	2	12	24	5	10	15	15	16	16
(b)	1	2	2	4	13	26	19	19	6	6
(c)	48	96	36	72	32	64	66	66	78	78

Comments:

1. This question attempted to test attitudes in a situation creating tension between kinship loyalty and adherence to an ethical ideal of strict truthfulness.

The results are, I feel, inconclusive since a number of questions, covering a wide range of possible situations, would be necessary to provide any convincing results. I can furnish no satisfactory reason for the difference in Roman Catholic and Methodist responses to this situation.

2. It should be kept in mind, of course, that the question calls for an ideal response, and is no indication of how the informants would in fact act if placed in such a situation.

QUESTION FIVE:

To drink beer: (a) Is a good thing.
              (b) Is good if you do not drink too much.
              (c) Is a sin.

Responses:

	Methodist		Catholic		Vapostori		Gentile		School Children	
	No.	%	No.	%	No.	%	No.	%	No.	%
(a)	7	14	15	30	1	2	22	22	1	1
(b)	13	26	25	50	2	4	49	49	47	47
(c)	30	60	10	20	47	94	29	29	52	52

Comments:

1. The word used for 'sin' is *chinyangadzo*, a term which has traditionally been used to refer to an offence against God, the Spirits or other people.

2. A large number of Methodists gave a response contrary to the disciplinary rules of their church, while the Vapostori were almost unanimous in their defence of total abstinence.

QUESTION SIX:

To smoke tobacco: (a) Is a good thing.
                 (b) Is good if you only smoke a little.
                 (c) Is a sin.

Responses:

	Methodist		Catholic		Vapostori		Gentile		School Children	
	No.	%	No.	%	No.	%	No.	%	No.	%
(a)	2	4	10	20	3	6	34	34	11	11
(b)	4	8	18	36	0	0	28	28	31	31
(c)	44	88	22	44	47	94	38	38	58	58

Comment:

Both Methodists and Catholics are stronger in their condemnation of smoking than they are of drinking: Methodists 88–60 per cent, Catholics 44–20 per cent, while the Vapostori remain constant at 94 per cent against both. One possible explanation for this may be that more of the informants were actually involved in beer drinking or at least beer making than in the use of tobacco. Beer drinking has an economic and social importance beyond that of the use of tobacco since it is an important part of the *nhimbe* (work parties), and is brewed for local sale in the Reserve.

QUESTION SEVEN:

To have many wives: (*a*) Is a good thing.
(*b*) Is all right if a man wishes it.
(*c*) Is a sin.

Responses:

	Methodist		Catholic		Vapostori		Gentile		School Children	
	No.	%	No.	%	No.	%	No.	%	No.	%
(*a*)	3	6	5	10	35	70	12	12	11	11
(*b*)	7	14	10	20	6	12	21	21	20	20
(*c*)	40	80	35	70	9	18	67	67	69	69

Comments:

1. The question should perhaps have been worded 'To have more than one wife', since the point of the enquiry was to enquire into attitudes concerning polygyny, not the abundance of wives.

2. The responses are remarkable for the close agreement of all the groups except the Vapostori. It is interesting that 67 per cent of the Gentile group condemned polygyny as a sin. It is useful to compare this figure with the percentage of married Gentile males in Budjga (77 per cent in the Tsutskwe community) who are monogamous.

3. On this issue the Vapostori group stands out in strong opposition to the rest. The Vapostori have apparently created a positive ethic of polygyny, a position quite different from mere permissiveness. The percentage of married Vapostori males who are polygynous in the Tsutskwe community is 57 per cent.

QUESTION EIGHT:

Tsonyo loved Nyasha who lived nearby. He asked his father to help him marry her. But his relatives did not think Nyasha was suitable for him, so they chose another girl for him to marry. What should he do?

(*a*) He should obey his parents and marry the girl they chose.
(*b*) He should refuse to marry anyone for a while.
(*c*) He should go and take the girl of his choice so that his parents will be forced to help with the bride-wealth and accept the situation.

Responses:

	Methodist		Catholic		Vapostori		Gentile		School Children	
	No.	%	No.	%	No.	%	No.	%	No.	%
(*a*)	14	28	33	66	44	88	51	51	72	72
(*b*)	9	18	7	14	1	2	9	9	14	14
(*c*)	27	54	10	20	5	10	40	40	14	14

N

Comment:

This question was designed to test whether religious affiliation had any effect on attitudes concerning the relative importance of a boy's wishes and those of his parents in the choice of his bride. Response (*a*) conforms to the Budjga stereotype of the 'old' way while response (*c*) typifies the individual choice thought 'modern'. Response (*b*) provided for an essentially neutral reply. It would have been useful to include another question concerning a girl's freedom of choice on the same issue.

QUESTION NINE:

Mr Mudiki and Mr Mukuru are both members of the church. The cattle of Mr Mudiki entered the garden of Mr Mukuru and destroyed his vegetables. What should they do?
(*a*) Settle the matter themselves.
(*b*) Go to the headman for the case to be judged.
(*c*) Go to the elders of their church for the judgement.

Responses:

	Methodist		Catholic		Vapostori		Gentile		School Children	
	No.	%	No.	%	No.	%	No.	%	No.	%
(*a*)	39	78	39	78	21	42	59	59	34	34
(*b*)	5	10	3	6	2	4	23	23	25	25
(*c*)	6	12	8	16	27	54	18	18	41	41

Comment:

This question sought to establish attitudes concerning the place of church leadership in disputes between members of a church. The type of situation described is a common occurrence, and the response of the majority in the Methodist, Catholic and Gentile groups (response (*a*)) would be considered a normal course of action in traditional Budjga society. To ascertain more accurately the position of these three groups on the matter of church authority versus village authority the question should have perhaps been rephrased to indicate that the two parties had failed to come to an agreement on their own and asked what should then be done in terms of responses (*b*) and (*c*). Fifty-four per cent of the Vapostori reacted in a manner consistent with their emphasis of the ethic that Christians should settle their own disputes and the fact that they do deal weekly with such matters at the *kireke* meetings (p. 101).

QUESTION TEN:

A Christian should:
(*a*) Not enter into matters of politics.
(*b*) Should be told by his church what to do in the political matters of the country.
(*c*) Disregard his church in this matter and pray to the family spirits who will direct him.
(*d*) Try his best to understand the politics of his country and to do his part.

Responses:

	Methodist		Catholic		Vapostori		Gentile		School Children	
	No.	%	No.	%	No.	%	No.	%	No.	%
(a)	6	12	5	10	38	76	24	24	31	31
(b)	5	10	8	16	10	20	19	19	35	35
(c)	1	2	6	12	2	4	19	19	14	14
(d)	38	76	31	62	0	0	38	38	20	20

Comment:

The passivity of the Vapostori Movement in Budjga is obvious from the responses recorded here; they are in fact categorically opposed to any participation by Christians in politics. (But it should be noted that this has not always been the reaction of the Vapostori to political issues; in 1958 in Pfungwe, to the north of Budjga, the Vapostori were among the leaders of the nationalist movement there.) The emphasis upon participation in politics found among the Methodist and Catholic groups is, I feel, a recent development resulting in part from the public stand that the leaders of both churches have taken in recent years on political issues.

QUESTION ELEVEN:

Is it true that there are witches?
  (a) Yes
  (b) No

Responses:

	Methodist		Catholic		Vapostori		Gentile		School Children	
	No.	%	No.	%	No.	%	No.	%	No.	%
(a)	45	90	45	90	46	92	93	93	76	76
(b)	5	10	5	10	4	8	7	7	24	24

QUESTION TWELVE:

Is it true that medicine made from human flesh is powerfully effective.*
  (a) Yes
  (b) No

Responses:

	Methodist		Catholic		Vapostori		Gentile		School Children	
	No.	%	No.	%	No.	%	No.	%	No.	%
(a)	26	52	22	44	29	58	55	55	45	45
(b)	24	48	28	56	21	42	45	45	55	55

* It is a commonly repeated assertion in Budjga that *nganga* use pieces of the human body in the preparation of their medicines.

QUESTION THIRTEEN:

Is it true that some sicknesses are brought by *ngozi*?★
  (*a*) Yes
  (*b*) No

Responses:

	Methodist		Catholic		Vapostori		Gentile		School Children	
	No.	%	No.	%	No.	%	No.	%	No.	%
(*a*)	45	90	45	90	49	98	88	88	75	75
(*b*)	5	10	5	10	1	2	12	12	25	25

★ An avenging spirit, p. 57.

QUESTION FOURTEEN:

Is it true that some sicknesses can only be healed by a *nganga*? (cf. pp. 53–5).
  (*a*) Yes
  (*b*) No

Responses:

	Methodist		Catholic		Vapostori		Gentile		School Children	
	No.	%	No.	%	No.	%	No.	%	No.	%
(*a*)	40	80	40	80	22	44	91	91	50	50
(*b*)	10	20	10	20	28	56	9	9	50	50

QUESTION FIFTEEN:

Is it true that some sicknesses can only be healed by prayer to God?
  (*a*) Yes
  (*b*) No

Responses:

	Methodist		Catholic		Vapostori		Gentile		School Children	
	No.	%	No.	%	No.	%	No.	%	No.	%
(*a*)	36	72	32	64	49	98	55	55	71	71
(*b*)	14	28	18	36	1	2	45	45	29	29

Comment (Questions 12–15):

These questions all cover Budjga attitudes to illness and its treatment, a
subject of great importance in Budjga religion. There is considerable uniformity
in the responses of all groups with the exception of the Vapostori. In their
response to Question Fourteen the Vapostori (here joined by the school
children) exhibit a hostility to the *nganga* far greater than that of the Methodists
and Catholics. This parallels their opposition to other elements of Traditional
Budjga religious beliefs concerning the *mhondoro* and *midzimu* (Questions 1, 2

and 3), an opposition much stronger than that of the Methodists and Catholics.

It would have been useful to include a question on the suitability of the use of European medicines, to test how strongly individual Vapostori accept the doctrine of their church at this point.

TABLE 11. Church Membership in Budjga

Churches with European connections

Methodist	3,992		
Catholic	1,680		
Anglican	52		
Seventh Day Adventist	45		
Salvation Army	45		
Apostolic Church of Pentecost of Canada	10		
	5,824	5,824	75·3%

Independent Churches

Johanne Maranke Vapostori	1,800		
Johanne Masowe Vapostori	20		
African Independent Church	40		
Watchtower	23		
Kruger Vapostori	35		
	1,918	1,918	24·7%
		7,742	100·0%

Notes

1. All figures represent estimates of 'active' membership in terms of the definition given this term on pp. 116–18.

2. The Methodist figure is from the *Journal of the Rhodesia Annual Conference*, 1964, Appendix. In the *Journal* the figure is broken down as follows: 'Full members': 1,673, 'Probationary members': 2,319.

3. All other figures are estimates made after consultation with members and leaders of the churches concerned. The Watchtower group being divided into two small congregations, it was easy for informants to name members and the figure given for this group is precise.

4. The Watchtower group is placed here with the Independents, since although this group does have connections with Europeans these connections amount only to the provision of literature from time to time.

5. The Roman Catholic figure of 1,680 is an estimate, made in consultation with the Catholic fathers at All Souls'. Attendance at Mass for all Catholic congregations in Budjga tabulated in one of the father's notebooks yielded a figure of 840, and it was estimated that this figure represented approximately 50 per cent of an 'active' membership paralleling that represented in the Methodist figures.

6. The 7,742 total church membership for the Reserve represents 12 per cent of the total Budjga population of 55,000. This compares with 30·1 per cent given for the Tsutskwe community. But it must be remembered that the Tsutskwe percentage is for adults and post-school-age adolescents only and includes an 'inactive' membership. Using the Tsutskwe ratio of adults–adolescents to children (1,505/1,450, or 55 per cent), we can posit that there are approximately 30,000 adults and adolescents in Budjga. If we add to this number approximately 5,000 school children old enough to figure in church estimates on membership as 'active' members a figure of 35,000 is achieved, and the 7,742 active church adherents represent 22·1 per cent of this figure. If we consider the figure of 7,742 active church members to represent 70 per cent of the total Christian figure for Budjga (the comparable percentage for Tsutskwe) we arrive at a figure of 11,000 (31·4 per cent) as being the total number of active and inactive Christians in the Reserve, which is similar to the 30·1 per cent found in Tsutskwe.

TABLE 12. School Enrolment in Budjga

Catholic Schools

Name	Boys	Girls	Total
1. All Souls'★	259	235	494
2. Nyakuchena★	233	232	465
3. Bwanya★	235	221	456
4. Kaunye★	153	122	275
5. Karonga	112	69	181
6. Mushimbo	151	110	261
7. Chipfiko	127	114	241
8. Chiunye	88	63	151
9. Chimoyo	111	61	172
10. Tsiko (St Mary's)	67	70	137
11. Gozi	103	54	157
Totals	1,639	1,351	2,990

★ Denotes Upper Primary school. All other schools have Lower Primary only. Figures are for 1964.

Methodist Schools

Name	Boys	Girls	Total
1. Danda	83	65	148
2. Kagande	100	110	210
3. Chindenga★	252	152	404
4. Curure	59	74	133
5. Nyamakope	84	57	141
6. Katsukunya★	240	172	412
7. Nyakabau	122	78	200
8. Manhemba	156	116	272
9. Muswaire	104	67	171

Methodist Schools (contd.)

Name	Boys	Girls	Total
10. Mtoko	163	137	300
11. Tsiga	78	66	144
12. Nyamuzuwe★	243	194	437
13. Kawazwa	68	39	107
14. Masenda	111	66	177
15. Chindoko	60	22	82
16. Nyamukowo	116	72	188
17. Chifamba	171	95	266
18. Kowo	237	102	339
19. Utonga	48	32	80
20. Bondemakara★	223	136	359
21. Mudzonga★	168	147	315
22. Masango	55	84	139
23. Chatiza	115	73	188
24. Nyamkosa	85	59	144
25. Musanhi	63	57	120
26. Makosa★	223	129	352
27. Chitekwe★	232	190	422
28. Kawere	285	107	392
29. Madimutsa	79	74	153
Totals	4,047	2,748	6,795

★ Denotes Upper Primary schools. All others are Lower Primary schools. In addition the Methodist Church runs the only Secondary school in Budjga, at Nyamuzuwe. There are 103 boys and 27 girls enrolled at this school. Figures are for 1964.

TABLE 13. Marriages registered at the Mtoko District Commissioner's Office, 1950–1960, under the 1950 Native Marriage Act

Year	Catholic	Methodist	Customary
1950	10	26	392
1951	8	26	737
1952	14	30	483
1953	22	28	197
1954	35	38	530
1955	26	33	870
1956	40	32	333
1957	43	39	3,134
1958	38	29	350
1959	53	33	219
1960	46	28	307
Totals	335	342	7,552

Notes:

1. The large number of customary marriages registered in 1957 is attributable to the attempt by the Administration in this year to implement the Native Land Husbandry Act (*supra*, p. 5) under conditions which favoured married men. As has been pointed out (*supra*, p. 6), the conditions of the Act have not as yet been fully carried out in Budjga.

2. Methodist ministers and Catholic priests are the only religious authorities at present registered as marriage officers in Mtoko.

3. Figures obtained from the District Commissioner's Office, Mtoko.

LIST OF WORKS CITED

A. BOOKS AND PERIODICAL ARTICLES

ALLAN, W., 1945. 'African Land Usage', *The Rhodes–Livingstone Journal*, **3**, pp. 13–20.

ANDERSSON, E., 1958. *Messianic Popular Movements in the Lower Congo*. Uppsala: Almqvist and Wiksells.

AQUINA, M., 1963. 'A Note on Missionary Influence on Shona Marriage', *The Rhodes–Livingstone Journal*, **33**, pp. 68–79.

BAETA, C. G., 1962. *Prophetism in Ghana*. London: Student Christian Movement Press.

BEATTIE, J. H., 1961. 'Group Aspects of the Nyoro Spirit Mediumship Cult', *The Rhodes–Livingstone Journal*, **30**, pp. 11–38.

BELL, E. M., 1961. *Polygons: A Survey of the African Personnel of a Rhodesian Factory*. Salisbury: University College of Rhodesia and Nyasaland, Department of African Studies, Occasional Paper No. 2.

BLAKE-THOMPSON, J. and R. SUMMERS, 1956. 'Mlimo and Mwari: Notes on a Native Religion in Southern Rhodesia', *Nada*, No. 33, pp. 53–58.

BOISSEVAIN, J., 1965. *Saints and Fireworks: Religion and Politics in Rural Malta*. London: The Athlone Press. London School of Economics Monographs on Social Anthropology, No. 30.

BRELSFORD, W. V., 1960. ed. *Handbook to the Federation of Rhodesia and Nyasaland*. Salisbury: The Government Printer.

BULLOCK, C., 1927. *The Mashona*. Cape Town.

BURBRIDGE, A., 1938. 'In Spirit-bound Rhodesia', *Nada*, No. 15, pp. 15–29.

DEVLIN, C., 1961. 'The Mashona and the Portuguese', *The Month*, Vol. 25, No. 3, pp. 140–51.

DOUGLAS, M., 1963. 'Techniques of Sorcery Control in Central Africa', in *Witchcraft and Sorcery in East Africa*, J. Middleton and E. H. Winters, eds. London: Routledge and Kegan Paul, pp. 123–41.

EISELEN, W. M., 1934. 'Christianity and the Religious Life of the Bantu', in *Western Civilization and the Natives of South Africa*, I. Schapera, ed. London: Routledge and Sons, pp. 65–82.

EVANS-PRITCHARD, E. E., 1937. *Witchcraft Oracles and Magic Among the Azande*. Oxford.

FIRTH, R., 1948. 'Religious Belief and Personal Adjustment' (Henry Myers Lecture), *Journal of Royal Anthropological Institute*, **78**.

——, 1961. *Conflict and Adjustment in Tikopia Religious Systems*. Unpublished manuscript. Cited by permission of the author.

FLOYD, B. N., 1959. 'Changing Patterns of African Land Use in Southern Rhodesia', *The Rhodes–Livingstone Journal*, **25**, pp. 20–39.

FORTUNE, G., 1959. *The Bantu Languages of the Federation: A Preliminary Survey*. Lusaka: Rhodes–Livingstone Institute.

FRIPP, C. and V. W. HILLER, 1959. *Gold and the Gospel in Mashonaland, 1888.* London: Chatto and Windus.

GARBETT, G. K., 1960. *Growth and Change in a Shona Ward.* Salisbury: University College of Rhodesia and Nyasaland, Department of African Studies, Occasional Paper No. 1.

——, 1961. 'The Land Husbandry Act of Southern Rhodesia', in *African Agrarian Systems*, D. Biebuyck, ed. London: Oxford University Press, pp. 185–202.

——, 1963. *Religious Aspects of Political Succession Among the Valley Korekore.* Lusaka: Rhodes–Livingstone Institute.

GEERTZ, C., 1960. *The Religion of Java.* Glencoe, Illinois: The Free Press.

GELFAND, M., 1956. *Medicine and Magic of the Mashona.* Cape Town.

——, 1959. *Shona Ritual.* Cape Town.

HOERNLÉ, W., 1927. 'Religion in Native Life', in *Thinking With Africa*, M. Stauffer, ed. London: Student Christian Movement, pp. 84–109.

HOLLEMAN, J. F., 1952. *Shona Customary Law.* London: Oxford University Press.

——, 1953. *Accommodating the Spirit Amongst some North-Eastern Shona Tribes.* Rhodes–Livingstone Paper No. 22. London: Oxford University Press.

HUGO, H. C., 1935. 'The Mashona Spirits', *Nada*, No. 13, pp. 52–8.

JAY, R., 1963. *Religion and Politics in Rural Central Java.* Yale University: Cultural Report Series No. 12, Southeast Asia Studies.

KAUFFMAN, R., 1960. 'Hymns of the Wabvuwi', *Journal of the African Music Society*, **11**, No. 3, pp. 31–5.

KRIGE, J. D. and E. J., 1943. *The Realm of a Rain Queen.* London: International African Institute.

KUPER, H., 1946. *The Uniform of Colour.* Johannesburg: Witwatersrand University Press.

——, 1955. 'The Shona' in *The Shona and Ndebele of Southern Rhodesia*, by H. Kuper, A. J. B. Hughes and J. van Velsen. London: International African Institute, pp. 9–40.

KUPER, L., 1965. *An African Bourgeoisie. Race, Class and Politics in South Africa.* New Haven: Yale University Press.

MARWICK, M. G., 1952. 'The Social Context of Cewa Witch Beliefs', *Africa*, **22**, No. 2, pp. 120–34.

MAYER, P., 1961. *Townsmen or Tribesmen.* Cape Town: Oxford University Press.

——, 1963. 'Some Forms of Religious Organization among Africans in a South African City', in *Urbanization in African Social Change*, K. Little, ed. Edinburgh: University of Edinburgh, Centre of African Studies, pp. 113–26.

MBEE, G., 1955. 'Letter from Mbugwe, Tanganyika', *Africa*, **xxv**, No. 2, pp. 198–208.

MITCHELL, J. C., 1960. 'The African Peoples', in *Handbook to the Federation of Rhodesia and Nyasaland*, W. V. Brelsford, ed. Salisbury: The Government Printer, pp. 117–81.

PARKER, FRANKLYN, 1960. *African Development and Education in Southern Rhodesia*. Ohio State University, International Education Monographs, No. 2.

PASCOE, C. F., 1901. *Two Hundred Years of the S.P.G.*, Vol. I. London: Society for the Propagation of the Gospel.

PAUW, B. A., 1960. *Religion in a Tswana Chiefdom*. London: International African Institute.

POSSELT, F. W. T., 1927. 'Some Notes on the Religious Ideas of the Natives of Southern Rhodesia', *South African Journal of Science*, Vol. 24, pp. 530–36.

POWELL, R. J., 1952. 'The Kuteurira Midzimu Ceremony at a Vashawasha Kraal', *Nada*, No. 29, pp. 87–9.

RANGER, T., 1964. 'The Early History of Independency in Southern Rhodesia', in *Religion in Africa*. Edinburgh: Proceedings of a Seminar held in the Centre of African Studies, University of Edinburgh, pp. 52–74.

ROBINSON, D. A., 1953. *Land Use Planning in Native Reserves in Southern Rhodesia*. Salisbury: Minister of Agriculture and Lands, Bulletin No. 1730.

ROTBERG, R., 1961. 'The Lenshina Movement of Northern Rhodesia', *Journal of the Rhodes–Livingstone Institute*, **29**, pp. 63–78.

SCHAPERA, I., 1934. 'Present-Day Life in the Native Reserves', in *Western Civilization and the Natives of South Africa*, I. Schapera, ed. London: Routledge and Sons, pp. 39–62.

——, 1958. 'Christianity and the Tswana', *Journal of the Royal Anthropological Society*, **88**, No. 1, pp. 1–9.

SHEPPERSON, G., 1963. 'Church and Sect in Central Africa', *Journal of the Rhodes–Livingstone Institute*, **33**, pp. 82–94.

SHEPPERSON, G. and T. PRICE, 1958. *Independent African. John Chilembwe and the Origins, Setting and Significance of the Nyasaland Native Rising of 1915*. Edinburgh: The University Press.

SIMMONDS, R. G. S., 1964. 'Charewa, Voice of the Rain God', *Nada*, **IX**, No. 1, pp. 60–3.

SUNDKLER, B. G. M., 1961. *Bantu Prophets in South Africa*. London: Oxford University Press.

TAYLOR, J. V., and D. LEHMANN, 1961. *Christians of the Copper-belt*. London: Student Christian Movement Press.

"TENDENGUWO", 1964. 'The Shona Rebellion in the Mrewa District as Told by Tendenguwo', *Nada*, **IX**, No. 1, pp. 4–6.

TORREND, J., 1921. *A Comparative Grammar of the South African Bantu Languages*. London: Kegan Paul (2nd ed.).

TRACEY, H., 1934. 'What are Mashawi Spirits?' *Nada*, 12, pp. 39–52.

——, 1963. 'The Hakata of Southern Rhodesia', *Nada*, 40, pp. 105–7.

TROELTSCH, E., 1931. *The Social Teaching of the Christian Churches*. (Translated by Olive Wyon.) London: George Allen and Unwin.

TURNER, V. W., 1961. 'Ritual Symbolism, Morality and the Social Structure among the Ndembu', *Rhodes–Livingstone Journal*, **30**, pp. 1–10.

——, 1962. *Chihamba, The White Spirit: A Ritual Drama of the Ndembu*. Manchester University Press: Rhodes–Livingstone Paper No. 33.

VAN DER MERWE, W. J., 1959. 'The Shona Idea of God', *Nada*, 34, pp. 39–63.

VAN VELSEN, J., 1961. 'Labour Migration as a Positive Factor in the Continuity of Tonga Tribal Society', in *Social Change in Modern Africa*. A. Southall, ed. London: Oxford University Press, pp. 230–41.

VON SICARD, H., 1944. 'Mwari, der Hochgott der Karanga', *Wiener Beiträge zur Kulturgeschichte und Linguistik*, Jahrg. 6, pp. 134–91.

WESTERMANN, D., 1937. *Africa and Christianity*. London: Oxford University Press.

WHITE, C. M. N., 1961. *Elements in Luvale Beliefs and Rituals*. Manchester University Press for the Rhodes–Livingstone Institute. Rhodes–Livingstone Papers, No. 32.

WILLOUGHBY, W. C., 1928. *The Soul of the Bantu*. London: Student Christian Movement.

WILSON, M., 1952. *Keiskammahoek Rural Survey*. Vol. III, *Social Structure*. Pietermaritzburg: Shuter and Shooter.

WISHLADE, R. L., 1965. *Sectarianism in Southern Nyasaland*. London: Oxford University Press.

WORSLEY, P., 1957. *The Trumpet Shall Sound*. London: MacGibbon and Kee.

B. REPORTS, PAPERS AND PAMPHLETS

British Parliamentary Papers. *The Command Papers*. C 6495 of 1891.

Catholic Church. *Rugwaro Rwokunamata Rwavanhu Vekirike Katolike*. Chishawasha Mission, 1962, 127 pp.

Catholic Mission Press, Gwelo:
  Nzira Yokudenga, 1958. 77 pp.
  Muchato Nemhuri, 1958. 27 pp.
  Chechi Imwe Chete Ie Chokwadi, 1959. 40 pp.
  Ushe HwaYawe, 1962. 98 pp.

Methodist Church.
  Journal of the Rhodesia Annual Conference. 1907–1964, *passim*.
  Ngoma dze Methodist Church ye Rhodesia. Old Umtali: Rhodesia Mission Press, 1928. Revised 1954. 299 pp.
  Doctrines and Disciplines of the Methodist Church. Africa Central Conference Edition. Cleveland, Transvaal: Central Mission Press, 1956, 200 pp.

Society for the Propagation of the Gospel, London. Archives: Letter from Knight–Bruce to Tucker, Nov. 25, 1889. J. Ms. Vol. 7, pp. 71–3.

Southern Rhodesia Government. *Report of the Native Education Inquiry Commission*, 1951. C.S.R., No. 6, Salisbury: The Government Printer.

Vapostori. *Humbowo Hutswa We Vapostori*. Mimeographed, 22 pp. No date but about 1955.

INDEX

LONDON SCHOOL OF ECONOMICS
MONOGRAPHS ON SOCIAL ANTHROPOLOGY

Titles marked with an asterisk are now out of print. Those marked with a dagger have been reprinted in paperback editions and are only available in this form. A double dagger indicates availability in both hardcover and paperback.

I, 2. RAYMOND FIRTH
The Work of the Gods in Tikopia, 2 vols., 1940. (2nd. edition in 1 vol., 1967.)

3. E. R. LEACH
Social and Economic Organization of the Rowanduz Kurds, 1940. (Available from University Microfilms Ltd.)

*4. E. E. EVANS-PRITCHARD
The Political System of the Anuak of the Anglo-Egyptian Sudan, 1940. (New edition in preparation.)

5. DARYLL FORDE
Marriage and the Family among the Yakö in South-Eastern Nigeria, 1941. (Available from University Microfilms Ltd.)

*6. M. M. GREEN
Land Tenure of an Ibo Village in South-Eastern Nigeria, 1941.

7. ROSEMARY FIRTH
Housekeeping among Malay Peasants, 1943. Second edition, 1966.

*8. A. M. AMMAR
A Demographic Study of an Egyptian Province (Sharquiya), 1943.

*9. I. SCHAPERA
Tribal Legislation among the Tswana of the Bechuanaland Protectorate, 1943. (Replaced by new volume, No. 43.)

*10. W. H. BECKETT
Akokoaso: A Survey of a Gold Coast Village, 1944.

11. I. SCHAPERA
The Ethnic Composition of Tswana Tribes, 1952.

*12. JU-K'ANG T'IEN
The Chinese of Sarawak: A Study of Social Structure, 1953. (New edition revised and with an Introduction by Barbara Ward in preparation.)

*13. GUTORM GJESSING
Changing Lapps, 1954.

14. ALAN J. A. ELLIOTT
Chinese Spirit-Medium Cults in Singapore, 1955.

*15. RAYMOND FIRTH
Two Studies of Kinship in London, 1956.

16. LUCY MAIR
Studies in Applied Anthropology, 1957. (Replaced by new volume, No. 38.)

†17. J. M. GULLICK
Indigenous Political Systems of Western Malaya, 1958.

†18. MAURICE FREEDMAN
Lineage Organization in Southeastern China, 1958.

†19. FREDRIK BARTH
Political Leadership among Swat Pathans, 1959.

†20. L. H. PALMIER
Social Status and Power in Java, 1960.

†21. JUDITH DJAMOUR
Malay Kinship and Marriage in Singapore, 1959.

†22. E. R. LEACH
Rethinking Anthropology, 1961.

23. S. M. SALIM
Marsh Dwellers of the Euphrates Delta, 1962.

†24. S. VAN DER SPRENKEL
Legal Institutions in Manchu China, 1962.

25. CHANDRA JAYAWARDENA
Conflict and Solidarity in a Guianese Plantation, 1963.

26. H. IAN HOGBIN
Kinship and Marriage in a New Guinea Village, 1963.

27. JOAN METGE
A New Maori Migration: Rural and Urban Relations in Northern New Zealand, 1964.

‡28. RAYMOND FIRTH
Essays on Social Organization and Values, 1964.

29. M. G. SWIFT
Malay Peasant Society in Jelebu, 1965.

†30. JEREMY BOISSEVAIN
Saints and Fireworks: Religion and Politics in Rural Malta, 1965.

31. JUDITH DJAMOUR
The Muslim Matrimonial Court in Singapore, 1966.

32. CHIE NAKANE
Kinship and Economic Organization in Rural Japan, 1967.

33. MAURICE FREEDMAN
Chinese Lineage and Society: Fukien and Kwangtung, 1966.

34. W. H. R. RIVERS
Kinship and Social Organization, reprinted with commentaries by David Schneider and Raymond Firth, 1968.

35. ROBIN FOX
The Keresan Bridge: A Problem in Pueblo Ethnology, 1967.

36. MARSHALL MURPHREE
Christianity and the Shona, 1969.

37. G. K. NUKUNYA
Kinship and Marriage Among the Anlo Ewe, 1969.

38. LUCY MAIR
Anthropology and Social Change, 1969.

39. SANDRA WALLMAN
Take Out Hunger: Two Case Studies of Rural Development in Basutoland, 1969.

40. MEYER FORTES
Time and Social Structure and Other Essays, in press.

41. J. D. FREEMAN
Report on the Iban, in press.

42. W. E. WILLMOTT
The Political Structure of the Chinese Community in Cambodia, in press.

43. I. SCHAPERA
Tribal Innovators: Tswana Chiefs and Social Change 1795–1940, in press.